BLACK AMERICA SERIES

WALTON COUNTY GEORGIA

BLACK AMERICA SERIES

WALTON COUNTY
GEORGIA

Lynn Robinson Camp and Jennifer E. Cheeks-Collins

ARCADIA
PUBLISHING

ISBN 978-0-7385-1528-1

Published by Arcadia Publishing
Charleston, South Carolina

Printed in the United States of America

Library of Congress Catalog Card Number: 2003104870

For all general information contact Arcadia Publishing at:
Telephone 843-853-2070
Fax 843-853-0044
E-Mail sales@arcadiapublishing.com
For customer service and orders:
Toll-Free 1-888-313-2665

Visit us on the Internet at www.arcadiapublishing.com

Contents

ACKNOWLEDGMENTS

Glory, honor, and praises to God—the almighty power that flowed through me so that this project could come to fruition.

My eternal gratitude goes to Katie White and the Arcadia Publishing team and my co-author, Jennifer E. Cheeks-Collins, for making my dream for Walton County a reality. Within the constraints of time, space, and availability of photos and documentation, a great deal of Walton County history could not be included in this work. Much of what is written in these pages is verbal lore. It is my sincere hope that others will be inspired to research and document family and local history.

God in his infinite wisdom has surrounded me with a loving, supportive family: my mother, Tessie Robinson; my soulmate, John Chambers; my son, Tarik Camp; Paige Camp; and Tate Camp. My support system also includes friends and co-workers who listened to me, encouraged me, and got excited with me. Barbara Simmons, Gloria Pruitt, Beverly Robinson, Carrie Duhart, Jennifer Wewers, Melinda Wyatt, MaryEllen Waiting, Ama Reynolds, Katie Kiernan, Tenequa Wildy, Mary Kottkamp, and Sue Hendrix—thanks for the support.

Thanks to all the contributors whose names will appear throughout the book. Special thanks to Teressa Sorrells, Camilla Mattox, Claudia Mae Hillman, Tommie Lee Hillman Sr. (in memory), Tommie Lee "Bro" Hillman Jr., Robbie Mapp Vaughn, Willie Smith, Geneva Locklin, Olia Pitts, and Larry Witcher, who contributed to this book with such a spirit of cooperation when we weren't sure we'd have enough photos to complete this project. You gave us hope. Thanks to my cousins who came through so that some of our family's history would be included: Herman Robertson, Emma Wiseman, Marilyn Williams, and Hazel and Governor Butler. Also, I'd like to thank George Marshall, Pastor Clarence Grier Jr., and Olia Pitts for providing me with reference material. I extend thanks to those I have interviewed over the past few years, including: Idell Locklin, Alberta Brown, Idora Battle (in memory), Catherine Jones, Lamar Howard, Earl Broughton Sr., Annie Bell Banks, Garo Sheats, Rufus Jackson, Cora Bell Cook, Robert Howard, Pastor Clinton Sorrells Sr., Lillian Perkins, George Marshall, and Thomas Thompson. You gave me such insight into what Walton County was like during the early years and I enjoyed hearing your stories. Thanks to Mary Ann Dotson, Nedra Malcom, Rachel Howard, Mary Durham, Geneva Ivey, Rachel Ivey, Debra Taylor, Irene White, Addie White, Evelyn Bush, MaMa Sarah Maddox, Ariel Young Sullivan, Elsa Barkley Brown, Mary Lee Jordan, Steven Conwell of the Monroe Police Department, John Kemp, Timothy Kemp, Fred Johnson, Cathy Spivey, John Robinson and Charlotte George of the Walton County Board of Education, Betty Foster, Patsy Vinson, Dorcas Jernigan, Ethel Kilgore, Trayse Price, Michael Hill, Flossie Hill, Barbara and William Knox, IDaniel Williams, Cherry Lee Roberts, Roger Hayes Sr., Rev. and Mrs. E.L. Ellis Jr., Evelyn Bush, The Georgia Department of Industry, Trade, and Tourism, and the Walton County Chamber of Commerce.

I used many biographies, church histories, articles, obituaries, notes, resumes, and souvenir booklets as resources. I acknowledge those whose work I referenced: Bessie Garrett, Linda Jones, Anita Brown, Jackie A. Gibson, Donald Hector, Sarah Nell Syphoe, Dr. Willie Enus, and Mollie Butler Lewis. I also acknowledge these websites and publications: Stony Brook website; First African Baptist Church website; *The Walton Tribune*; *The Atlanta Journal and Constitution*; *The Atlanta Daily World*; Souvenir Program 100th Session of the Northwestern Baptist Association No.1; Souvenir Program 1877–1977 Northwestern Baptist Association; Souvenir program 123rd Anniversary Browns Hill Baptist Church; Fellowship Missionary Baptist Church, Macedonia Baptist Church, Spring Hill A.M.E. Zion, Good Hope Baptist Church, and Triumph The Church of God histories; minutes of meetings of the Walton County Board of Education; and *Reflections*, the Georgia African American Historic Preservation Network Newsletter October 2002.

I would also like to thank the following organizations, businesses, and individuals for supporting this and other local history projects that I initiated over the past few years: Emory University, Avondale Mills, Inc., Standridge Color Corporation, Young Funeral Home, Mollie's Learning Center, Dr. and Mrs. Wendell Smith, Walton Electric Membership Corporation, Rich and Janice Rusk, The Moore's Ford Memorial Committee, Inc., Fellowship Missionary Baptist Church, The A.P. Henderson Foundation, The Herndon Foundation, The Monroe Art Guild, The McDaniel-Tichenor House, The Monroe Walton County Library, The Detroit Library, The Auburn Avenue Research Library, Monroe Water, Light, & Gas, The Martin Luther King Jr. National Historic Site, and Georgia Council for the Arts.

Finally, I acknowledge the memory of my father, Huel Robinson, who made many sacrifices so that I could develop the talents, abilities, and skills that I use today. And my godfather, Daniel W. Young Sr.—a dynamic businessman and activist who inspired me greatly.

Love, Peace, and Joy,
Lynn Robinson Camp

This vision has come full circle and is now a sure reality. I thank my co-author, Lynn Camp, for you were the true backbone of this publication.

To Katie White and the Arcadia Publishing team I thank you for giving historians an outlet to tell our stories. Thanks again for your help and endless support.

To the citizens of Walton county I pray this publication portrays your legacy in a true and honorable light. I have learned a great deal about this county, its people, and the community. I sincerely appreciate you opening your doors and letting us into your lives.

To every contributor within this publication I say thank you and God bless you. We could have never done this without you.

To my family and friends, I thank you for always supporting and encouraging me even when I was at my wit's end. Joseph and Gail Basar, Tiana A. Cheeks-Budgewater, Janet Cheeks, Lee and Joyce Collins, Sharon Collins, Yolanda Jackson, LaShonda E. Johnson, James and Thelma Myers, Jamila Myers, Keah Myers, Corey Riley and Shundra C. Summers—I am eternally grateful to all of you.

To my mother, Alice, you are such a ray of light in my life. I thank you for always giving, encouraging, and guiding me. You have no idea the profound impact you have had in my life. I can only hope to become half the parent to my children that you are to me.

Keith, what can I say? Your love is amazing. You have a heart that just keeps on giving and for that I love you and adore you. May our love and hearts never part. I thank you for our two wonderful children.

Kamryn and Karson, Mommie loves you two. I fell in love with you both the day you two graced this world. I thank God for allowing me to be your mommie.

I pray for world peace and may all men on this earth love one another. God Bless.

Lord, I thank you for all your greatness . . .

Jennifer E. Cheeks-Collins

Georgia Council for the Arts
OFFICE OF THE GOVERNOR

FOREWORD

Lynn Robinson Camp and Jennifer E. Cheeks-Collins's book is an important addition to Arcadia's *Black America* Series. They have made a commendable effort to document the history of this community. It is obvious that the authors value the stories shaped from the lives of each member of the Walton County community. This work will ensure that generations to come will learn these stories.

Peace and Blessings,

Andrew Young

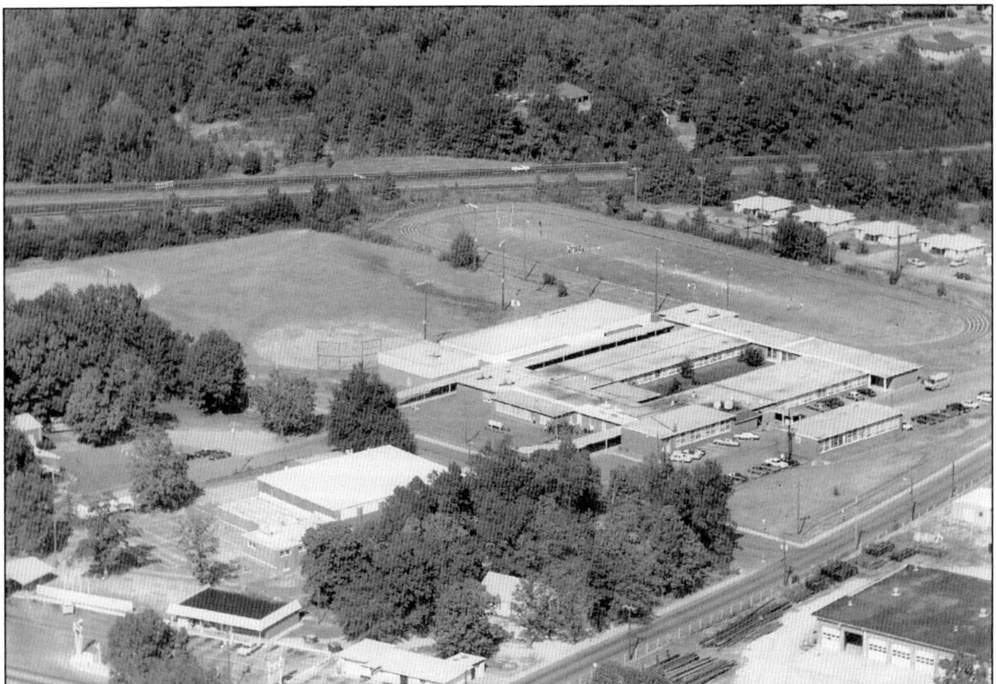

Carver High School and gym, First African Baptist Church, Broad Street, and several other streets in the African-American community of Monroe, Georgia are depicted in this aerial view. (Courtesy of Lynn Camp.)

INTRODUCTION

Walton County was carved from a parcel of land once belonging to Jackson County. In the infancy years of this county, the black community consisted generally of slaves. The slave population gradually increased during the establishment of the county in 1818 through 1860. The county was built largely at the expense of slave labor. Many residents, farmers, and businessmen relied on the till of their slaves for most of their economic wealth. In regard to the treatment of slaves in Walton County, very little is documented. Views of the slaves and the slave-owners almost always differ and are quite controversial in this county. Various documents disclose facts that some slaves had amicable relationships with their owners. Some slaves were even granted freedom upon their owners' deaths and others were included in their owners' wills. These instances reflect the humane hand of slavery in Walton County, but there was the cruel face of slavery displayed to many in the county. Reports show cases of runaways, beatings, and mistreatment of slaves.

Walton County changed dramatically during and after the Civil War. Many men left their farms and took up arms to protect the Confederacy. Women, children, and slaves were left behind, pondering over an uncertain future. Once the war ceased, Southern men came home to rebuild their lives and the South. The new South meant life without slaves and slave labor. Farmers now had to rely on themselves, tenant farmers, and sharecroppers to make ends meet. The newly freed slaves in Walton County took advantage of their freedom. Many migrated to Atlanta. Others moved to the North. A part of the population stayed in the county and built new lives, predominately as businessmen and farmers.

The 20th century was one of a new outlook for the blacks of Walton County. Many people had high hopes and endless dreams of a better future. These aspirations were nearly diminished by the failing economy and the racism blacks were confronted with daily. The county was scorned nationally when a white mob lynching took the lives of two black couples in Walton County. The black and white communities became more and more racially divided due to the fact that no one was convicted of the crime until more than 50 years after it occurred. Known as the Moore's Ford Lynching, this tragedy is one that Walton County residents still mourn, and the healing process continues today.

This publication focuses on the lives of African Americans from Walton County and the legacy they share with the world. The intent is to take the reader on a pictorial journey, one that begins in the early days and travels through years to highlight the daily traditions and lives of blacks. Images of school houses and churches shed light on the community's desire to grow in mind and spirit. We pay homage to the people who fell victim to racial violence in Walton County, and celebrate the men and women who actively participated in the Civil Rights Movement. Within these pages, the spirit of Walton County's African-American community is brought to life. Enjoy.

One

Early Days

Post-Slavery to Post–World War II

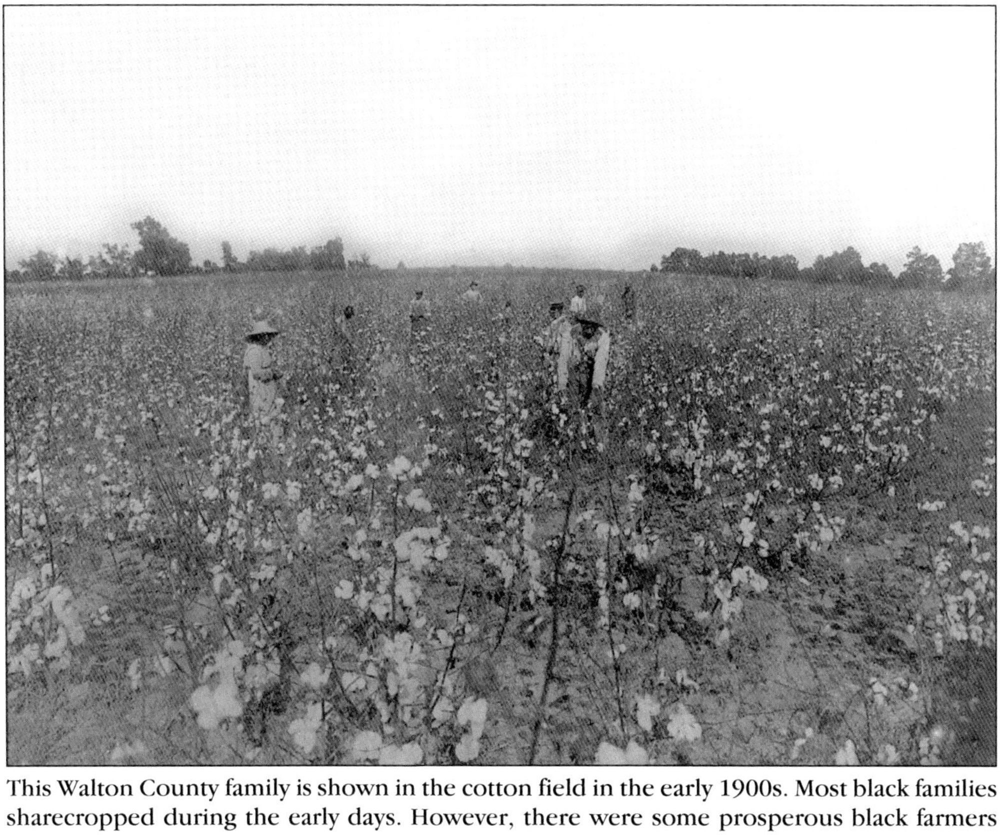

This Walton County family is shown in the cotton field in the early 1900s. Most black families sharecropped during the early days. However, there were some prosperous black farmers who owned large farms. (From the E.M. Carnes Collection; Courtesy Larry Witcher.)

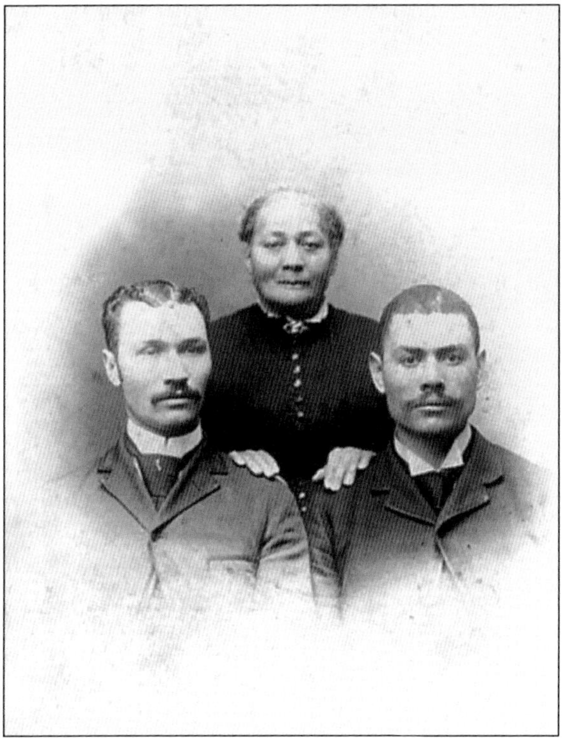

Alonzo Franklin Herndon (left), Walton County's most famous native son, is pictured with this mother, Sophenie, and brother, Thomas. Herndon was born a slave in Walton County in 1858 near Social Circle, Georgia. He left Walton County at age 16 and went on to become a successful businessman, a member of the Niagara Group (which later became the NAACP), the founder of Atlanta Life Insurance, and Atlanta's first black millionaire. (Courtesy the Herndon Foundation.)

These unidentified Walton County men are enjoying a ride in a Model T Ford. (The E.M. Carnes Collection; Courtesy Larry Witcher.)

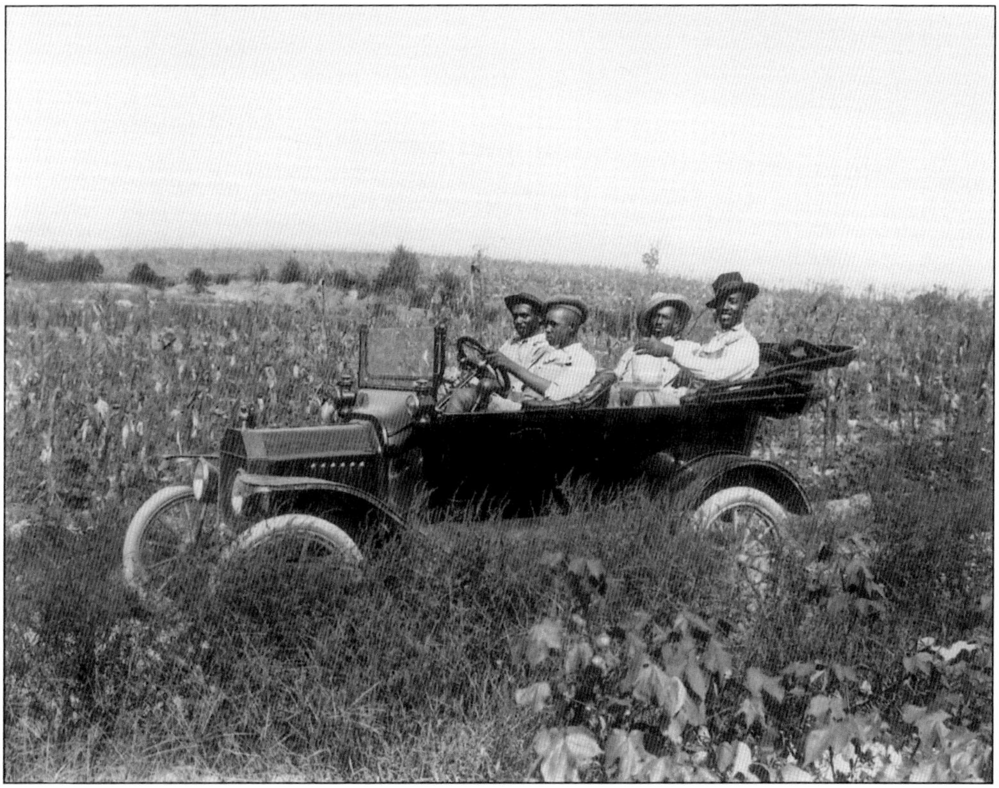

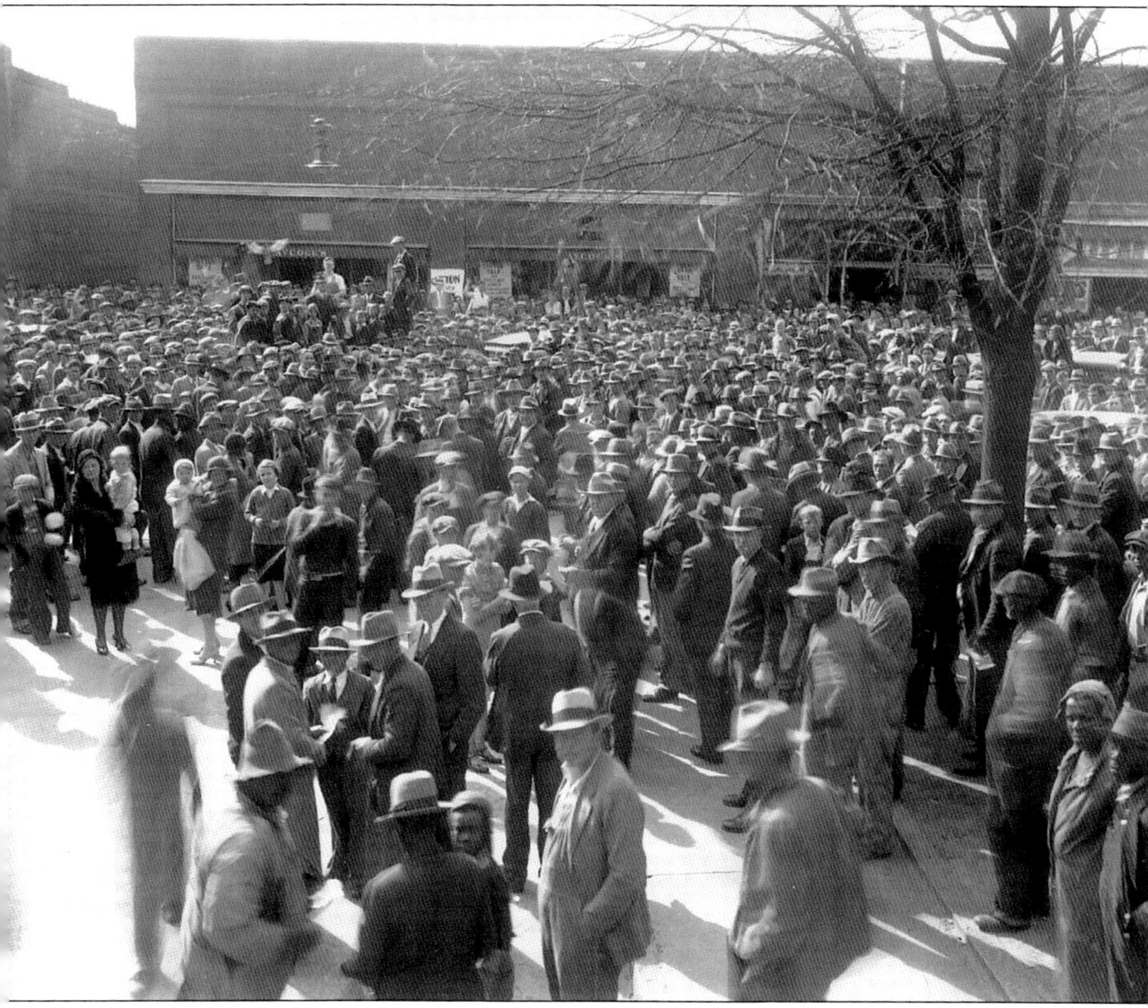

This crowd, which included several African-American residents of the county, gathered at the courthouse in downtown Monroe in the 1940s. (From the E.M. Carnes Collection; Courtesy Larry Witcher.)

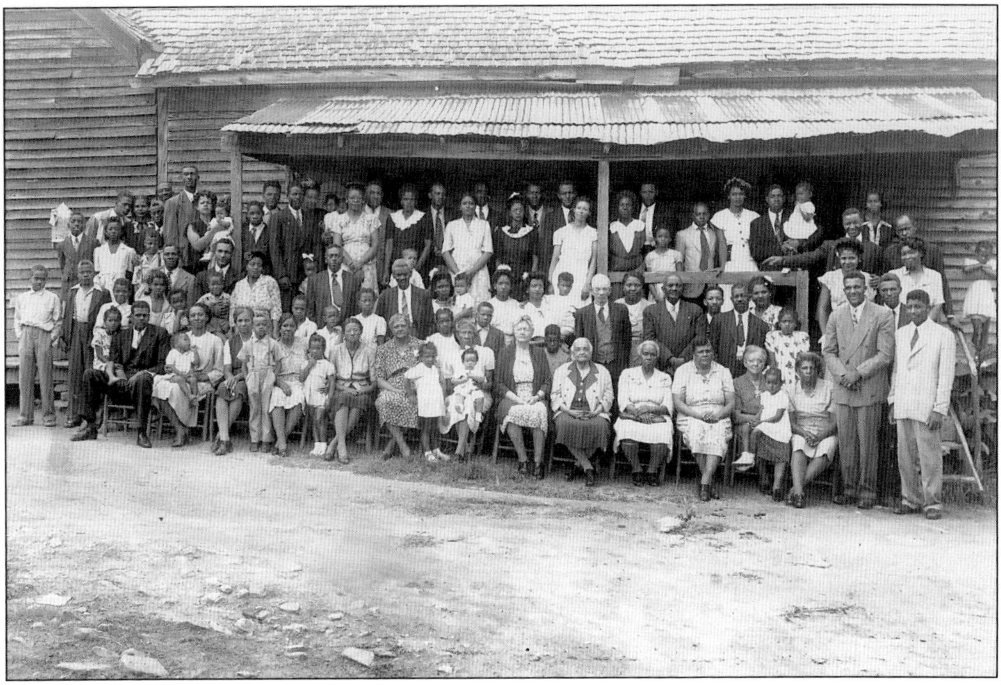

This is an unidentified Walton County family posed in front of their "home house" at a family gathering in the 1900s. (From the E.M. Carnes Collection, Courtesy Larry Witcher.)

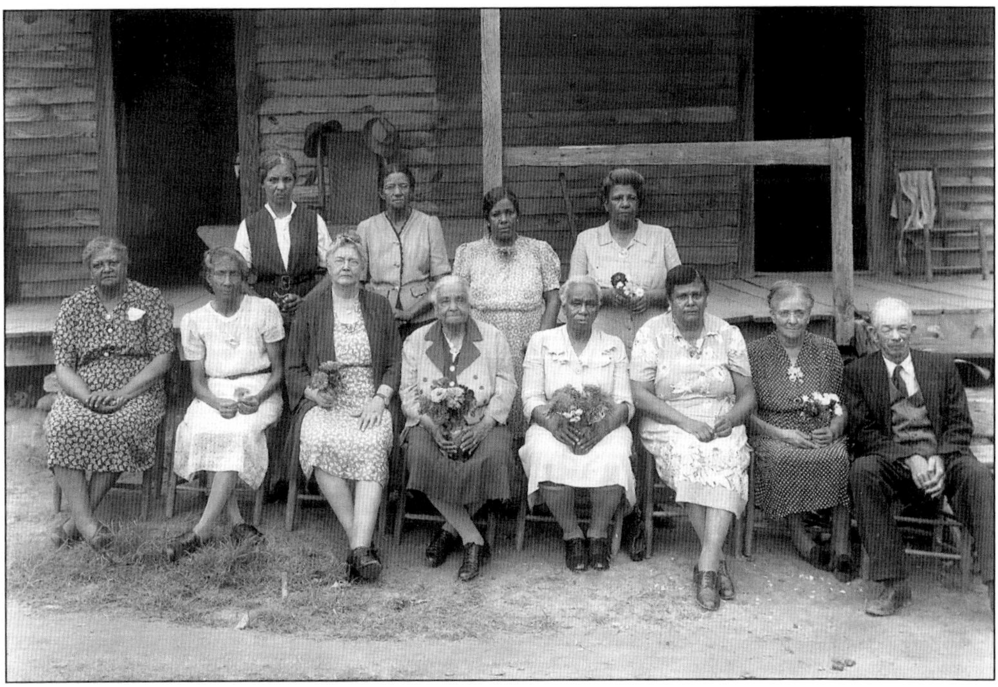

The elders of the family pictured at the top of the page pose together in this early 1900s photograph. Most of the females are holding flowers. (From the E.M. Carnes Collection; Courtesy Larry Witcher.)

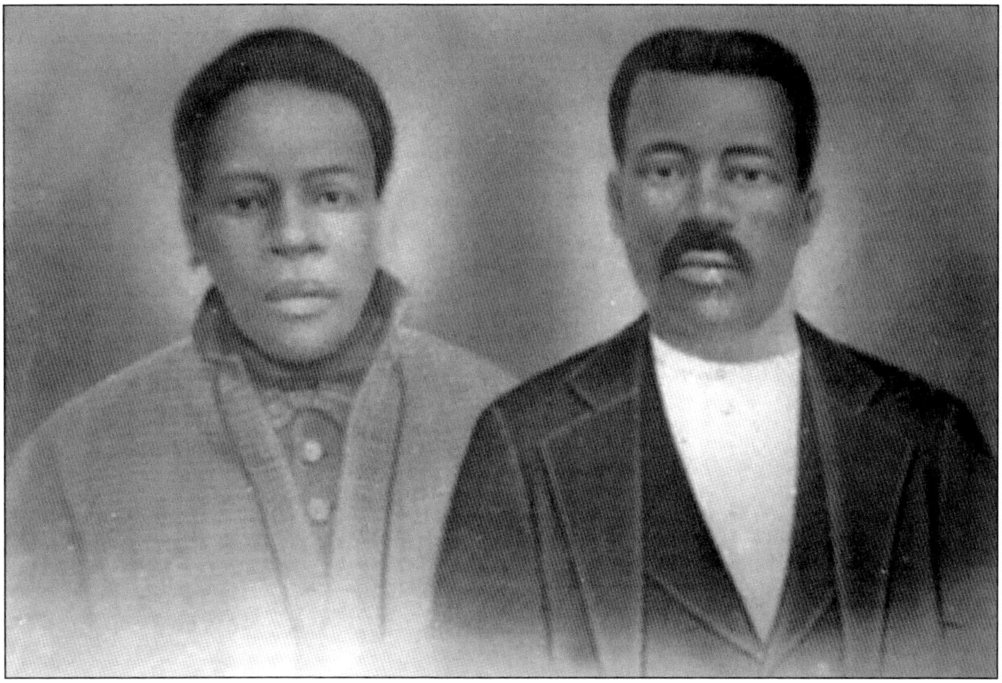

Laura Butler, Alex Butler's mother, and Mole Robinson, Alex Butler's uncle, are shown in this *c*. 1880 photograph. Alex Butler married Emily Hawk. (Courtesy Emma Wiseman and Marilyn Williams.)

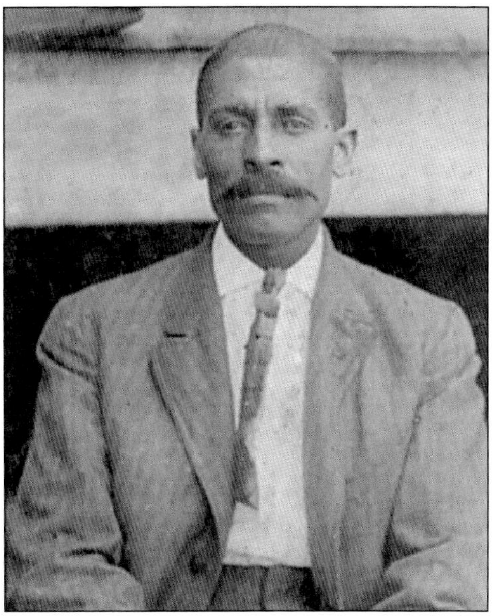

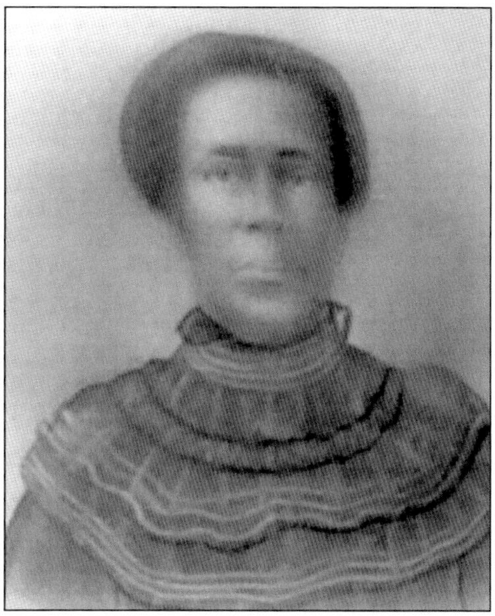

(*above, left*) William "Cap" Jackson opened Jackson Funeral home in 1926 in Walton County. Mr. Jackson was one of the county's most well-known businessmen. (Courtesy Evelyn Bush.) (*above, right*) This is Margaret Hawk *c*. 1890. She is the mother of Emily Hawk Butler, whose son Clifton Butler became a very respected farmer and deacon in the Good Hope community. (Courtesy Emma Wiseman and Marilyn Williams.)

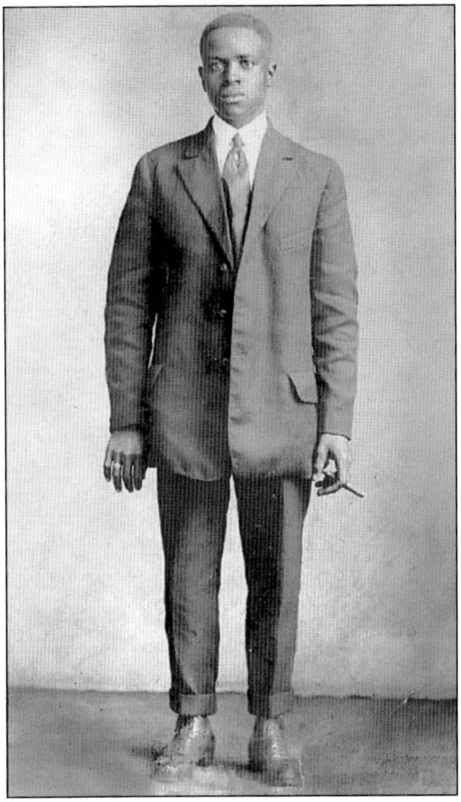

Goodway Robertson is shown here in the early 1900s. (Courtesy Willie Smith.)

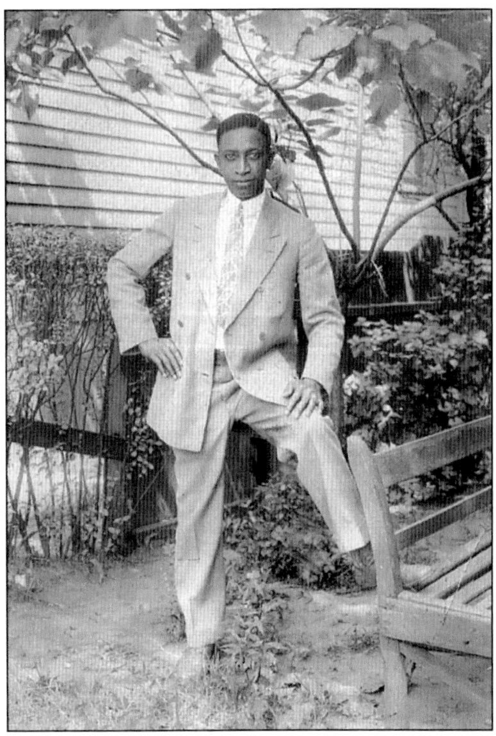

Hope Robertson posed for this early 1900s photograph. (Courtesy Willie Smith.)

Deacon John Bell was one of the founders of Mars Hill Baptist Church. He was the father of Sarah E. Knox. (Courtesy the Knox Family.)

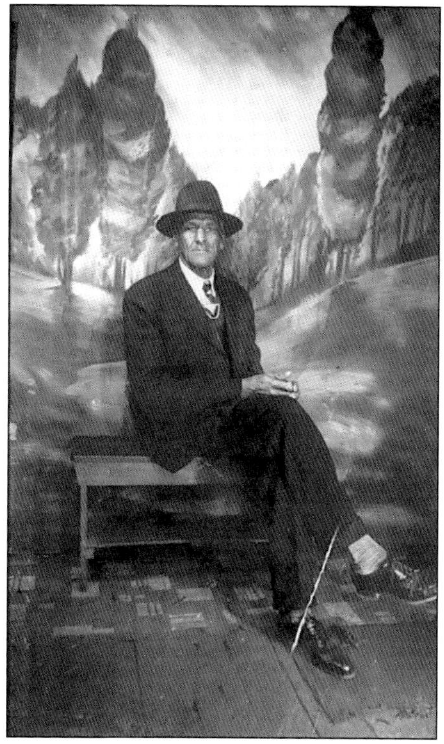

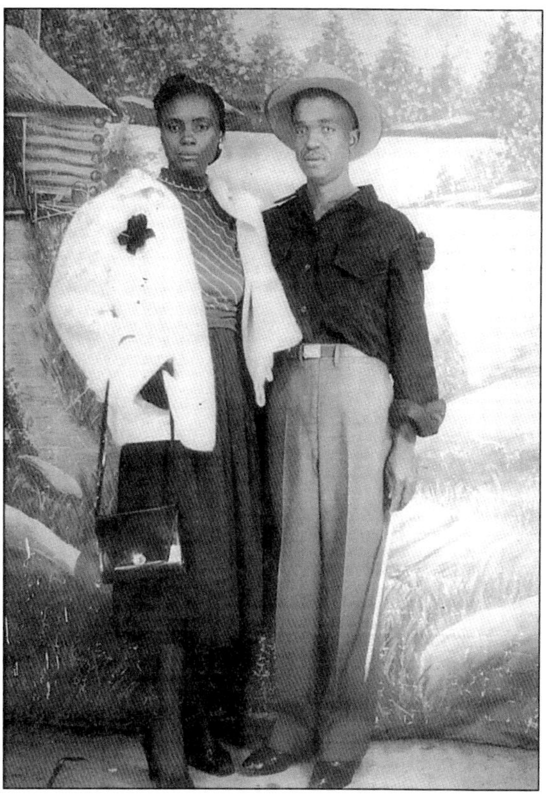

Francis and R.L. Sorrells moved to Walton County in the 1940s from Oconee County. Francis was one of the nine children of Mary and William "Lil' Pa" Jones. She was known in the community for the fancy hats and clothes she made. She also plowed a two-acre garden to produce vegetables for her family and to share with neighbors. (Courtesy Teressa Sorrells.)

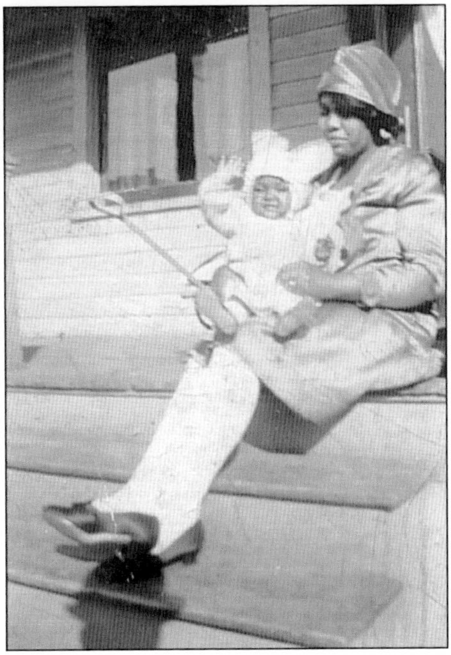

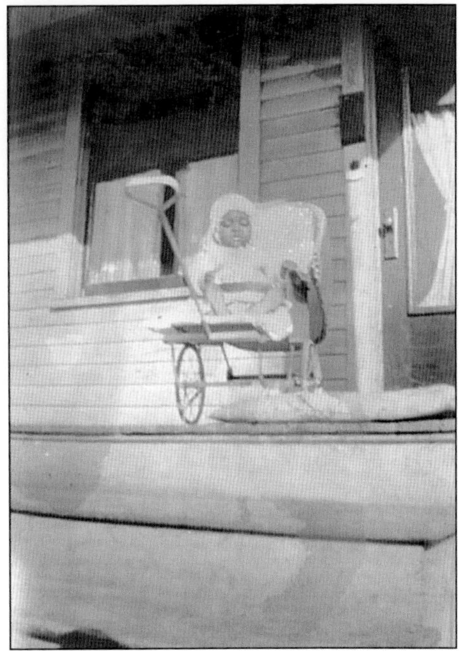

(above, left) Grace Jackson Rakestraw is holding her infant daughter, Evelyn Rakestraw, on the front porch in 1928. (*above, right*) Evelyn Rakestraw, age 8 months, is seen on the porch in her baby carriage in 1928. (Both images courtesy Evelyn Bush.)

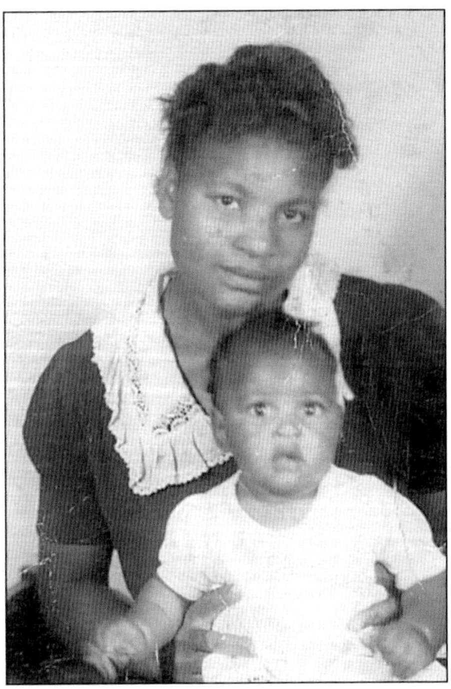

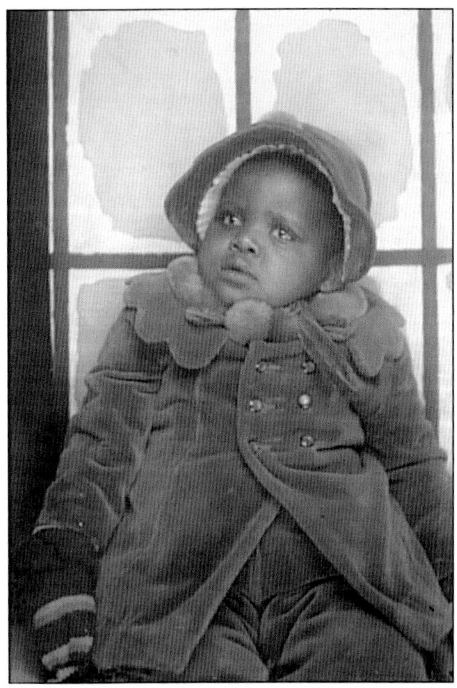

(*above, left*) This is an unidentified Walton County woman and child, *c.* 1940. (Courtesy of Camilla Mattox.) (*above, right*) This unidentified Walton County baby is dressed warmly in a coat, hat, and gloves, *c.* 1935. (Courtesy of Willie Smith.)

The twin daughters of A.D. and Cleo Bradley, Ola (left) and Hattie (right), were placed in chairs for this *c.* 1950 photograph. (Courtesy of Tessie Robinson.)

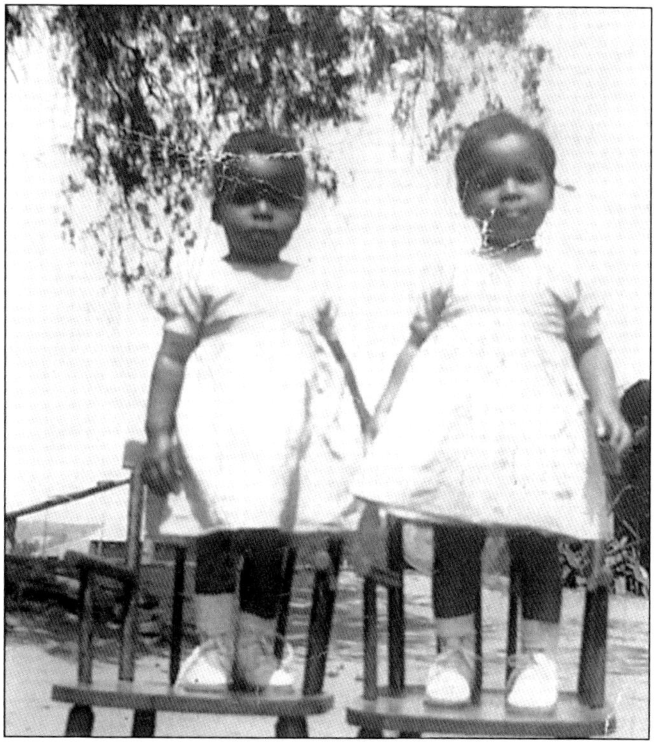

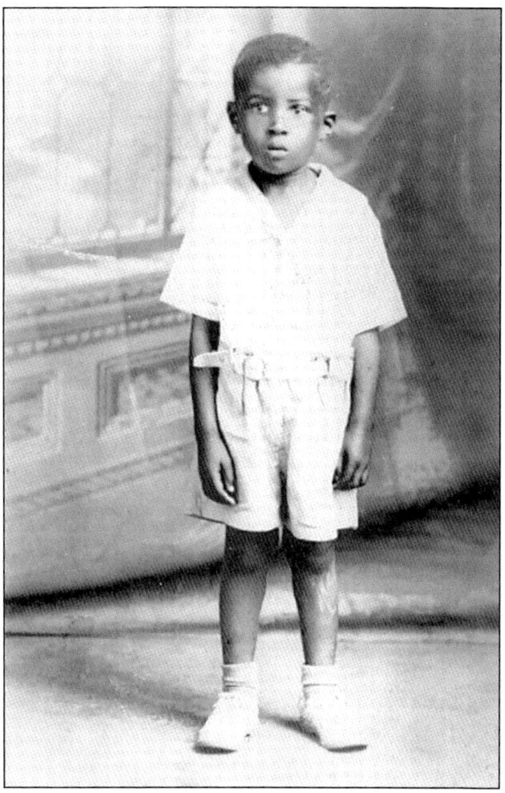

Justin Smith's son is shown in this *c.* 1920 photograph. (Courtesy of Willie Smith.)

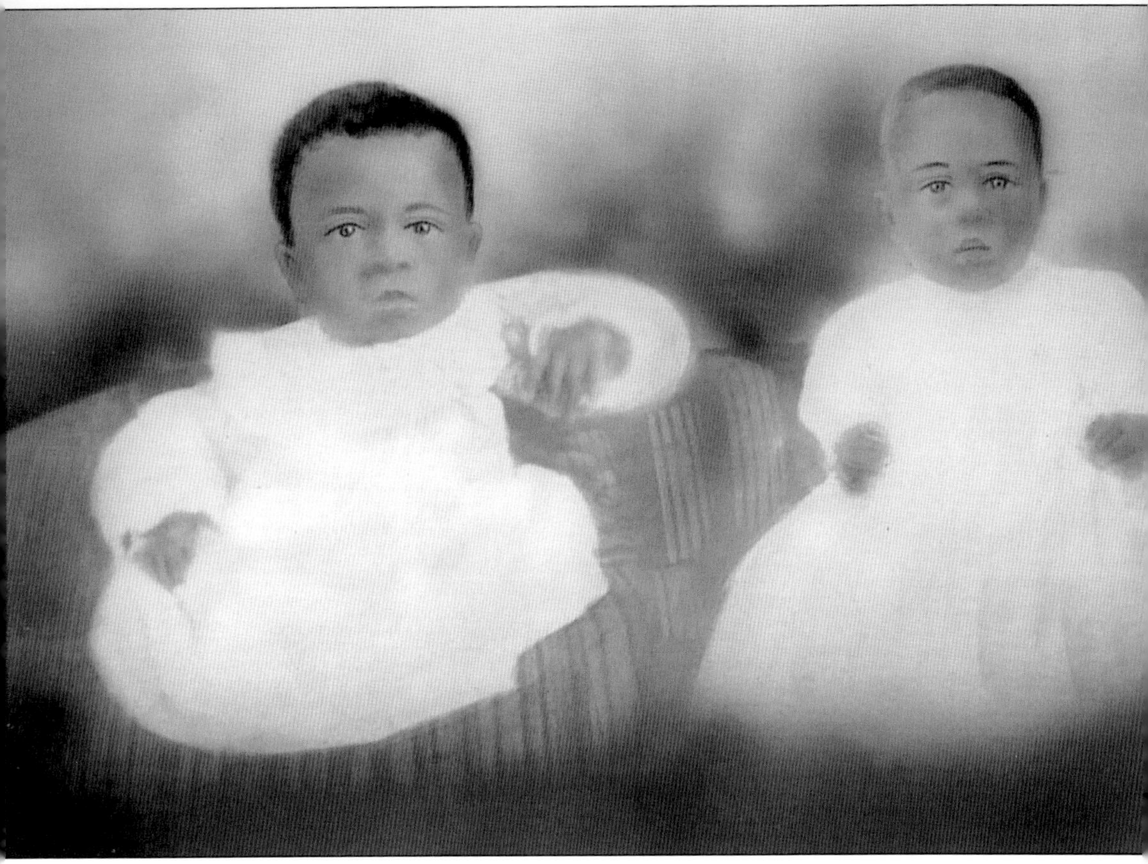

Willie Smith and his Uncle Hope Robertson appear in this painting. Both boys were born in 1908. Large families, with ten or more children, were common during the early days. The youngest siblings would often end up with nephews and nieces close to their own age as the older siblings married and started families. (Courtesy of Willie Smith.)

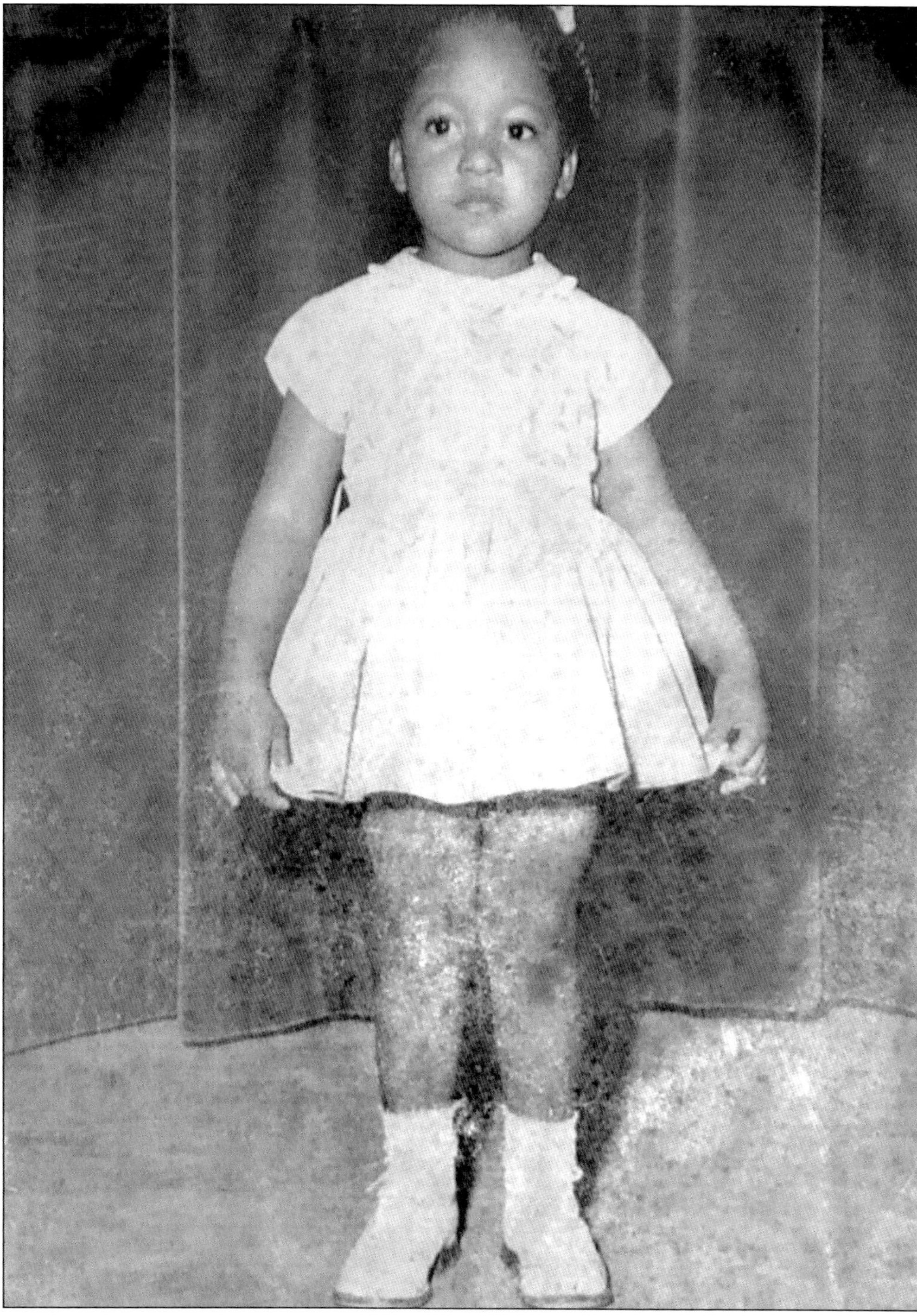

Ze Ester Michele Bush is the granddaughter of Grace Jackson. Ze Ester often modeled for photographs printed on church fans and calendars distributed by Jackson Funeral Home. (Courtesy Evelyn Bush.)

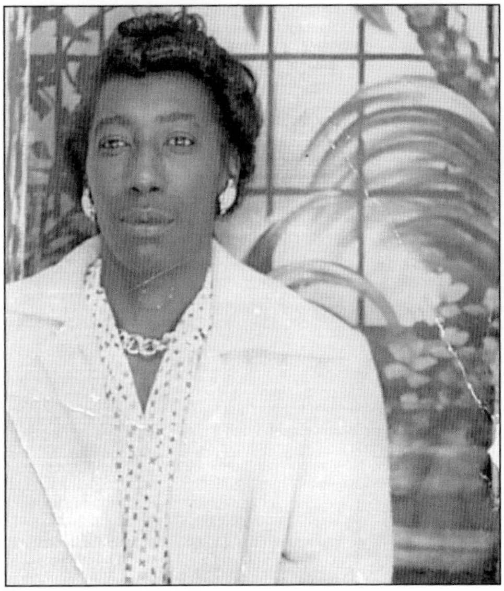
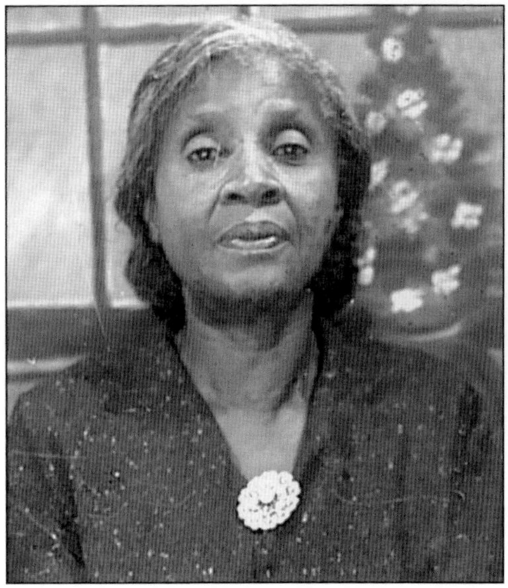

(*above, left*) Susie Mae Branch is shown in this *c*. 1950 photograph taken at the county fair. The fair was one of the few opportunities for blacks in the county to be photographed. (Courtesy Tessie Robinson.) (*above, right*) Genie Nolan (1897–1980) was the daughter of Alex and Helen Goodwin. She married Sam Nolan and raised her children in the Mount Enon community. Her children are Modris Preston, Grady Akridge, Laddie Bailey, and Geneva Locklin. (Courtesy Geneva Locklin.)

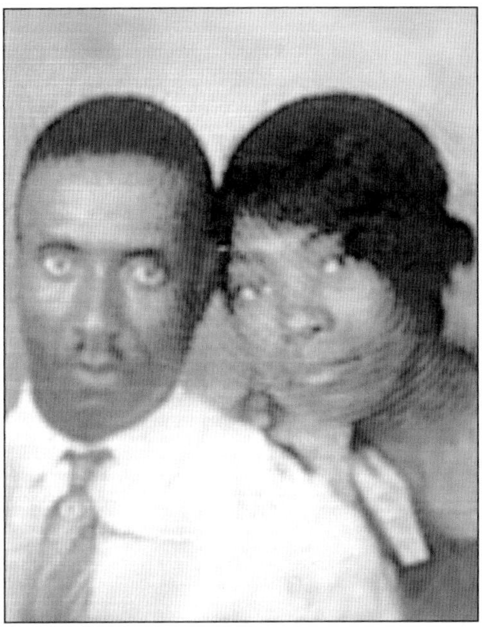
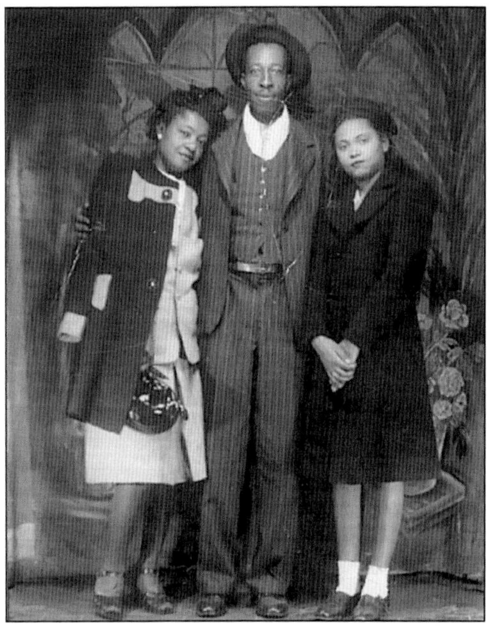

(*above, left*) Joe "Man" Adams and Rosie Robinson are shown in this *c*. 1920 photograph. Rosie enjoyed crocheting dollies, hats, and gloves. (Courtesy Tessie Robinson.) (*above, right*) Pictured from left to right are Stella Thurman Few, Frank Few, and Ruthie Manuel. These sisters and their brother, the children of Anna and Will Thurman, lived in the Mt. Enon Community and attended Mt. Enon Church *c*. 1930. (Courtesy Claudia Mae Hillman.)

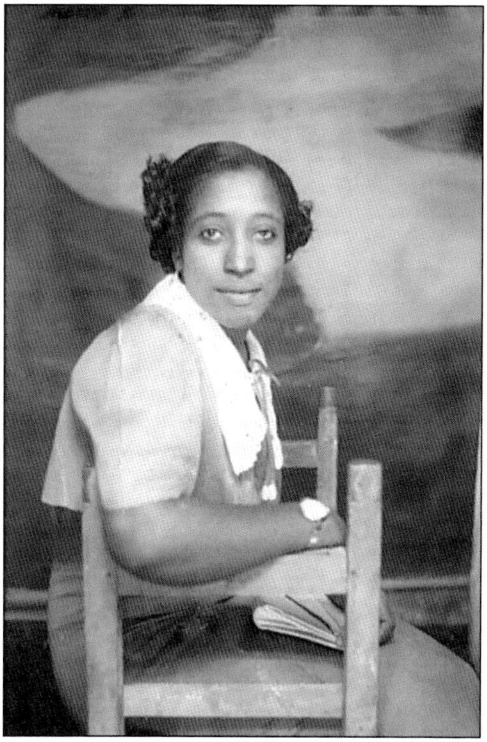

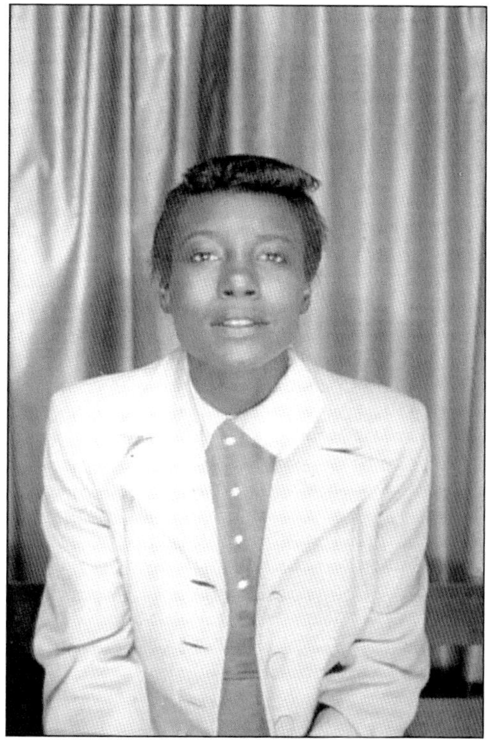

(*above, left*) This unidentified woman, pictured *c.* 1940, lived in the "Turner Town" community. "Turner Town" was a popular community for blacks who moved from farms during the 1940s and 1950s. (Courtesy Camilla Mattox.) (*above, right*) Claudine Tory is shown in this *c.* 1950 photograph, which was taken at the county fair. Young people would save money they earned picking cotton to go to the fair. (Courtesy Tessie Robinson.)

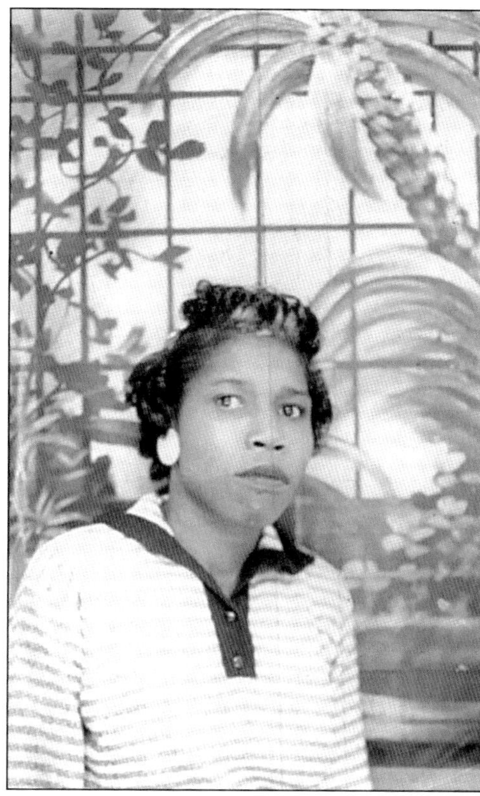

Pictured here is Gladys Henson, *c.* 1955. (Courtesy Camilla Mattox.)

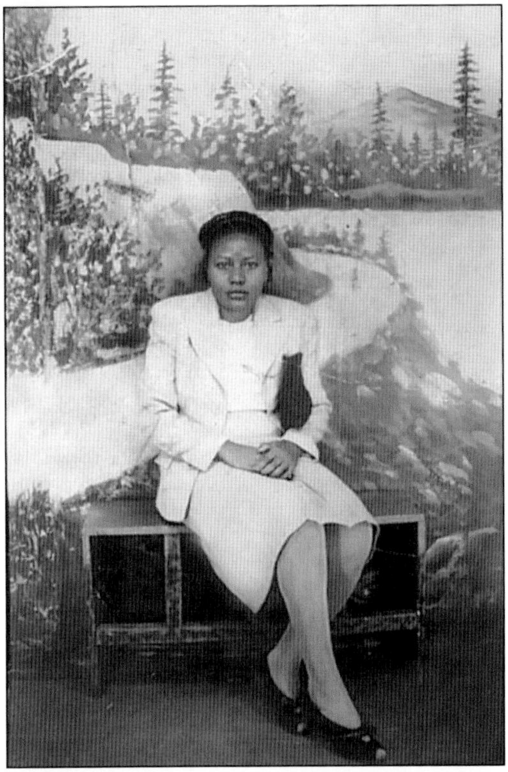

This wife of Otis Brown is pictured *c.* 1940. (Courtesy Camilla Mattox.)

Francis Maddox and her brother-in-law, Eddie Mattox, are seen in this 1930s photograph at a train depot. (Courtesy Camilla Mattox.)

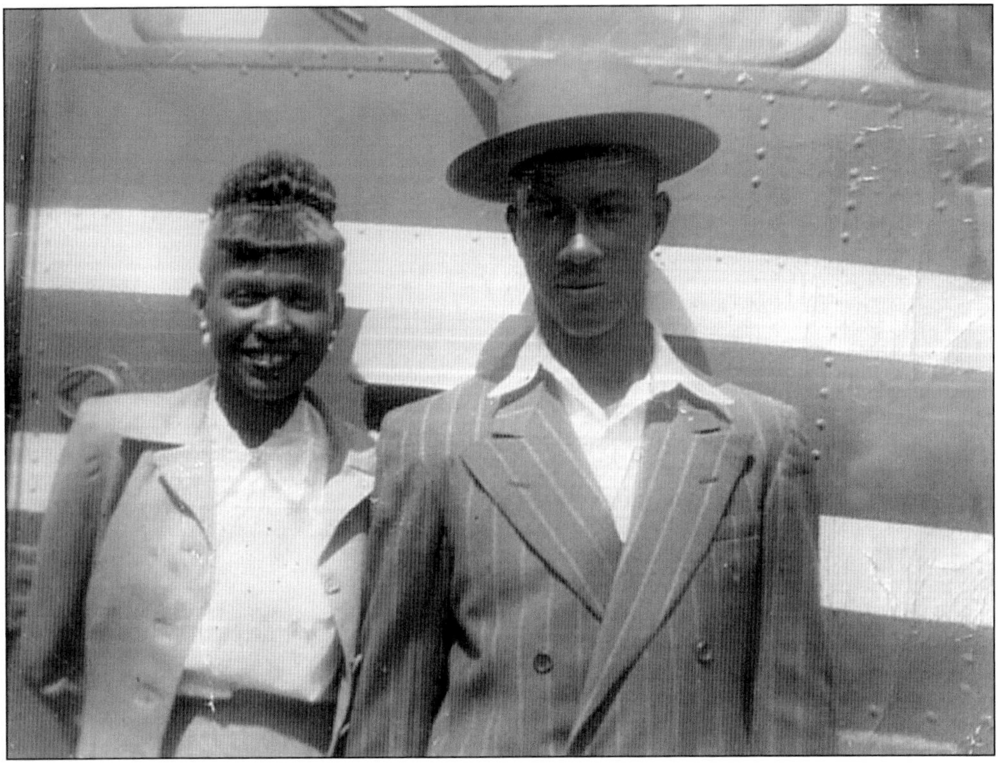

This is Jewel Thurman Glenn, the daughter of Anna and Will Thurman, *c.* 1940. Jewel moved to Pittsburgh in the 1940s like many other Southern blacks. (Courtesy Claudia Mae Hillman.)

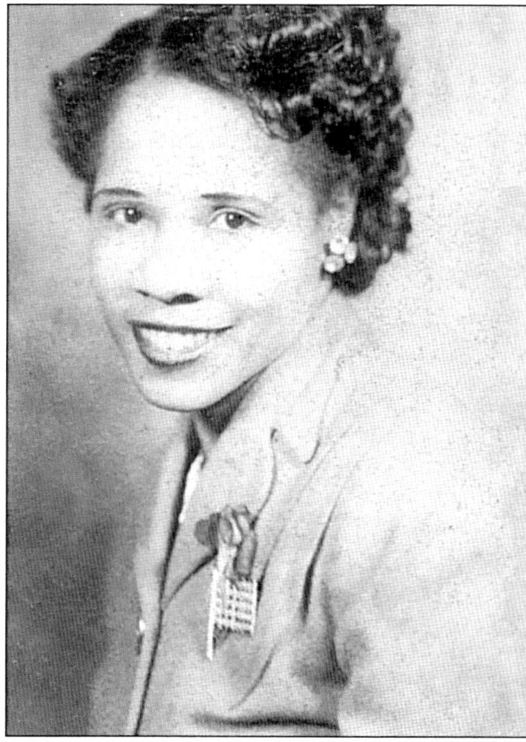

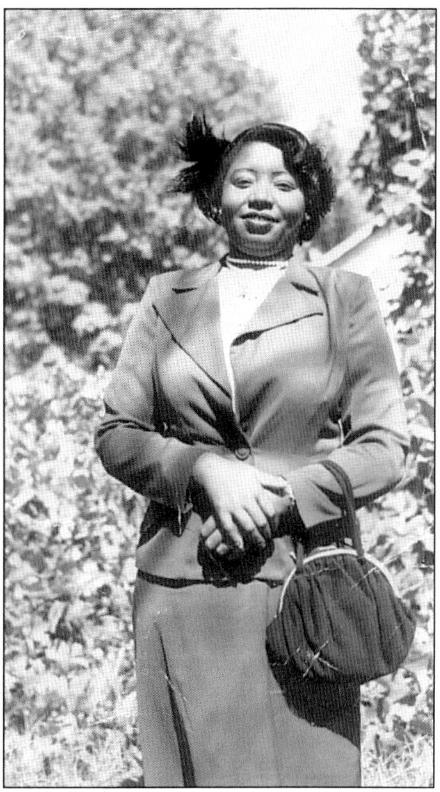

Camilla Mattox of Walton County posed for this 1950s photograph. (Courtesy Camilla Mattox.)

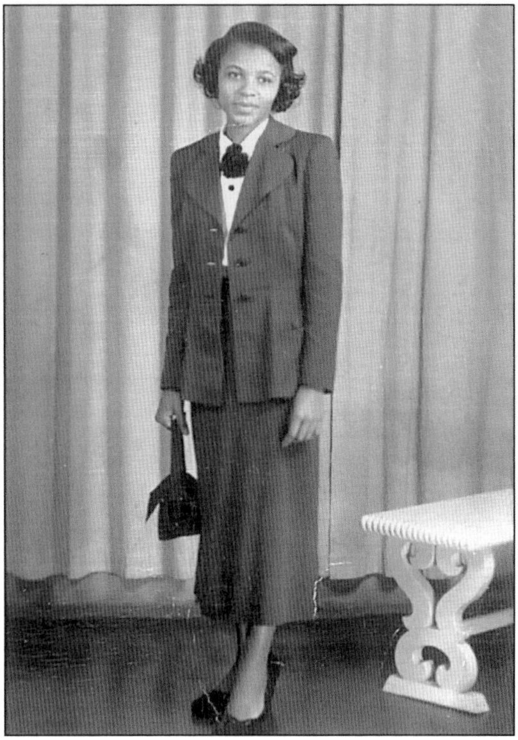

Miss Heard is the subject of this *c.* 1955 photograph. (Courtesy Camilla Mattox.)

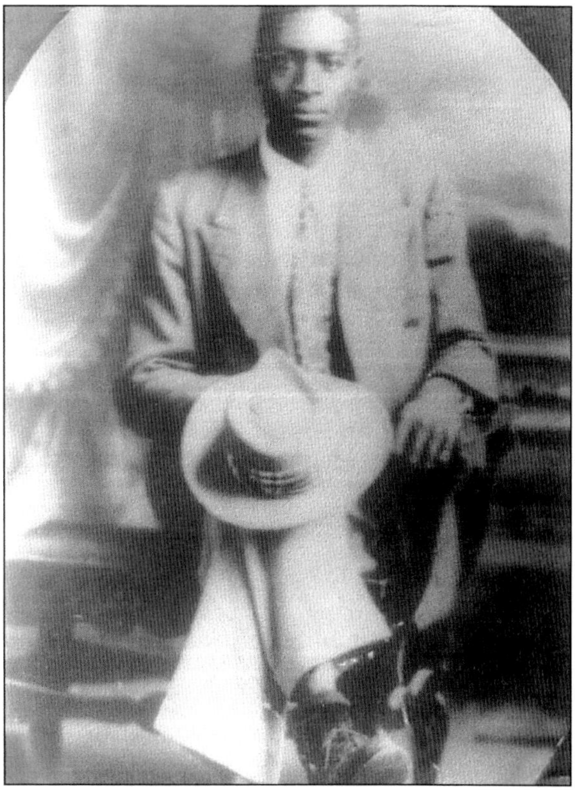

Clifton Butler (September 21, 1921–March 20, 1995) is pictured as a teen in the 1930s. He lived in Walton County all his life. (Courtesy Emma Wiseman and Marilyn Williams.)

Jack Simmons strikes a pose for the camera in front of a bedspread hanging on a clothes line, *c.* 1930. (Courtesy Catherine Jones.)

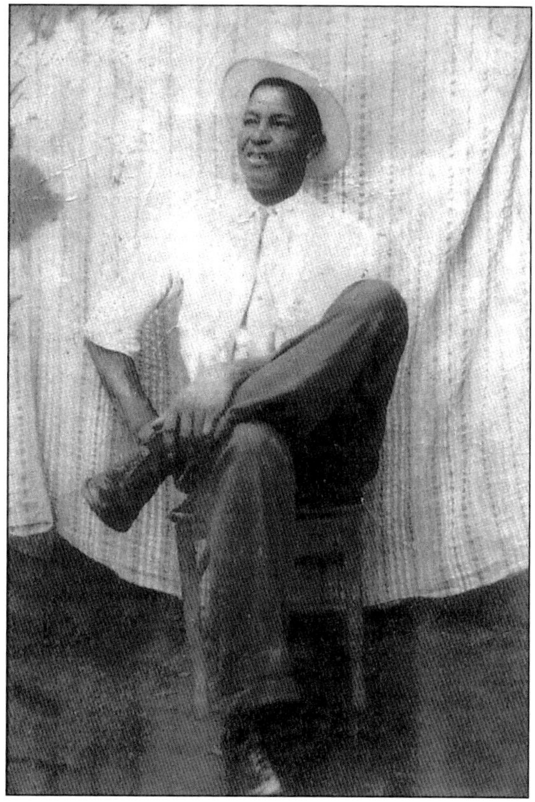

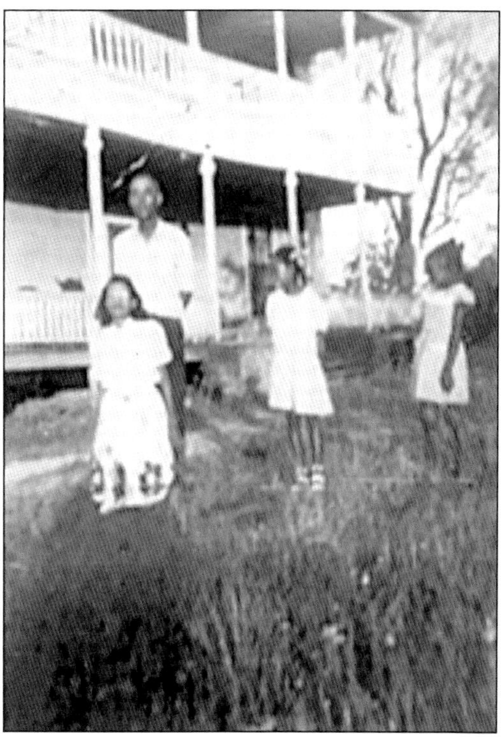

Idora Battle, Opal Jackson, Thorn Carroll, and Gladys Battle are pictured in front of the Jackson-Bush farm house in this 1945 photograph. William "Cap" Jackson was the original owner of the 600-acre farm in the Gratis community. He had crops of cotton, wheat, oats, corn, and rye, as well as 12 mules and 4 cows. Mrs. Battle lived on a nearby 85-acre farm, which she inherited from her father, Wes Patterson, who was born in Africa and brought to Georgia as a slave. Patterson purchased his farm in 1885 and Mrs. Battle was born on that farm in 1909. She lived on the property until her death in 2001. (Courtesy Evelyn Bush.)

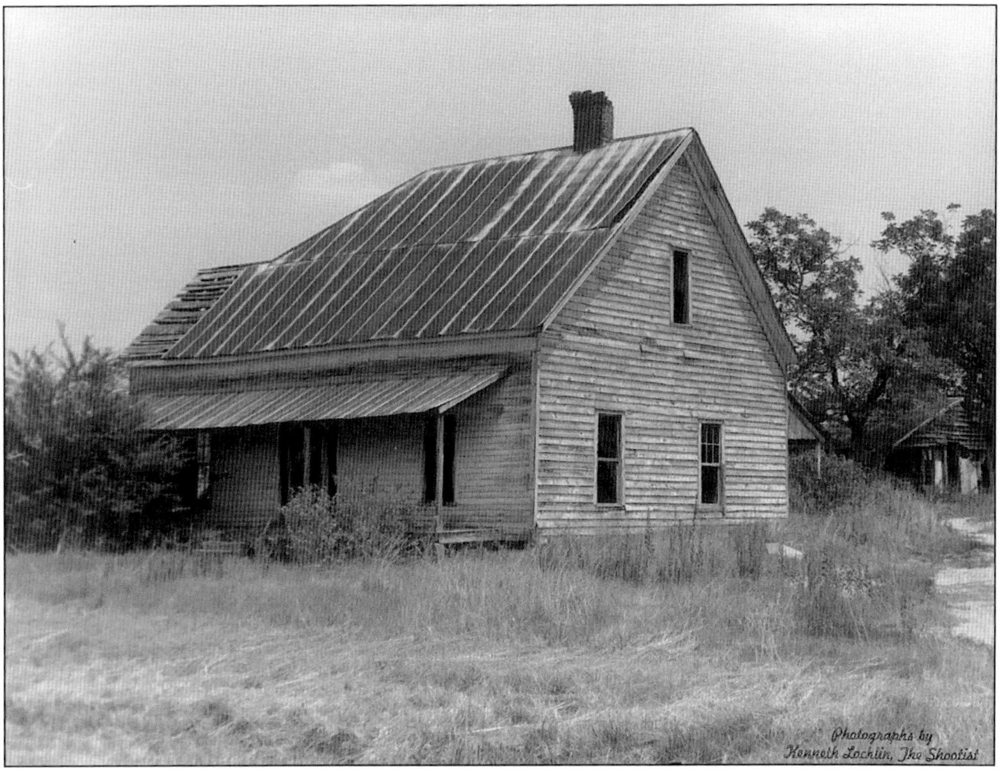

This house on Jacks Creek Road off Highway 78 in Monroe is where Geneva and Orell Locklin raised their family. (Photograph by Kenneth Locklin; Courtesy Geneva Locklin.)

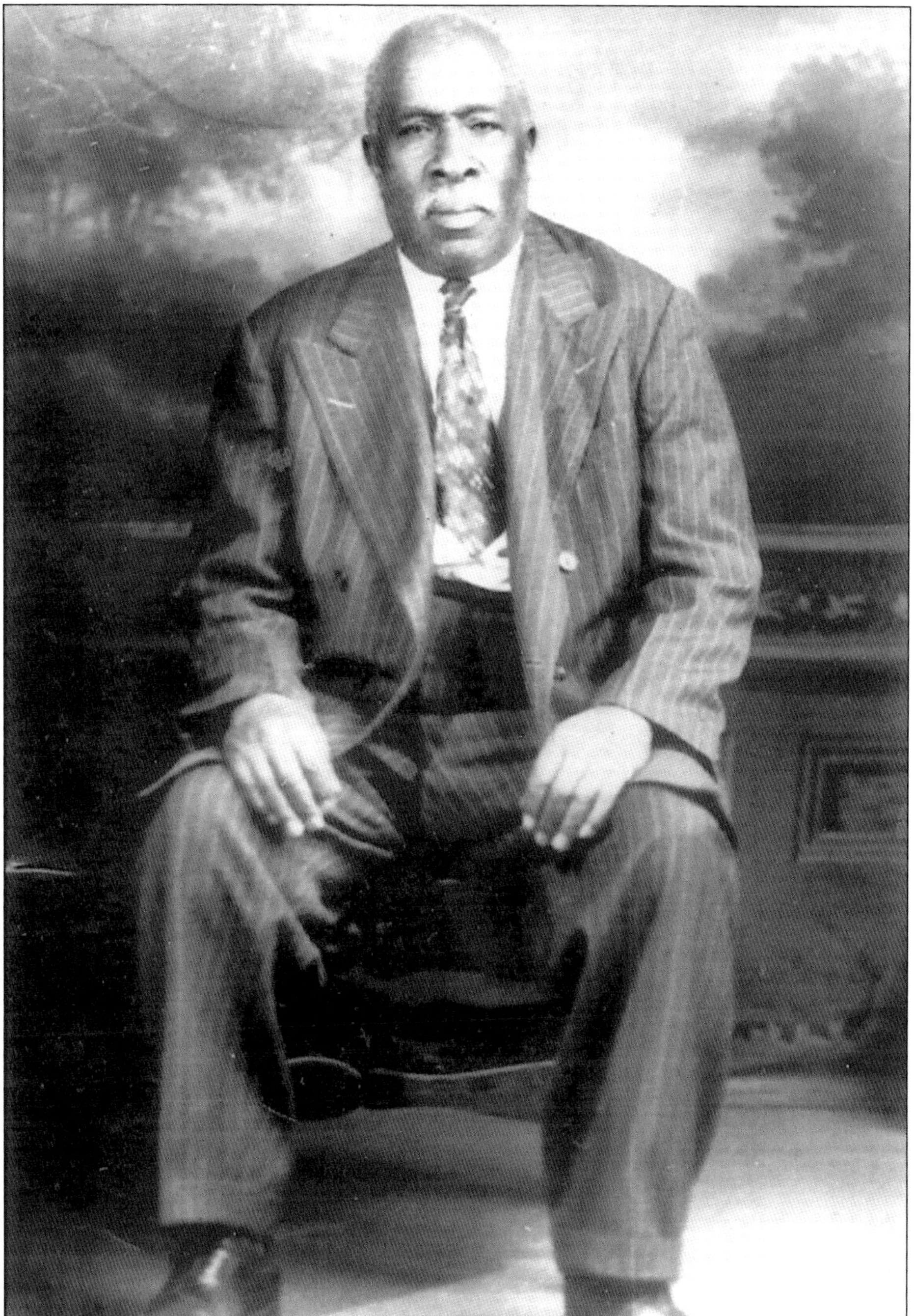

Alex Butler of Walton County was born May 12, 1878 and died December 11, 1973. Throughout his long life he was a man known to many in Walton County. He was the husband of Emily Hawk Butler and was the father of Pecolia Butler Smith, Carlton Butler, Charlie L. Butler, Curtis Butler, Norlean Butler Boals, Elsie Butler Crawford, Louise Butler Leslie, and Clifton Butler. (Courtesy Emma Wiseman and Marilyn Williams.)

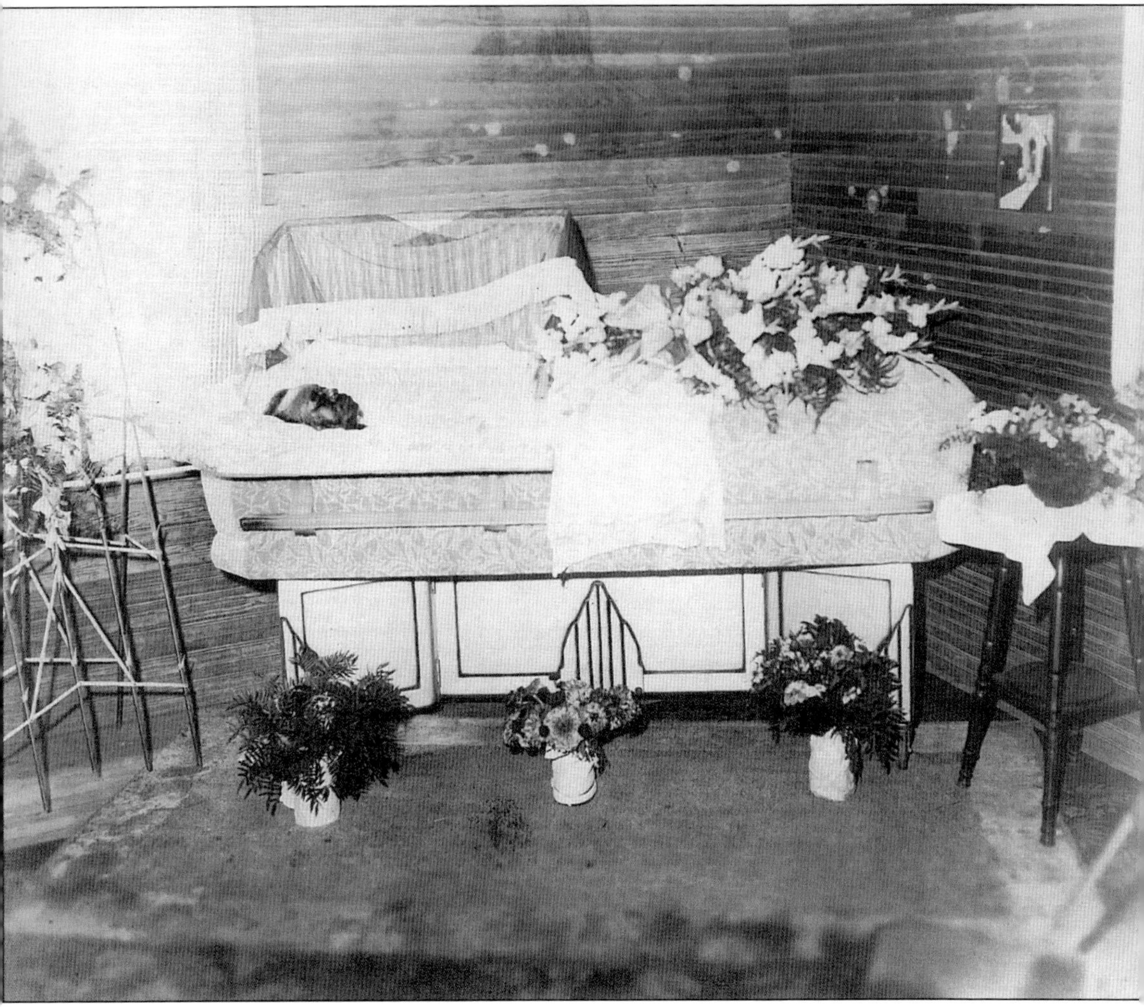

Emily Hawk Butler (May 21, 1889–September 1, 1945) is pictured in her casket in 1945. It was customary for families to lay deceased family members in state at their homes before the funeral. Emily Hawk Butler was the mother of Clifton Butler, Charlie L. Butler, Carlton Butler, Curtis Butler, Norlean Boal, Elsie Crawford, Pecolia Smith, and Loise Leslie. (Courtesy Emma Wiseman and Marilyn Williams.)

Two

Church and Religion

Keeping The Faith

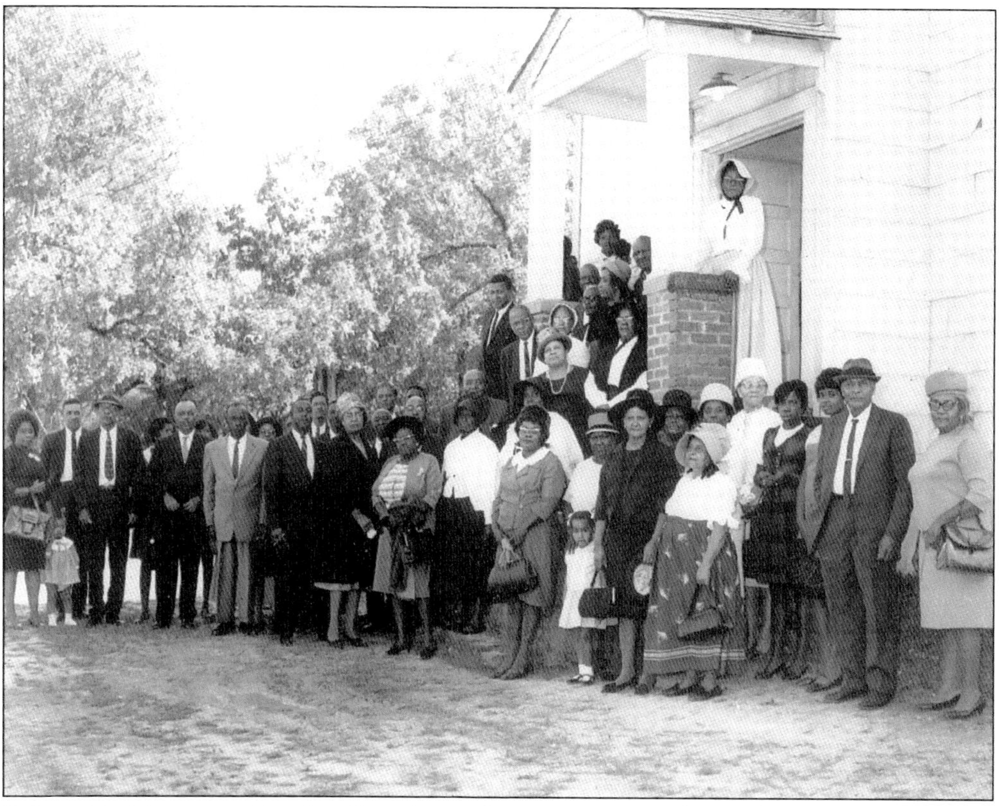

Fellowship Missionary Baptist Church members are seen in front of the church in 1968. (Courtesy Fellowship Missionary Baptist Church.)

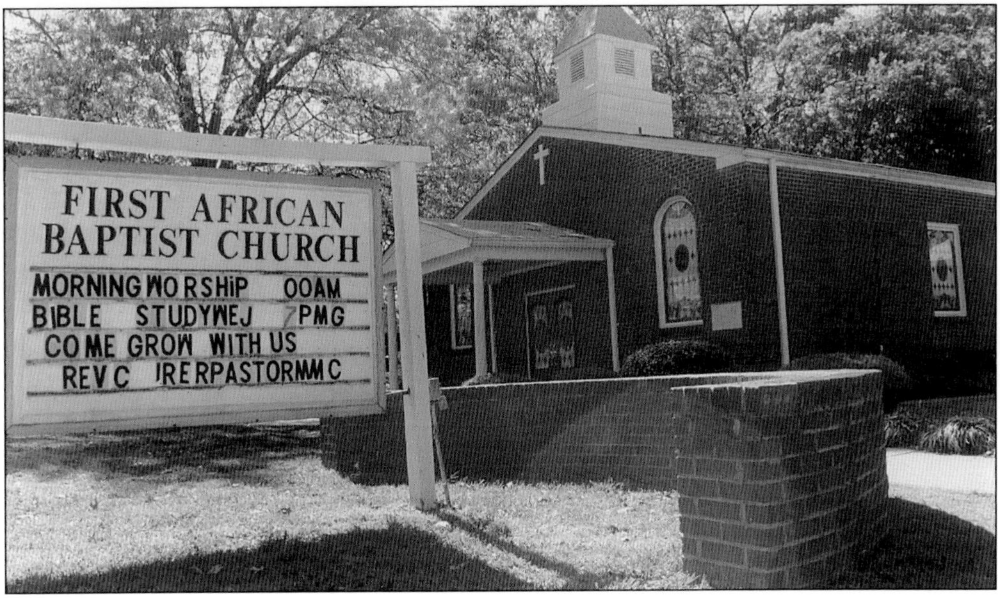

First African Baptist Church, located at 130 Tyler Drive, was established in 1868. A log cabin was built on one-half acre of land on Alcova Street. A guarantee was made by George Selman that a piece of land south of the log cabin would be used for worship in 1870. The log cabin was replaced by a wooden structure and the church was given the name the Colored Baptist Church; its first pastor was Rev. Jesse Gilbert. Later, it was renamed Zion Hill. In 1949 two Baptist churches, Tabernacle Baptist and Zion Hill Baptist, decided to unite under the name the First African Baptist Church ("First A.B."). The merger did not last long, however. The church has experienced noteworthy growth in church programs, auxiliaries, and official staff over the years. (Photograph courtesy Wes Swietek, *The Walton Tribune*.)

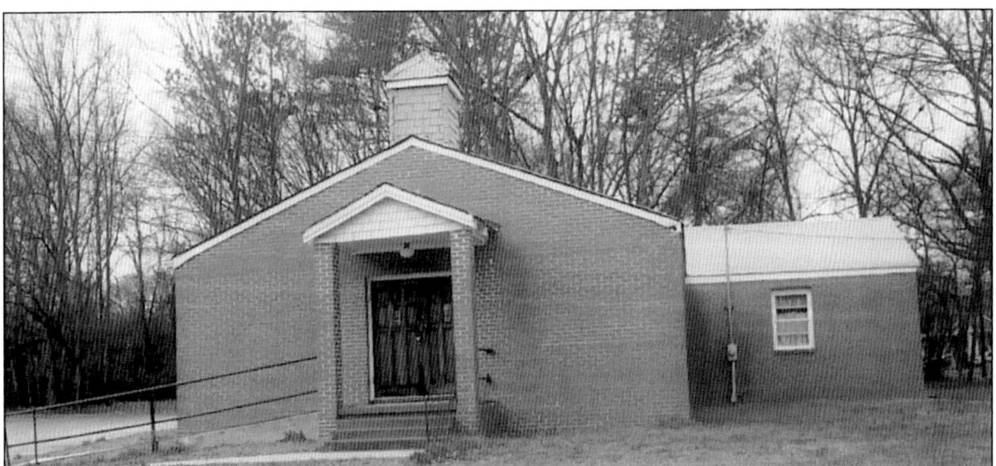

Triumph the Church and Kingdom of God in Christ, located at 443 Ash Street in Monroe, was established January 20, 1902 by the constituent assembly under the administration of Father Elias Dempsey Smith. Fr. Dempsey Smith became an apostle, priest, and king of Triumph the Church and Kingdom of God in Christ in 1915. Presently Bishop Zephaniah Swindle is the Head Apostle and District Apostle W.R. Malcolm is over District 1. (Photograph by Lynn Camp.)

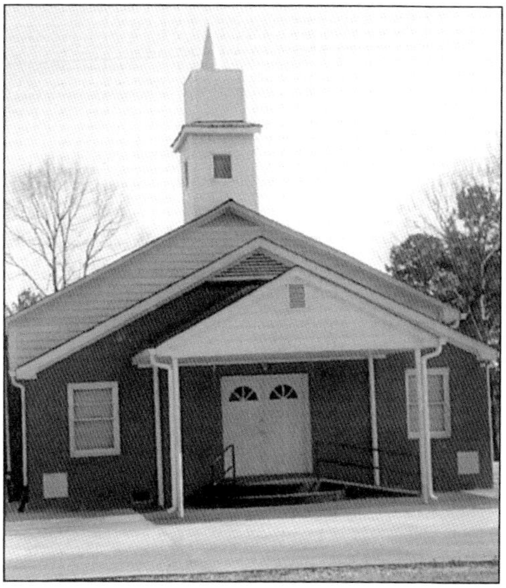

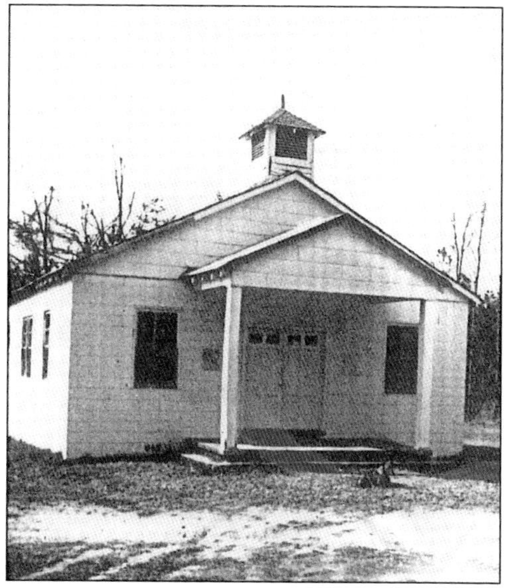

(*above, left*) Mount Enon Baptist Church was organized around 1864 on land given to Solomon Locklin for a home site. Locklin asked J.B. Locklin, a white man, to give the land for a church and he agreed. A brush arbor was erected and eight slaves who were members of the white church transferred their membership. (Photograph by Lynn Camp). (*above, right*) Pictured here is the early Prospect A.M.E. Zion Church of Walton County. (Courtesy Mollie Butler Lewis.)

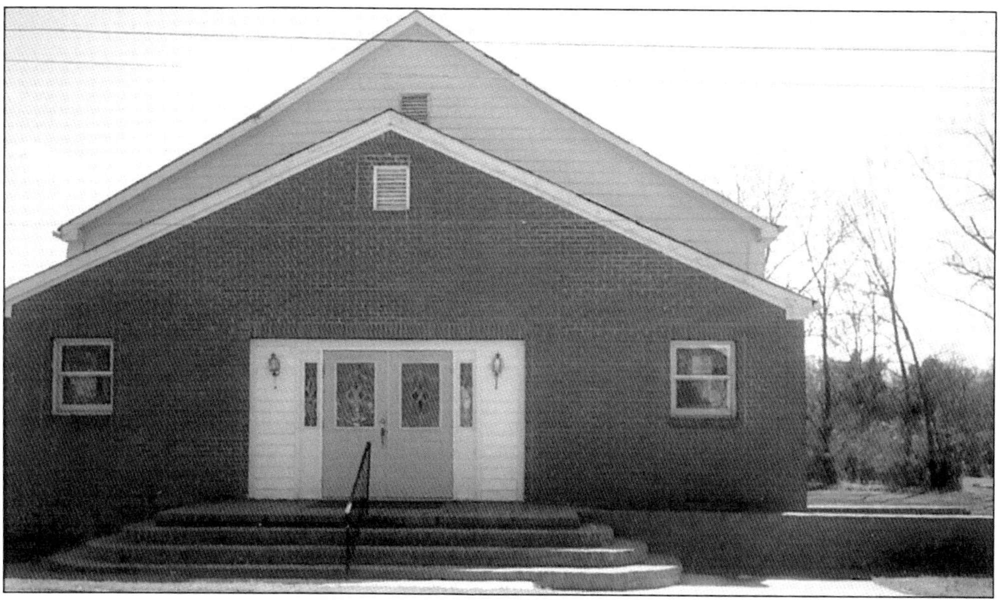

This is Cargle Chapel African Methodist Episcopal Church of Social Circle. During the 1800s a congregation known as African Methodist met in a cotton gin beside the railroad track. One of the members, Deacon Howard Cargill, donated a parcel of land at 300 Popular Street in Social Circle and William Hill drew the blueprints for the church. The members saved their nickels, dimes, and quarters to build the church in 1919. Charter members were William Hill, Susan Hill, Prisilla Walker, and Howard Cargill. (Photograph by Lynn Camp.)

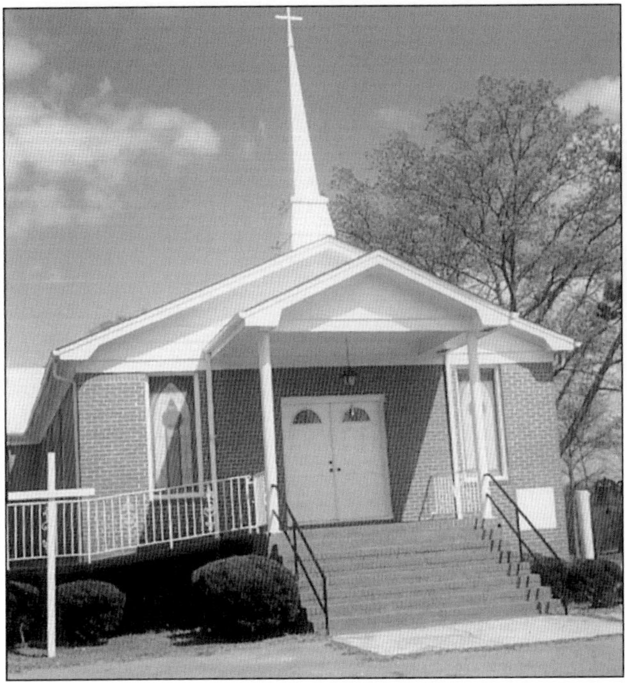

Spring Hill A.M.E. Zion Church was founded in 1885 when two ministers and a few "god-fearing people who were concerned about their souls and those of others" began meeting under a brush arbor down at a spring. The two ministers, Rev. Joe Hendricks (Methodist) and Rev. Kelly Lewis (Baptist), preached alternately and decided the church would follow the denomination of the minister who was first to take in a member. Lula Ansley joined the church under Rev. Joe Hendrich, so the church was named Spring Hill A.M.E. Zion Church. (Photograph by Lynn Camp.)

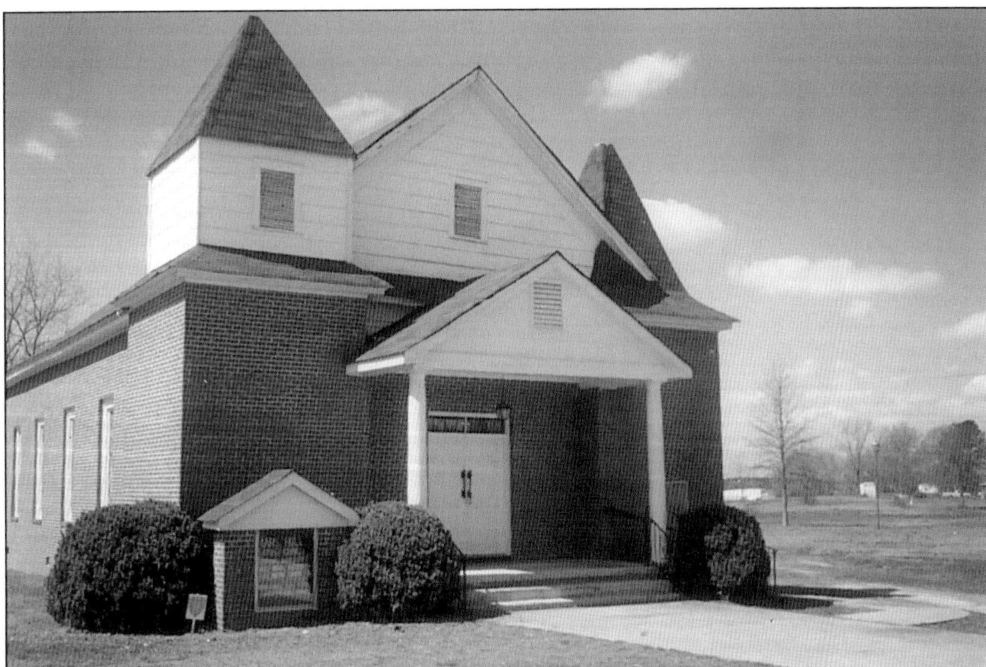

Mars Hill Baptist Church in Social Circle was organized in 1868. A small group decided to organize a Baptist church as the John Wesley A.M.E. Zion Church was the only black church in town at the time. They met under a brush arbor until they built their first church building. Early pastors included Rev. Terrell Abercrombie, Rev. Josh Henderson, Rev. W.A. Crittenden, I.J. Means, Rev. Joe Harris, and Rev. J.T. Saxton. (Photograph by Lynn Camp.)

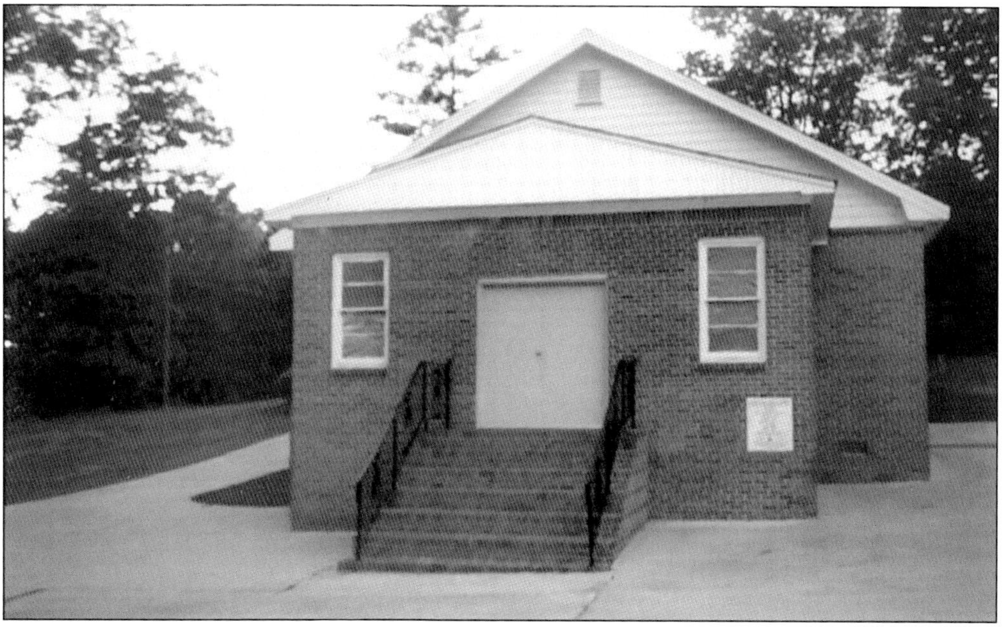

Browns Hill Baptist Church, located on Browns Hill Church Road in Monroe, was founded in 1867 when "a few of God's children came together down by the creek and began worshipping and praising God under an old brush arbor." A church was built later on land donated by a neighbor. That structure was destroyed by a storm; the second was destroyed by fire. The third one is the structure used today. Early pastors included Rev. John Henry Barnes, Rev. John Henry Price, Rev. John Henry Stephens, Rev. O.F. Maddox, and Rev. J.L. Byrd, who pastored the church from 1949 to 1982 (33 years). (Courtesy of Olia Pitts.)

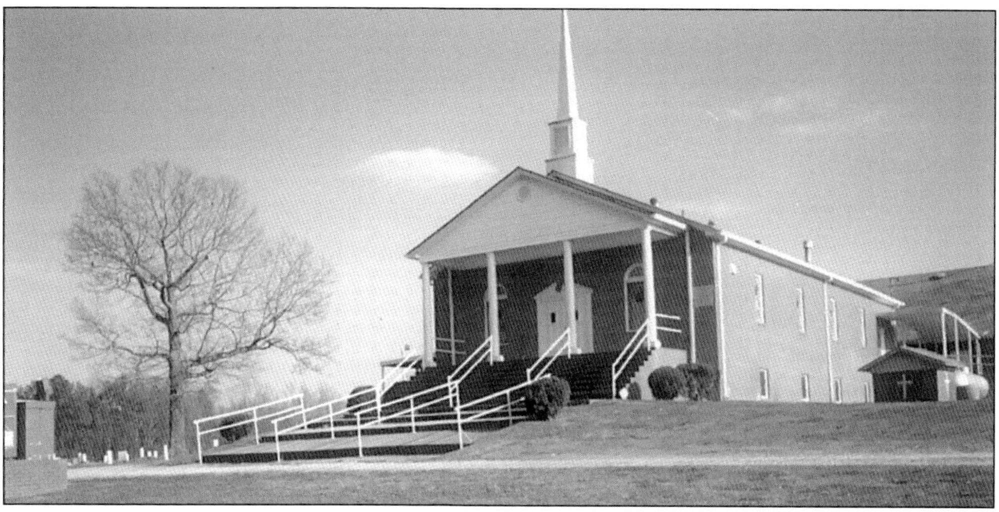

Macedonia Baptist Church, located at 1519 Macedonia Church Road in Monroe, was organized in the 1880s by Pastor Kelly Lewis. The first church was built on land purchased from Isaac Keeton. A second church was constructed during the 1890s. In 1914 a wooden structure was purchased from First Baptist Church of Monroe and moved in sections using mules and wagons. Rev. Grady H. Henricks Jr. was installed as pastor of Macedonia Baptist Church in 1993 and continues to serve in 2003. (Photograph by Lynn Camp.)

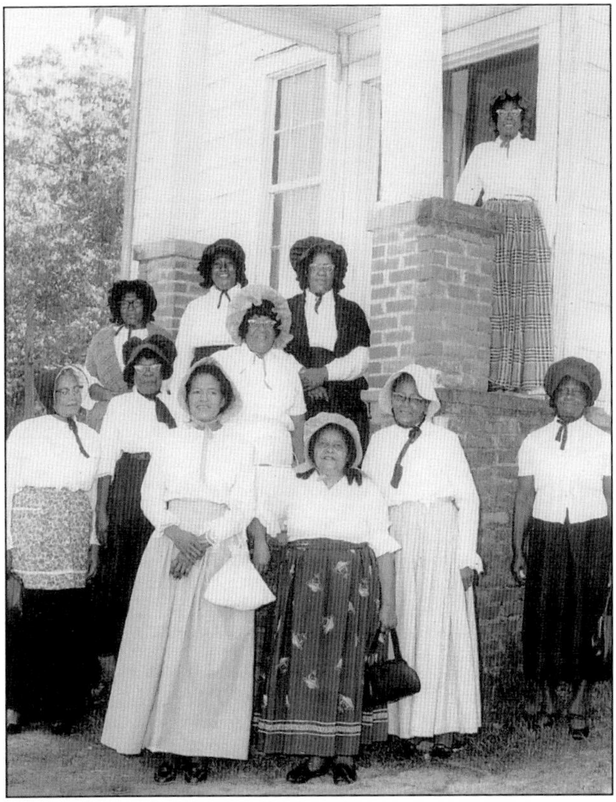

The Fellowship Missionary Baptist Church 1968 Mother's Board included Ruth Knox, Minnie Caudle, Marie Hill, Flossie Gober, Popie Wright, Inell Brown, Effie Caudle, Inez Ivey, Jessie Ivey, Gladys Jackson, and Gwendolyn Smith. (Courtesy Fellowship Missionary Baptist Church.)

The Fellowship Missionary Baptist Church 1968 Deacon' s board included Willie Taylor, Sanford Ivey, David Hyman Sr., Calvester Gober, Herman Strickland, Eddie Pitts, Willie Ivey, Arthur Jackson, and Rev. Philip Culbreath, pastor. (Courtesy Fellowship Missionary Baptist Church.)

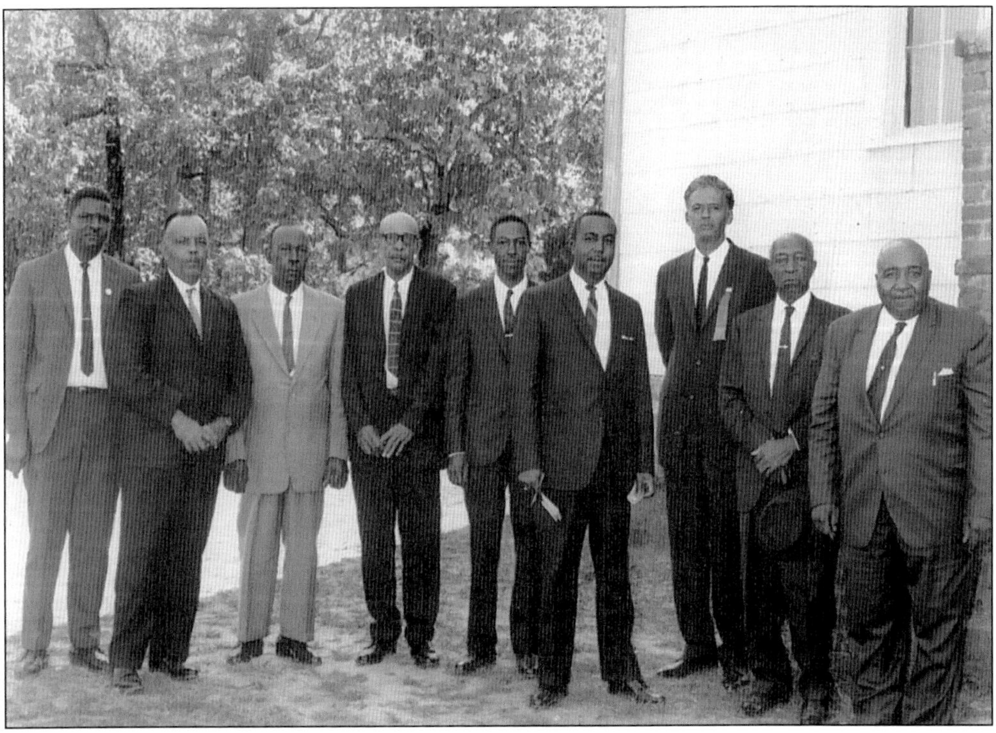

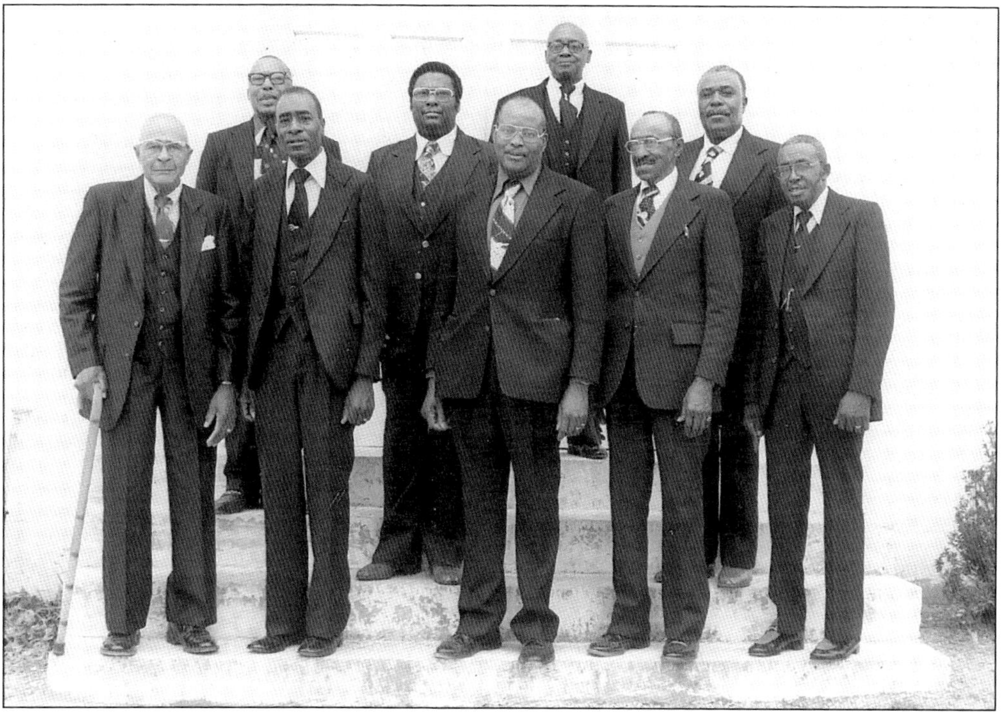

Pictured are the deacons of Good Hope Baptist Church in the 1970s. From left to right are (front row) John Hillman, Clifton Butler, Arthur Akridge, and James (Peter) Perkins; (middle row) Joseph Biggs and John L. Locklin; (back row) Euell Byrd and Rev. J.L. Byrd. (Courtesy Emma Wiseman and Marilyn Williams.)

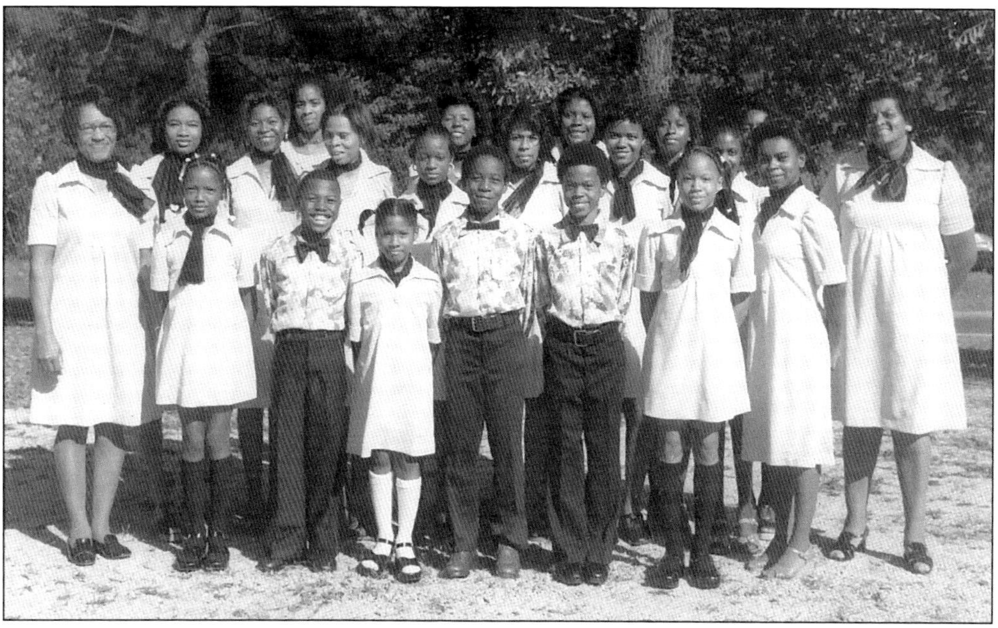

The Youth Choir of Good Hope Baptist Church is shown in this 1970s photograph. (Courtesy Emma Wiseman and Marilyn Williams.)

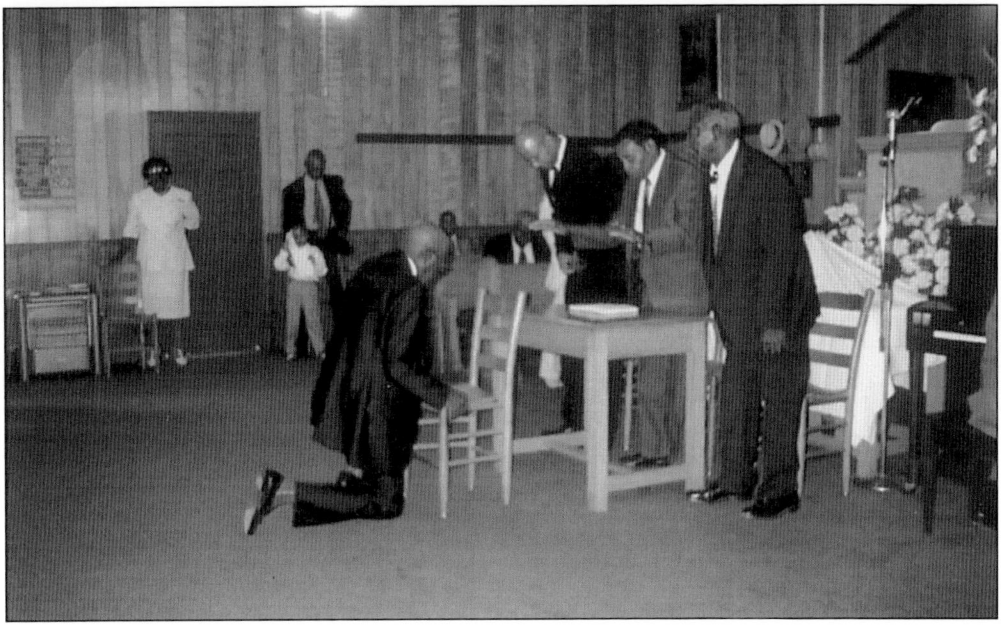

Deacons of Good Hope Baptist Church are shown during morning devotion. Deacon James Perkins (kneeling) is pictured praying. An enduring tradition in some churches in Walton County, the devotion featured the deacons kneeling at a chair and praying "a speech prayer" and leading the congregation in "lined hymns." (Photograph by Lynn Camp.)

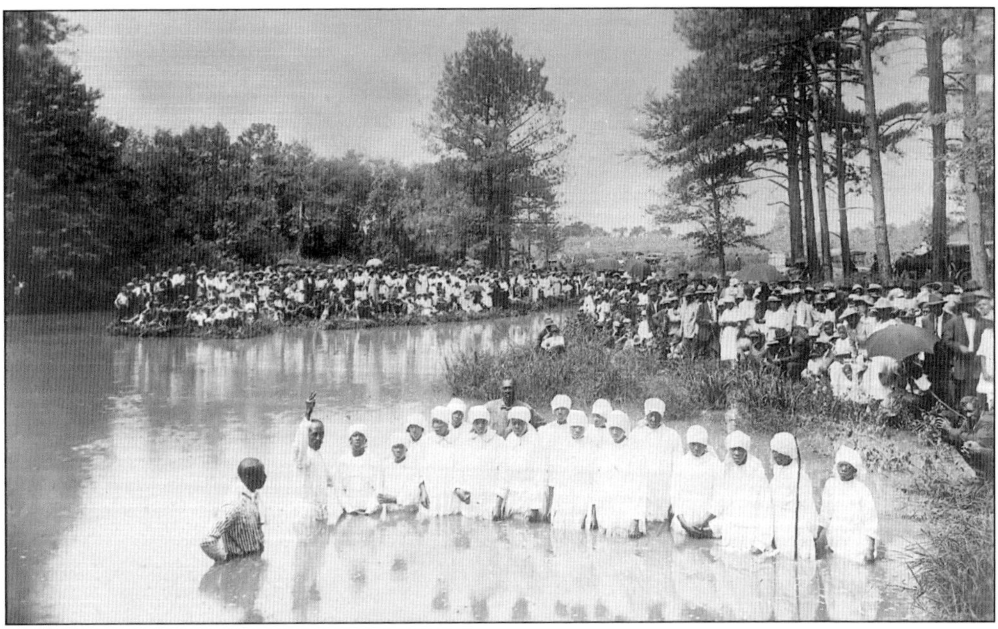

River baptisms are a lost tradition in Walton County as churches now have indoor pools. One minister in nearby Barrow County will still perform a river baptism upon request in the Appalachee River, which spans the Walton-Barrow County lines. This *c.* 1930 photograph, believed to have been taken on the Appalachee River, shows a congregation on the riverbanks during a baptism. (From the E.M. Carnes Collection; Courtesy Larry Witcher.)

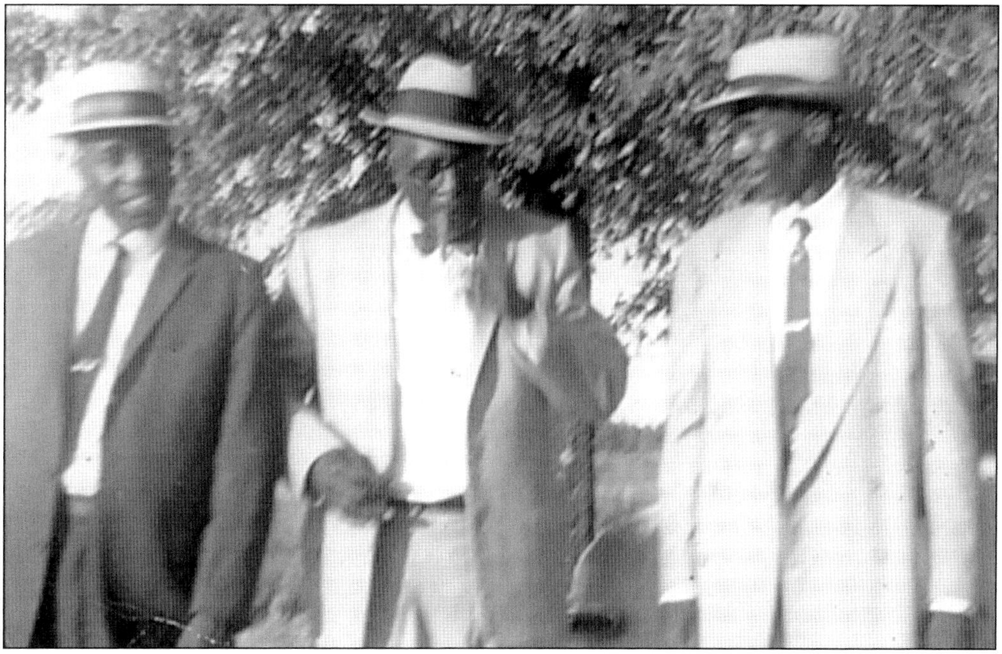

This photograph was taken on Homecoming Day at Good Hope Baptist Church in Good Hope, Georgia, in the 1960s. From left to right are Carlton Butler, Charlie L. Butler, and Clifton Butler. Family and friends anticipate this annual gathering on the fourth Sunday in August. (Courtesy Emma Wiseman and Marilyn Williams.)

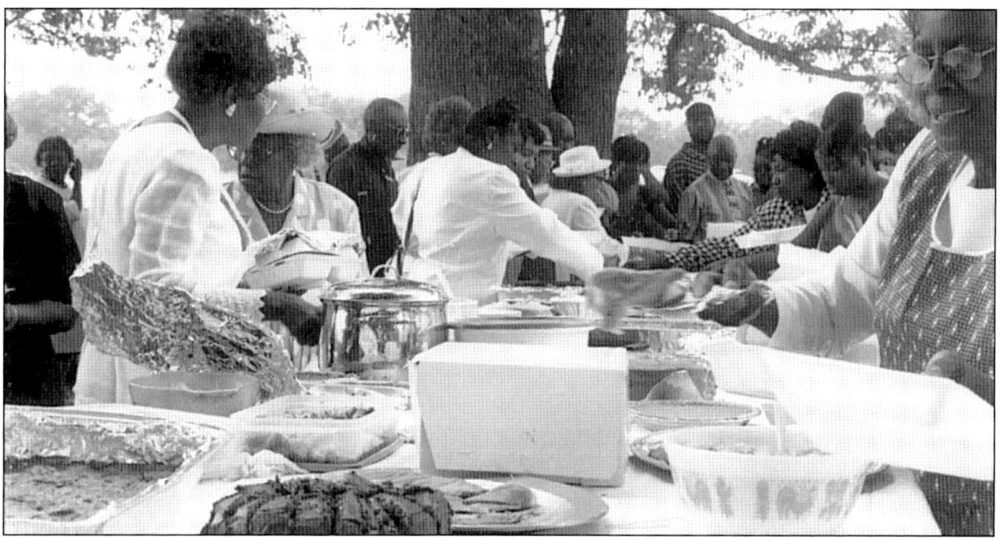

This is a picture of Homecoming Day with Dinner on the Grounds at Good Hope Baptist Church in Good Hope, Georgia. The church was established in 1873 under a brush arbor with Richard Baldwin, Cobb Harris, and Pete Colquitt. Members of the Mt. Perry Missionary Baptist Church in nearby Bishop, they felt a need to organize a church in this community because worshippers had to travel so far in their wagons to attend the nearest church. Pictured to the far right is Lillian Perkins, who joined the Good Hope Baptist Church in 1944. (Photograph by Amiee Schmidt, Georgia Council for the Arts.)

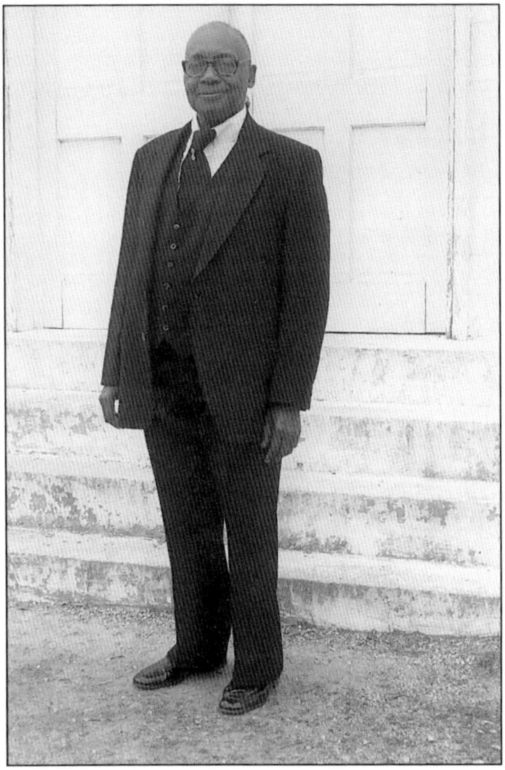

Rev. J.L. Byrd, beloved pastor of Good Hope Baptist Church 1947–1995 and Pastor Emeritus from 1995 until his homegoing in 1999, is shown here. The church has had only seven pastors, including Rev. Jessie Gilbert 1876–1885, Rev. Square Hull 1884–1892, Rev. Harrison Vincent 1892–1946, Rev. J.L. Bryd, Rev. W.L. Norman 1995–1996, Rev. Andrew L. Howard, and present pastor Rev. Nathan Durham. (Courtesy Emma Wiseman and Marilyn Williams.)

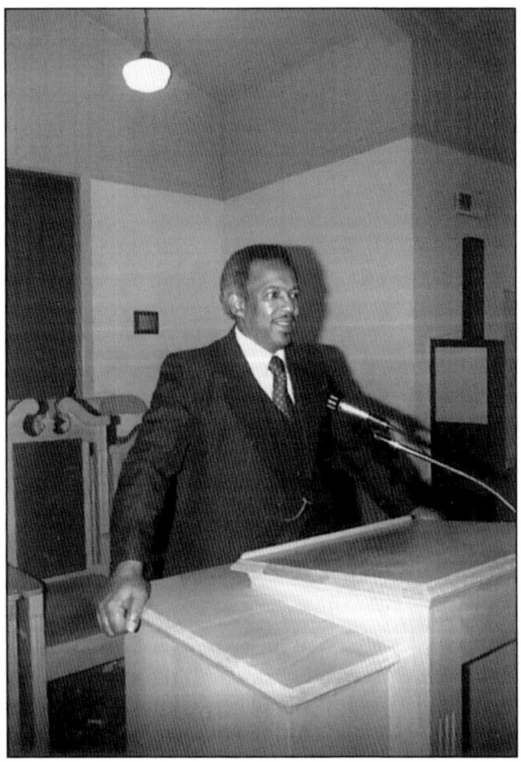

Rev. Clarence Grier Jr. is pictured *c.* 1968. He is the 19th pastor of First African Baptist Church and has served as pastor since 1968. He succeeded Rev. E.L. Ellis Jr., who served for three years. Under Reverend Grier's leadership the church has grown tremendously to become one of the largest black congregations in Monroe. (Courtesy Rev. Clarence Grier Jr.)

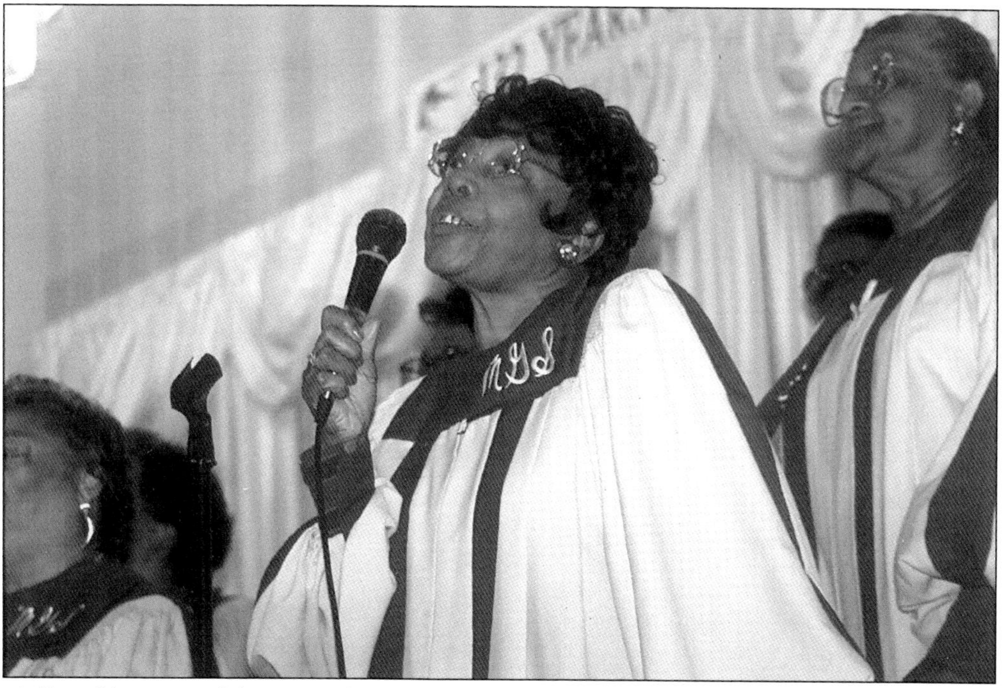

Idell Locklin, one of the original members of the Missionary Gospel Singers, is seen singing at the 45th anniversary celebration in 2000. Also pictured in Consa Vella Shields. (Courtesy Wes Swietek, *The Walton Tribune*.)

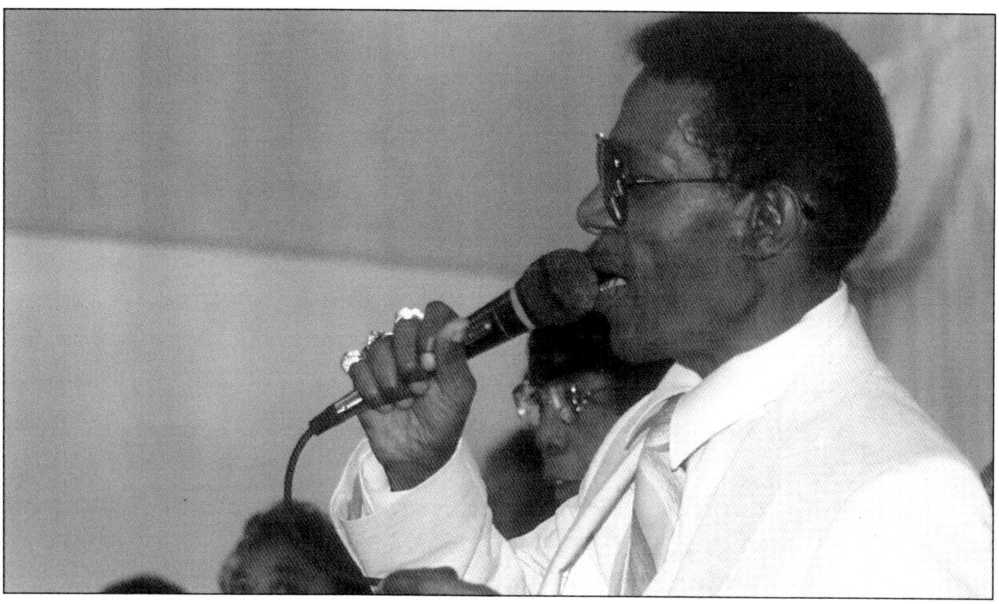

Bobby Whitlock, the only male member of the Missionary Gospel Singers, leads a song for the 45th anniversary celebration. Bobby, who once sang with the Christianaires of Chicago, says he enjoys being the ladies' escort. The Missionary Gospel Singers celebrated having been together as a group singing in the community for 45 years in April 2000. (Courtesy Wes Swietek, *The Walton Tribune*.)

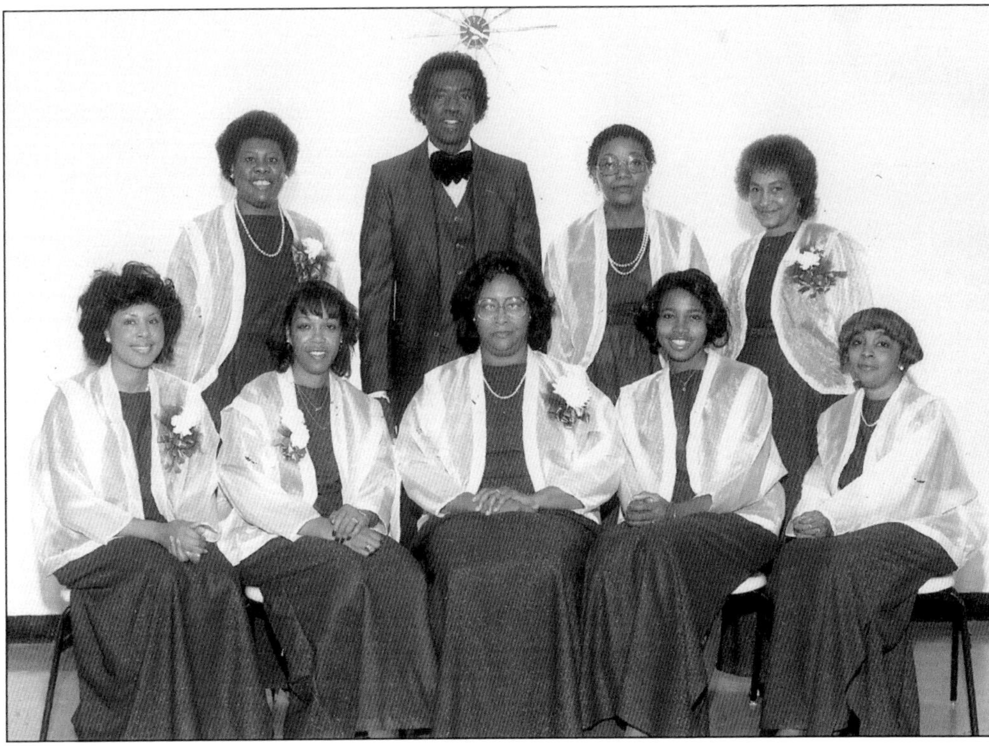

The Floyd Family Fan Club is pictured here. From left to right are (front row) Teressa A. Sorrells, Evelyn Floyd, Iunice Foster, Rosie Johnson Crawford, and Patsy Sanders; (back row) ? Smith, Albert Floyd, Annie Meadows, and Betty Foster. (Courtesy of Teressa Sorrells.)

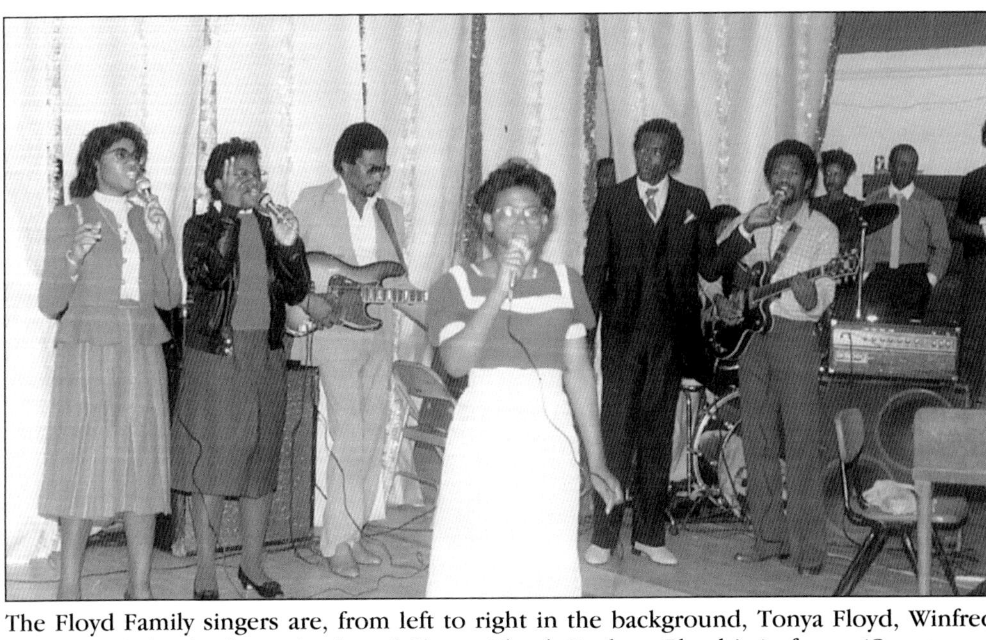

The Floyd Family singers are, from left to right in the background, Tonya Floyd, Winfred Floyd, Paul Floyd, Albert Floyd, and Shawn Floyd; Paulette Floyd is in front. (Courtesy of Teressa Sorrells.)

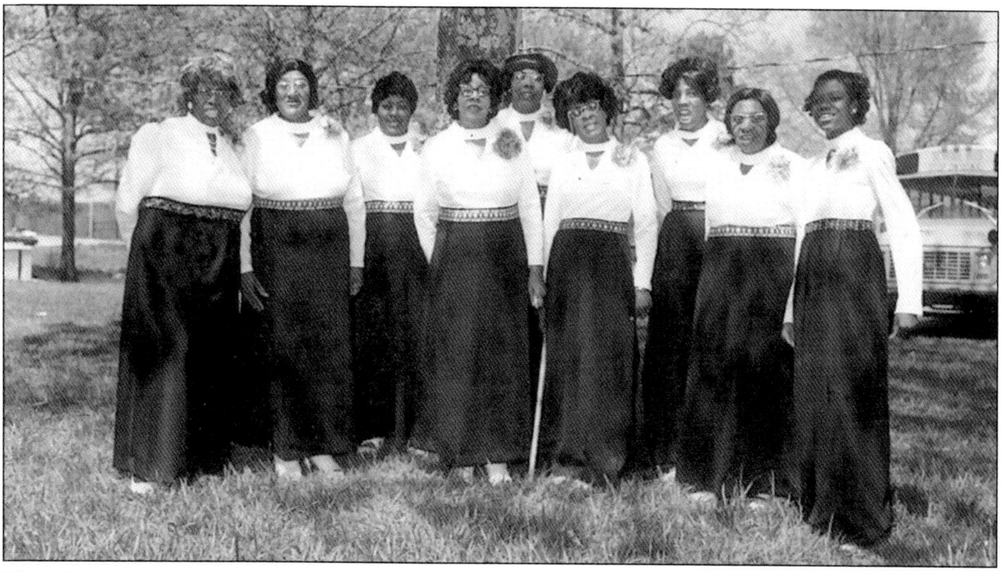

The Missionary Gospel Singers are shown in this 1960s photograph in front of First African Baptist Church. From left to right are Emma Rome Jackson, Isabell Spearman, Margaret Manuel, Zelma Biggs, Idell Locklin, Myrtice Perkins, Jennie Landers, Gertrude Witcher, and Sharon Phillips. The group organized in 1950 when Idell Locklin began singing with her mother, Gertrude Witcher, and sister-in-law, Cora Witcher. They made their first public appearance in 1955 at the Fire Baptized Holiness Church, which was holding service in a tent, on Maple Street. Lola Mae Smith was their pianist when the group started, but after her death the group became popular as a cappella singers. (Courtesy Idell Locklin.)

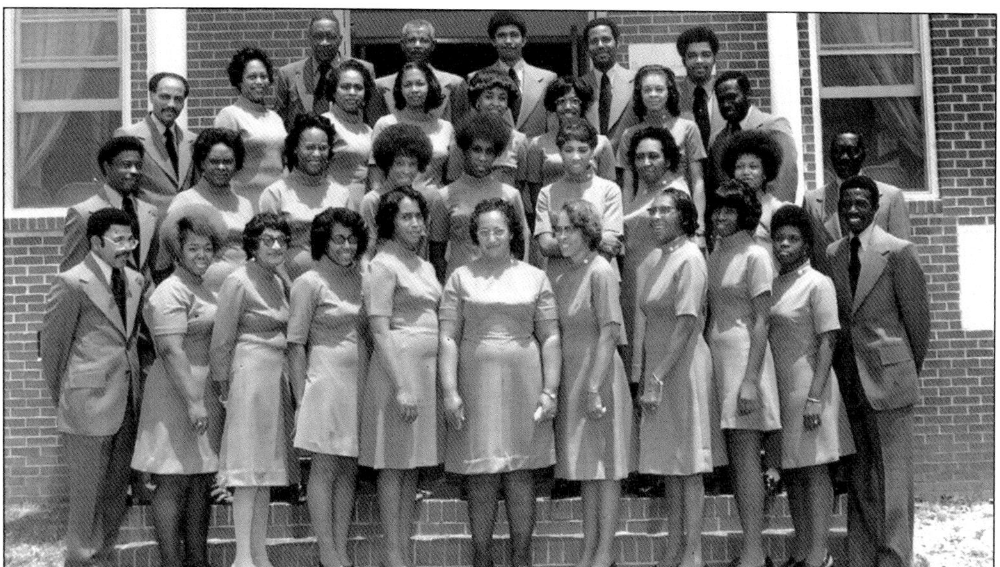

The Campton Gospel Chorus was founded by Earl Broughton Sr. in 1955. Broughton wanted to "bring the Methodists and Baptists together." Macedonia Baptist Church, Prospect A.M.E. Church, and Spring Hill A.M.E. Church members joined to form the chorus, which sang alternately at the three churches. (Courtesy Donald Hector.)

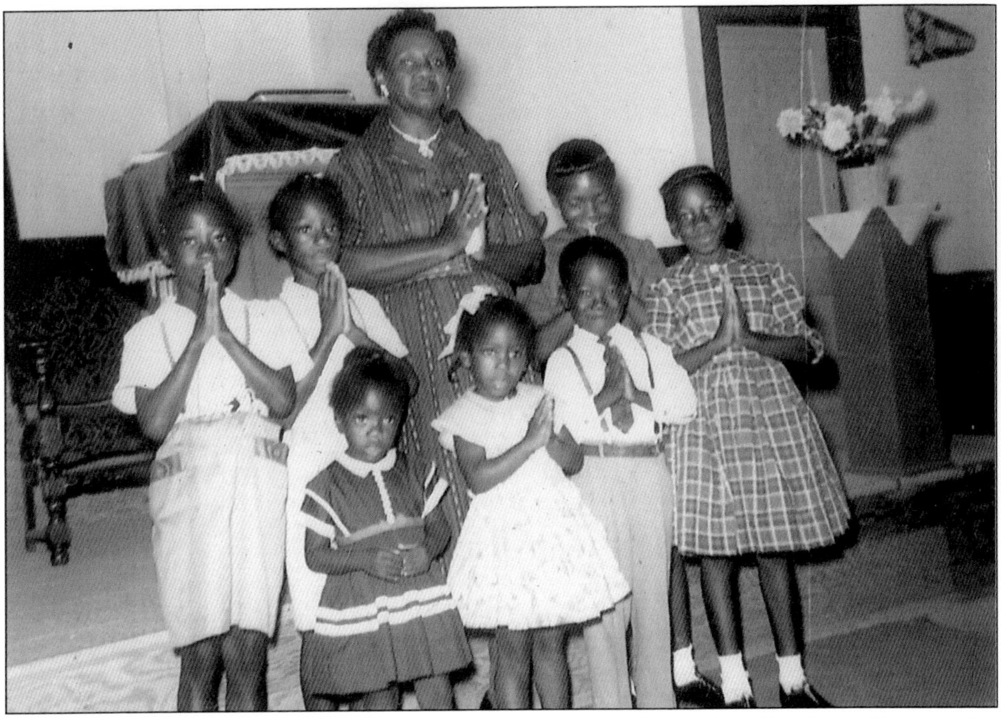

Mrs. Lovie Akridge's Sunday School class is shown with praying hands, reflecting the community's strong belief in prayer. (Courtesy Robbie Mapp Vaughn.)

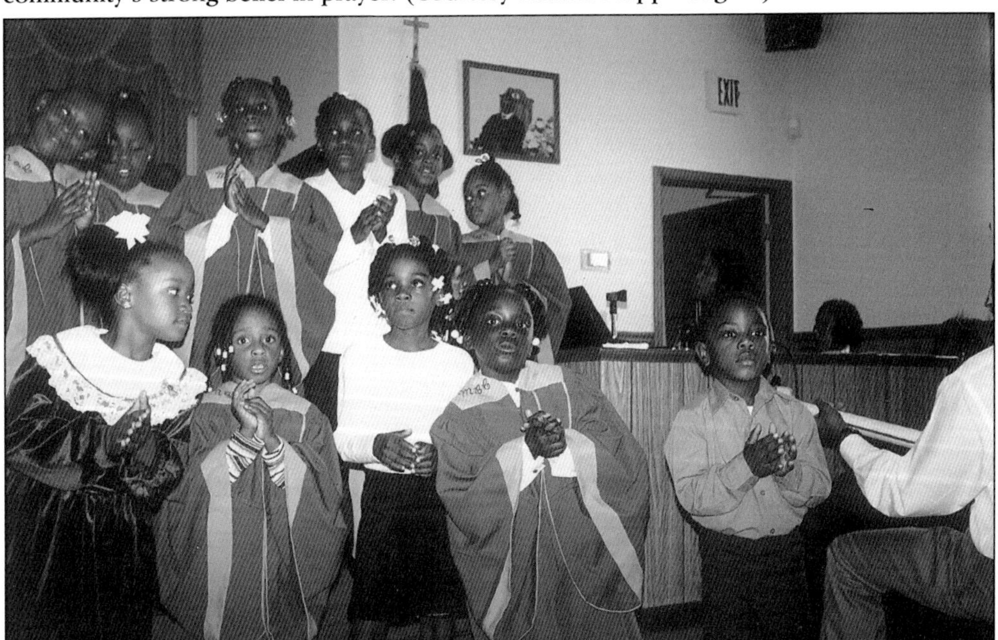

The Children's Choir of Macedonia Baptist Church is pictured in concert. The children learn the traditional songs of the church as well as contemporary songs. (Photograph by Lynn Camp.)

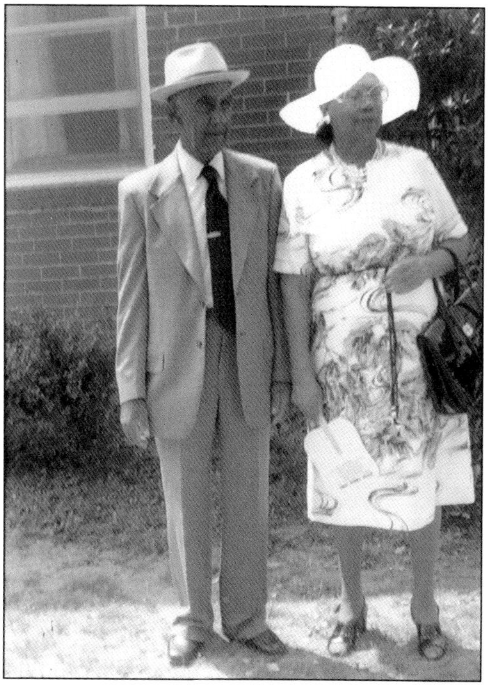

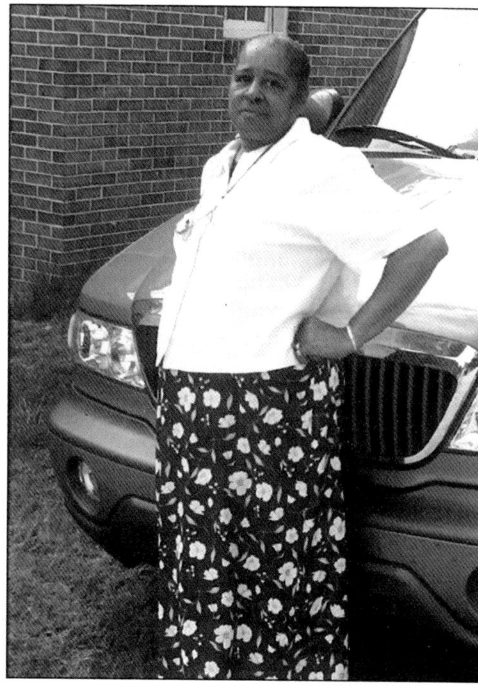

(*above, left*) Guy Locklin and Cleonious Locklin are seen in front of the Mount Enon Baptist Church *c.* 1980 (Courtesy of Geneva Locklin.) (*above, right*) Sarah Brown was reared in the Good Hope community of Walton County. She came from a large family that attended Browns Hill Baptist Church. In her early years Mrs. Brown was a farmer and she later moved to "town" and became a day laborer. (Courtesy Olia Pitts.)

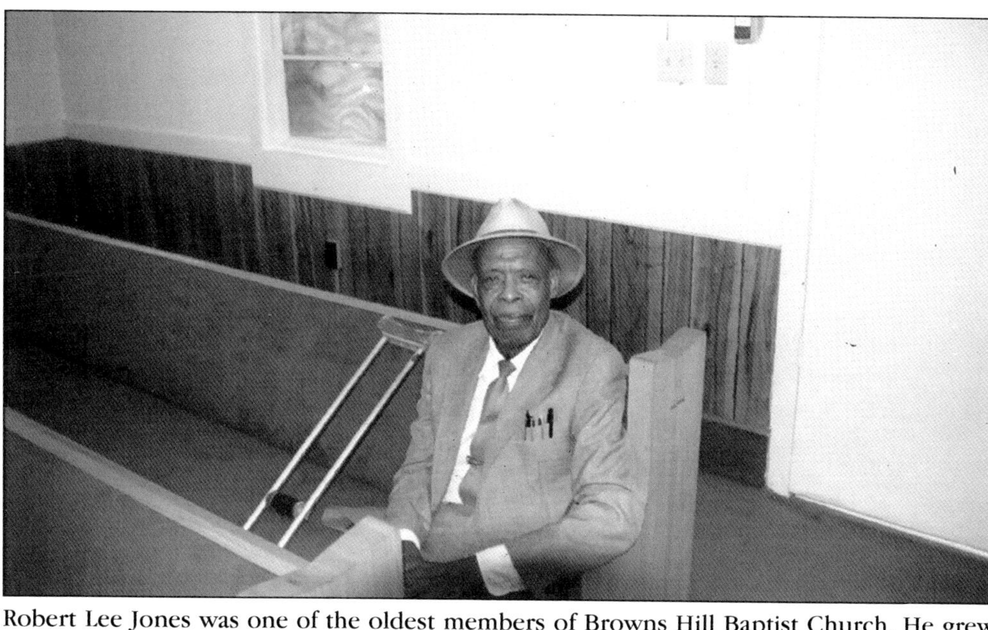

Robert Lee Jones was one of the oldest members of Browns Hill Baptist Church. He grew up in the Browns Hill community. Particularly known for his farming, he grew a variety of beans and yielded many ears of corn in Walton County. (Courtesy Olia Pitts.)

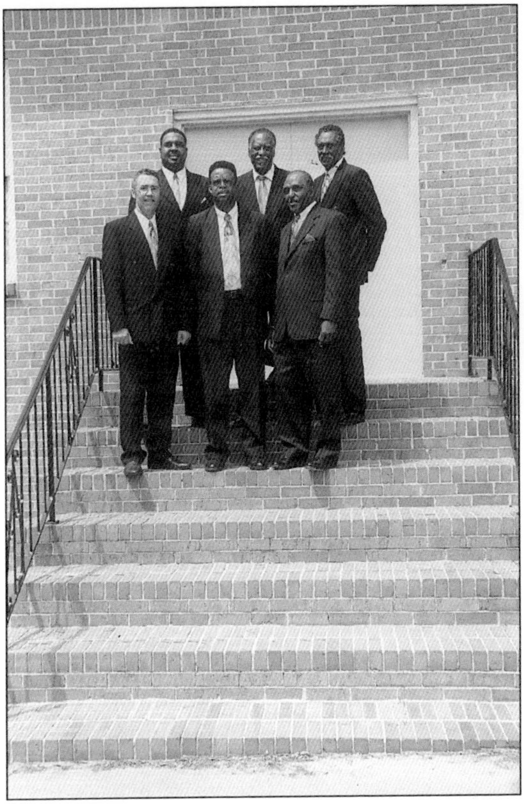

Deacons at the Browns Hill Baptist Church in 2001 include Dee A. Hopkins (chairman), Albert Floyd, Clifford Floyd, Horance Floyd Jr., Wayne Sills, Samuel Floyd, and Anthony Williams. (Courtesy Olia Pitts.)

Deaconesses at the Browns Hill Baptist Church in 2001, "Ladies on the move for Christ," include Fannie Giles, Olia Pitts, Evelyn Eulene Hopkins, Dorothy Sills, Evelyn Floyd, Monica Williams, and Bernice Floyd. (Courtesy Olia Pitts.)

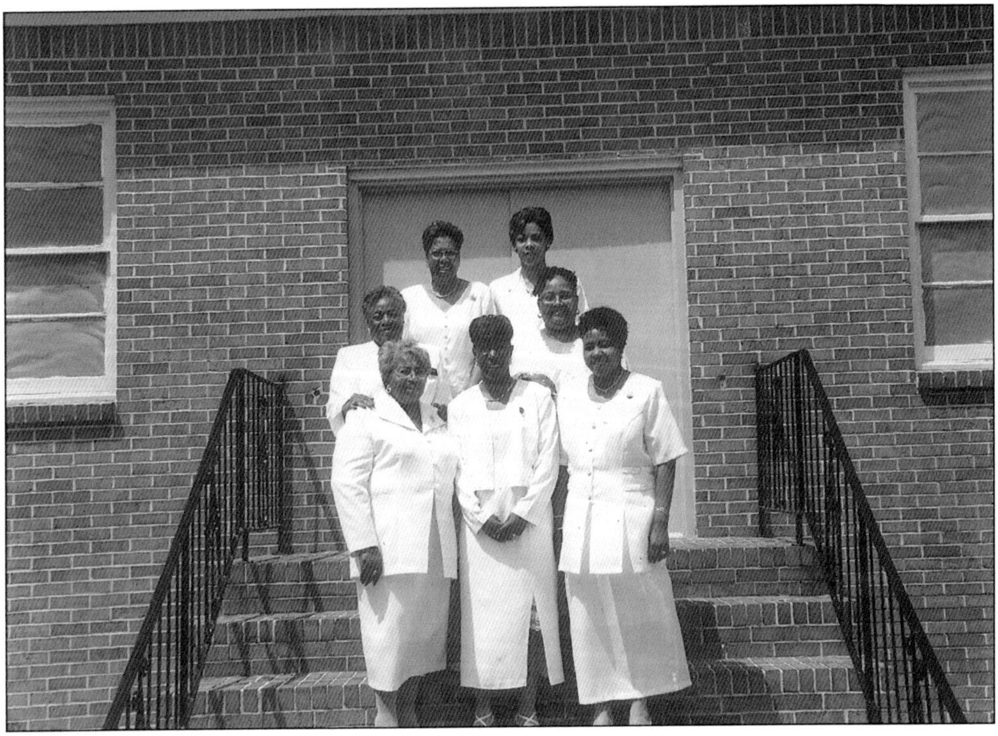

Three

Social Events, Family, and Community Activities

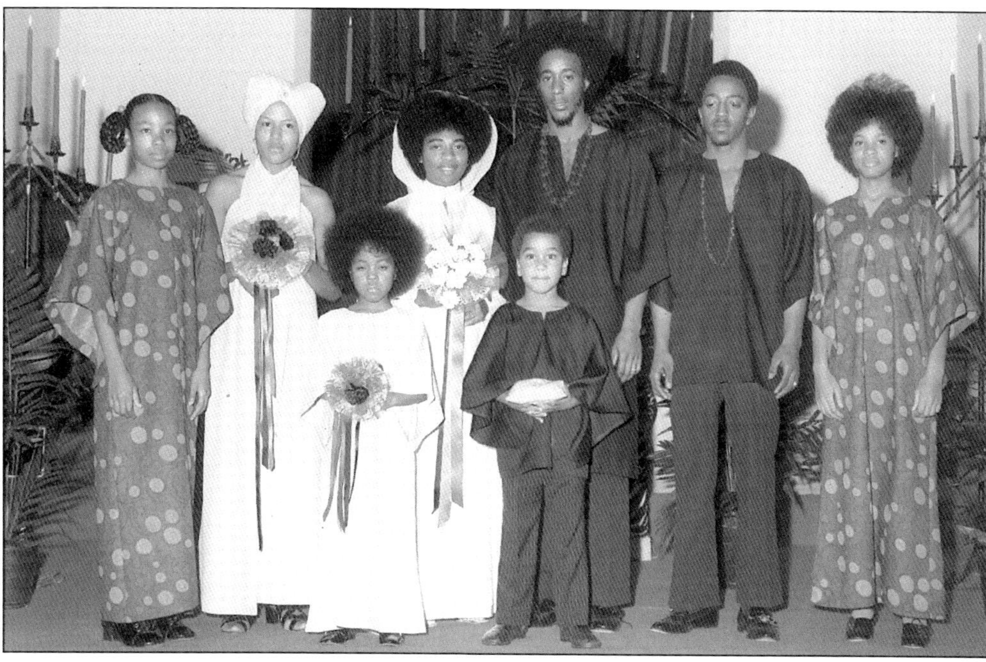

Ruby Lynn Robinson married Charles Camp during an African-American ceremony in 1971 at First African Baptist Church in Monroe. Pictured with the couple are, from left to right, Mayla Brown, Mary Ann Hill, Robin Robertson, Joey Flint, Rufus Camp, and Patricia Hester. (Courtesy Lynn Camp.)

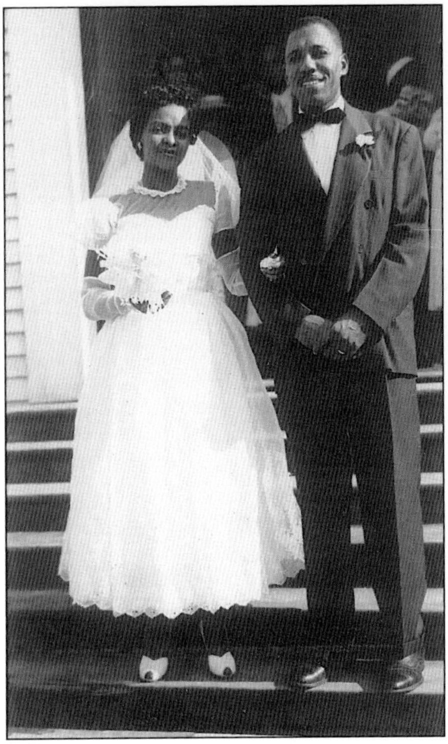

Evelyn and William Bush Sr. are pictured on their wedding day in 1952. The wedding was held at Macedonia Baptist Church in the Gratis Community in Monroe. (Courtesy Evelyn Bush.)

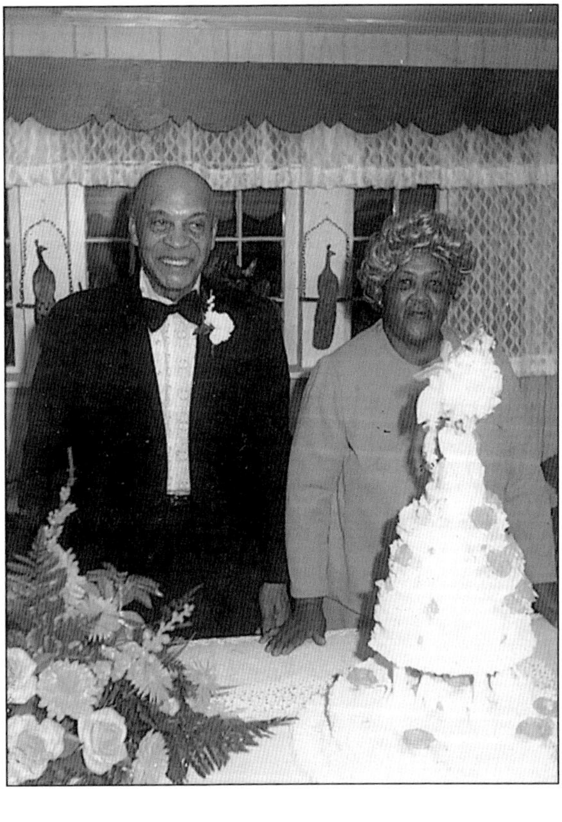

Deacon Rupel Knox and Sarah Emma Knox celebrate their 50th wedding anniversary. Considered "pillars of Mars Hill Baptist Church," the couple had 14 children. (Courtesy the Knox family.)

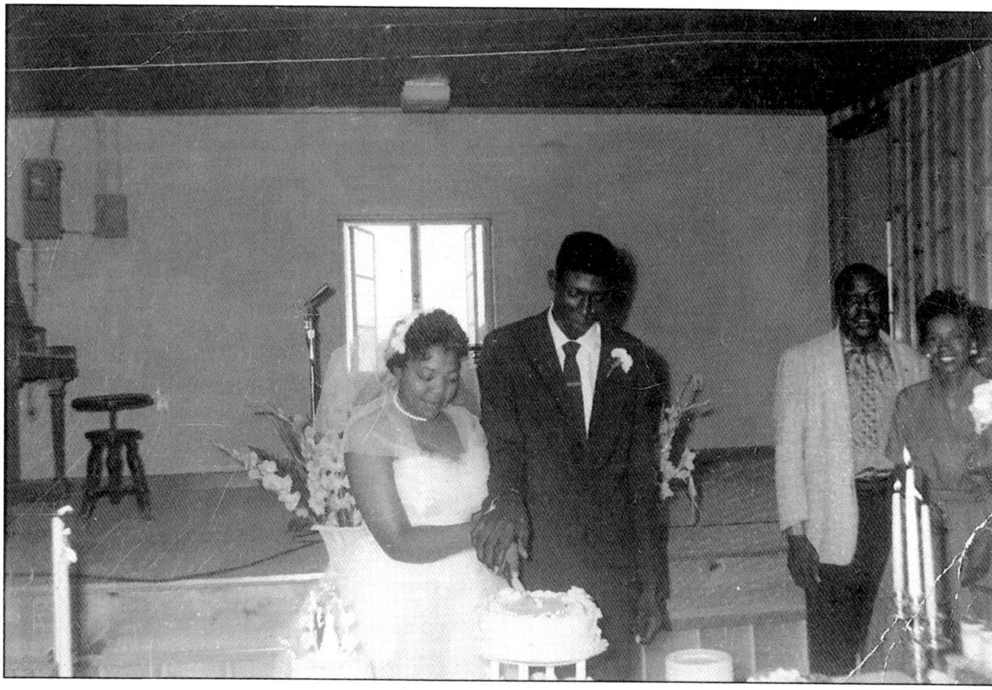

McLeroy and Mary Nell Malcom are shown cutting the cake at the reception at the American Legion Post 531 in Monroe in 1958. (Courtesy Camilla Mattox.)

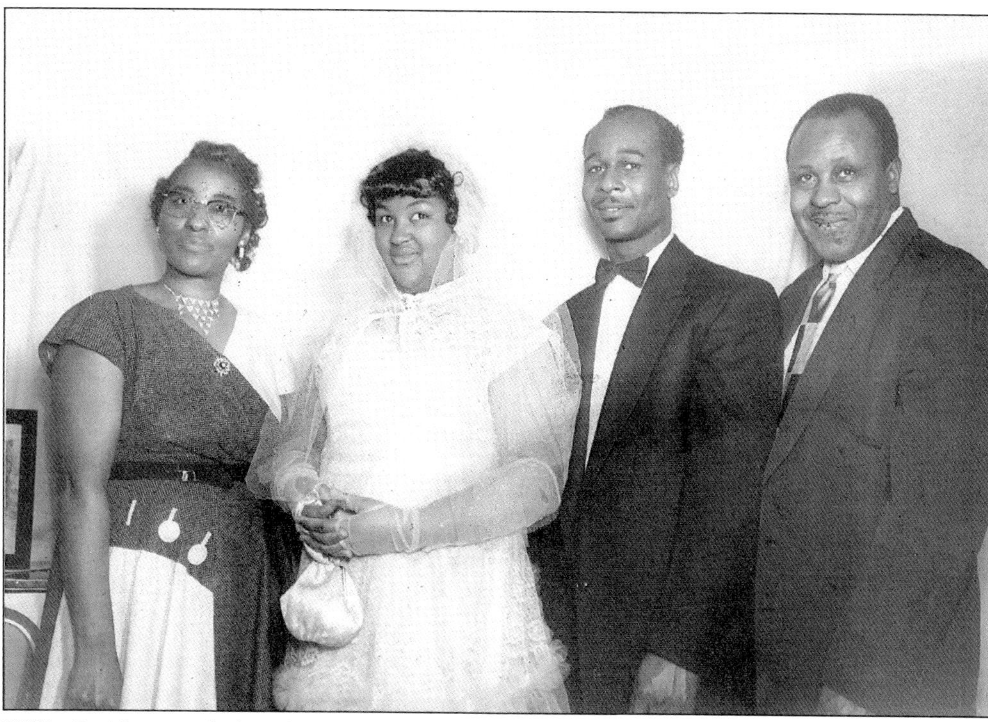

Willie Smith attends his daughter Mary's wedding to Joseph Woodridge. Also pictured is Mary Francis Church, *c.* 1960. (Courtesy Willie Smith.)

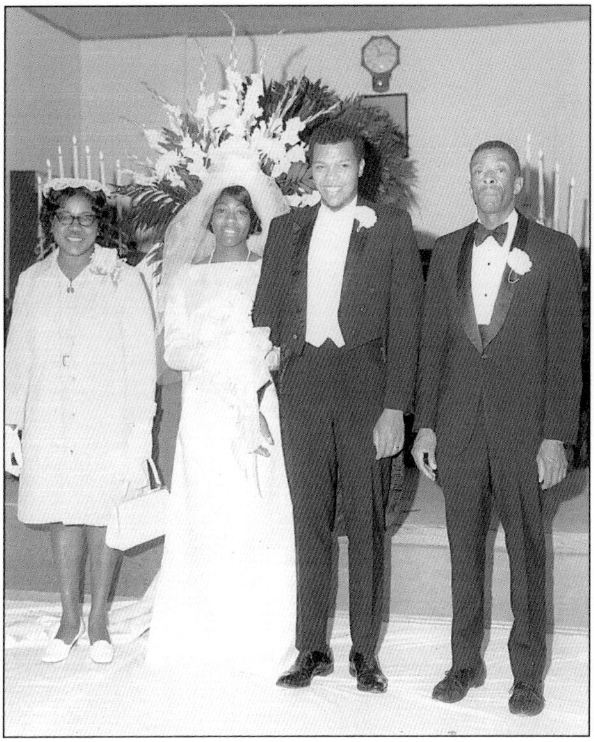

Robbie Jewel Mapp married Michael Etchison at Mount Enon Baptist Church in Monroe, 1971. Pictured with the couple are Robbie's parents, Annie Ruth and Clarence Mapp. (Courtesy Robbie Mapp Vaughn.)

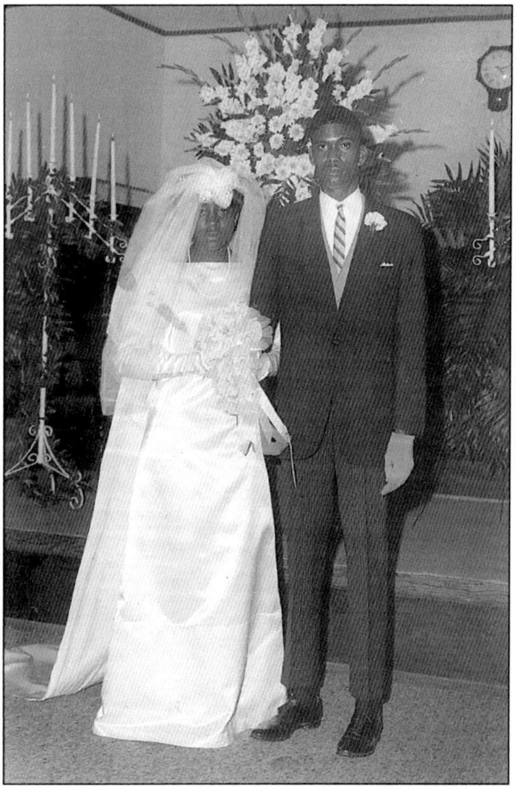

Robert and Anna Ivey's wedding was held in 1966 at Mt. Enon Baptist Church. (Courtesy of Robbie Mapp Vaughn.)

Brandon and Denise Cheeks are shown with bridesmaids and the flower girl in the 1980s. (Courtesy Robbie Mapp Vaughn.)

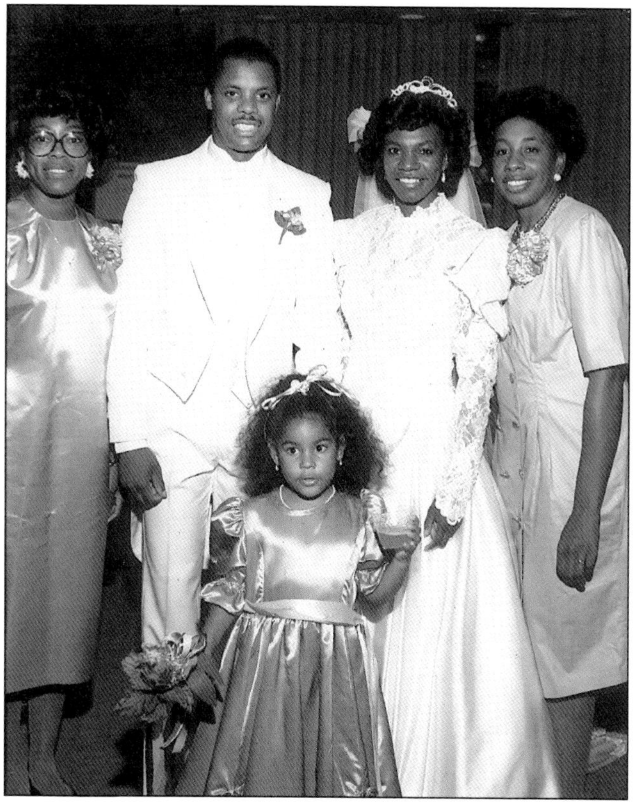

The wedding ceremony of Larynee Ridgeway and Willie Norman (*c.* 1988) was performed by Rev. B.Z. Daniel, who has performed pastoral duties in Walton County for over 50 years. Larynee's bridesmaid was Joy Lewis and Willie's best man was Rodney Jones. (Courtesy Teressa Sorrells.)

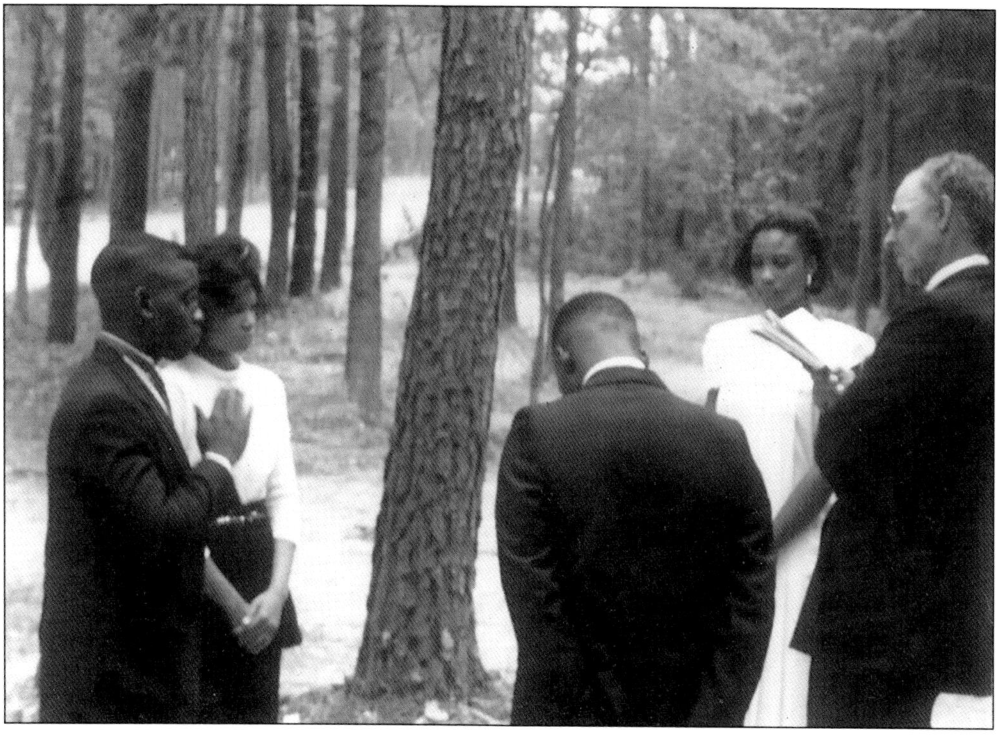

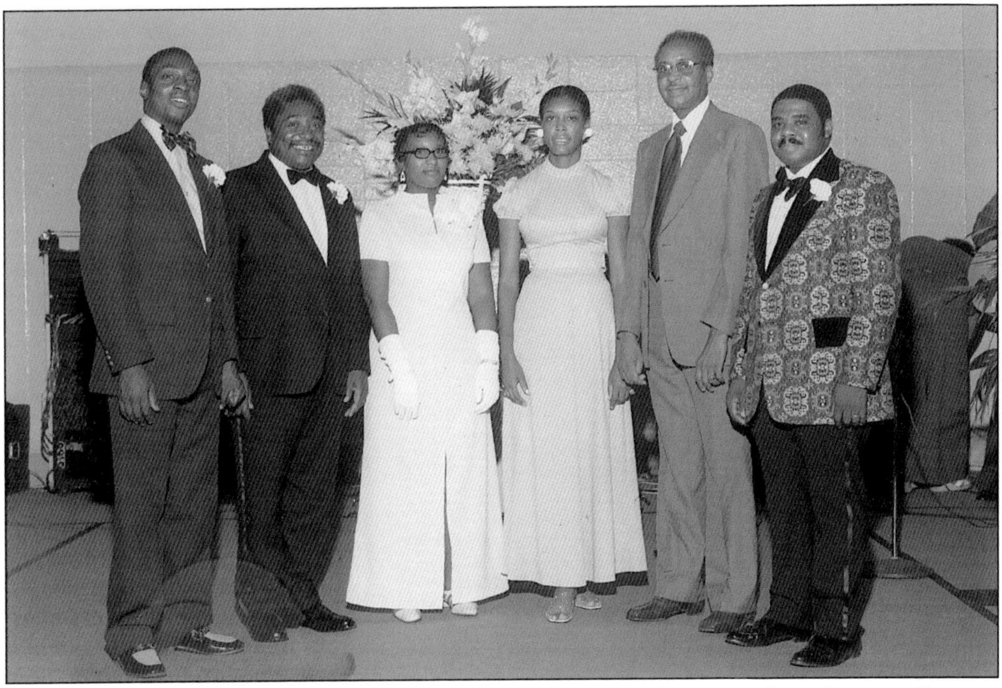

Pictured here are members of the Fort Valley State College Alumni, Walton County Chapter, *c.* 1965. From left to right are Dr. Willie Enus, George Marshall, Mary Britton, Bobbie Sue Morris, C.P. Cochran, and Carl Britton. (Courtesy George Marshall.)

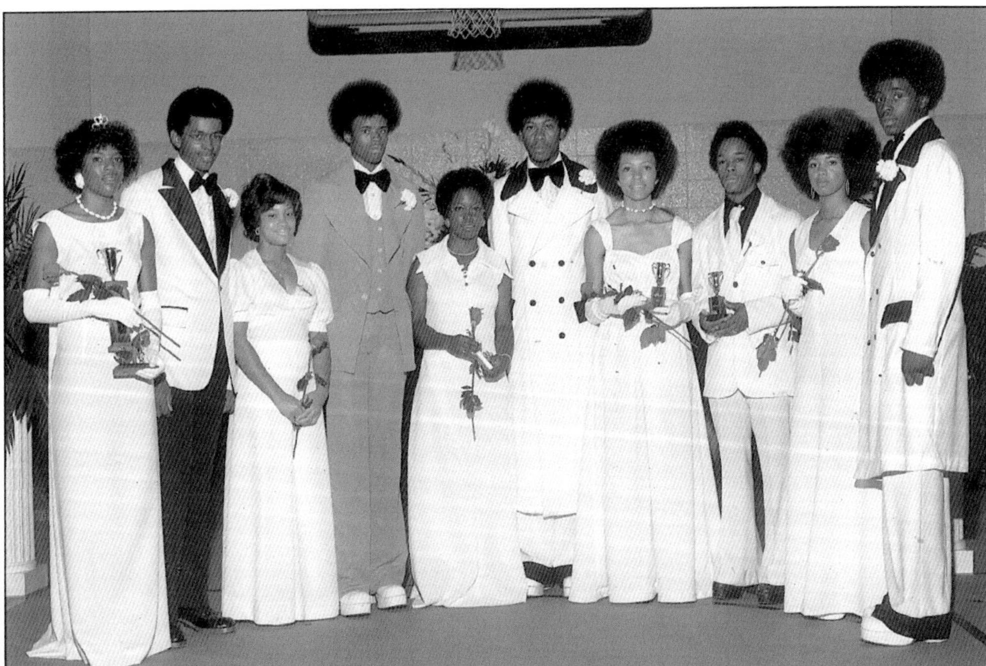

These young ladies and their escorts were participants in the Débutante Ball held at the Loganville High School gym *c.* 1970. (Courtesy George Marshall.)

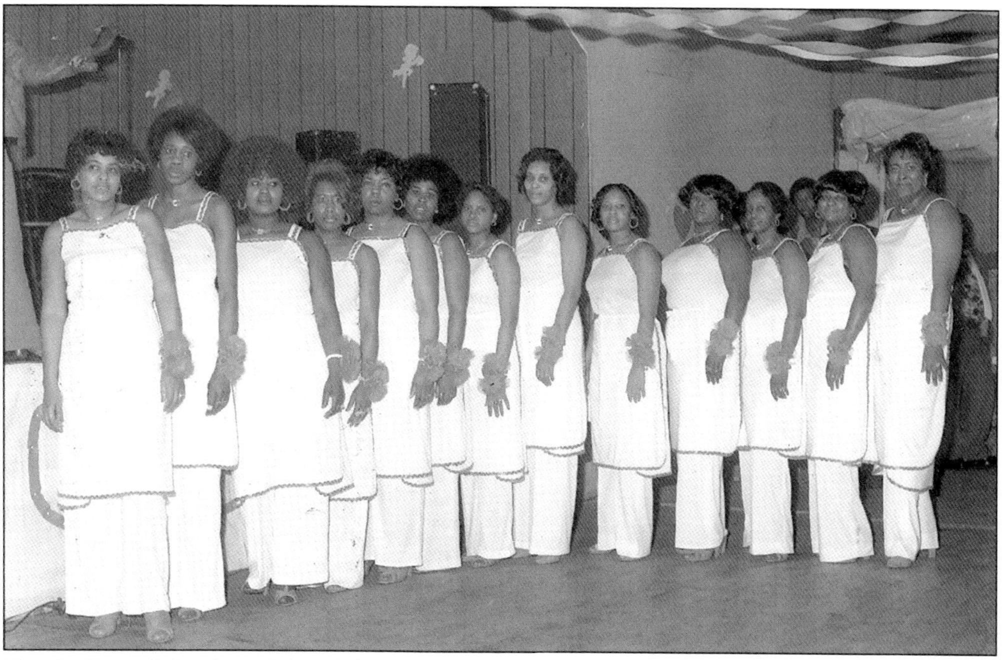

The Ladies of Soul (L.O.S. Club) are shown in this *c.* 1970 photograph. The club was organized to provide a social outlet for Walton County women of color. The organization also did charity work in the county. (Courtesy Claudia Mae Hillman.)

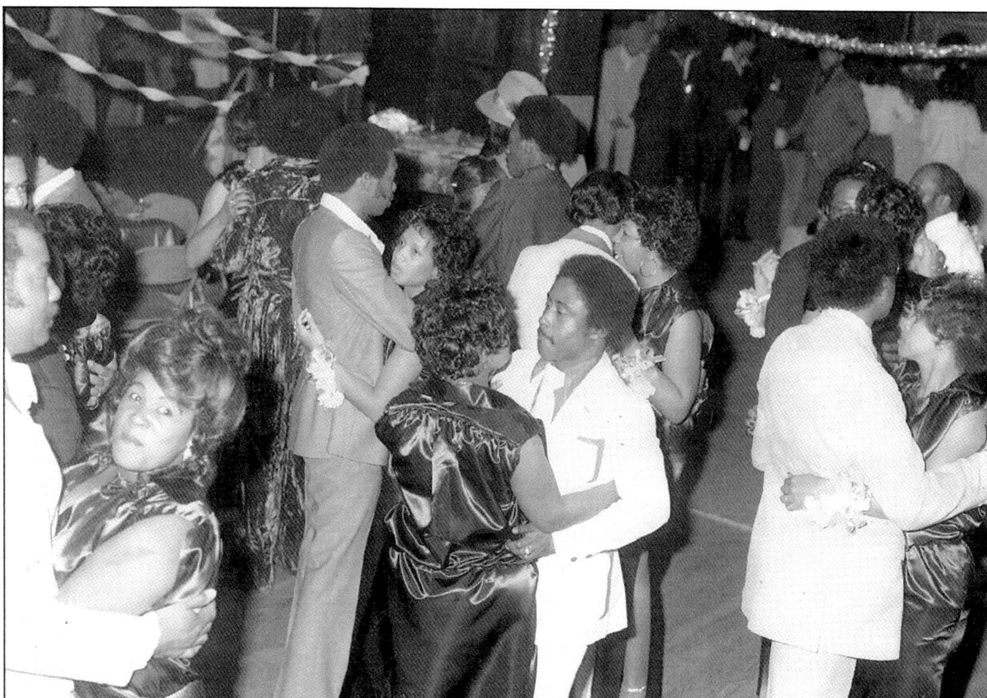

The Ladies of Soul's anniversary was a much-anticipated social event. This photograph is from the 1970s. (Courtesy Claudia Mae Hillman.)

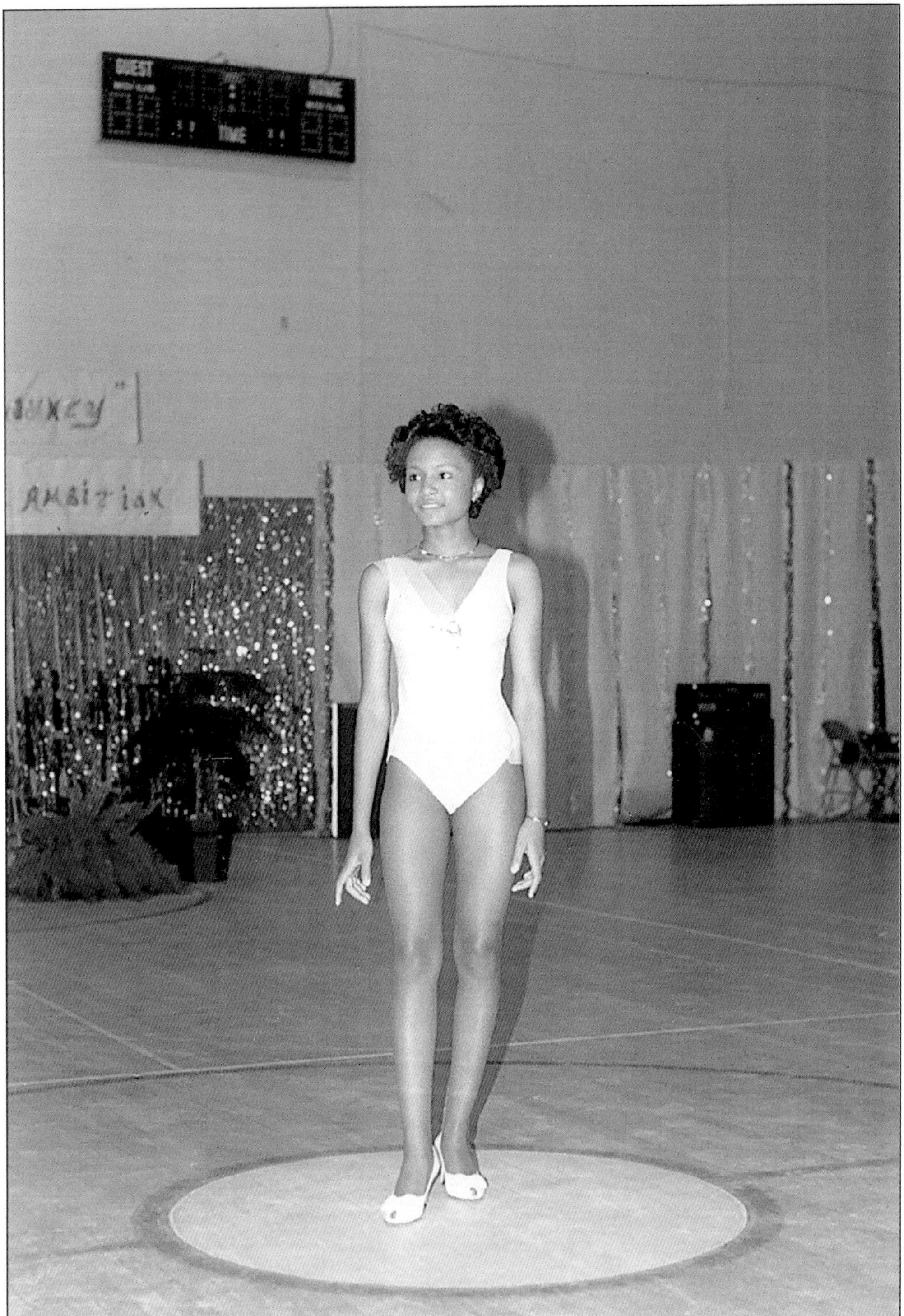

The 1984 Miss Black Walton County Pageant was held in the Carver Middle School gym. Larynee Ridgeway is pictured in the swimsuit competition. (Courtesy Teressa Sorrells.)

Matrons of the Zebulon Star Chapter #166 Order of Eastern Stars, from left to right, are Ethel Kilgore, Gladys Summerour, Willie Marshall, and Catherine Thompson, pictured in the 1970s. The Eastern Stars is a sister organization to the Masons. They support the Masons in their activities, sponsor youth programs and scholarships, and perform charitable community work. (Courtesy George Marshall.)

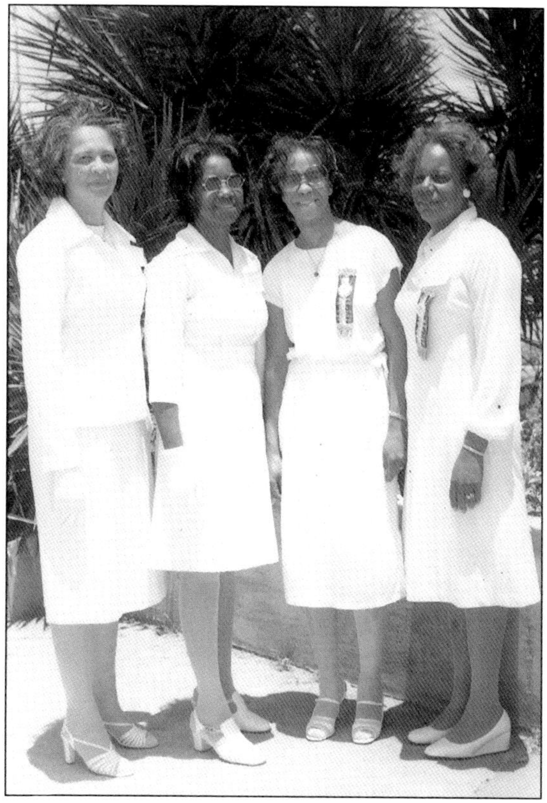

The Brownie Girl Scout Troop #157 is pictured with troop leaders. In the back row from left to right are Helen Booker, Estella Bell, and Robbie Vaughn. It is interesting to note here that Bazoline Usher, who was born in Walnut Grove in 1880, was instrumental in integrating Girl Scouting in Georgia. (Courtesy Robbie Mapp Vaughn.)

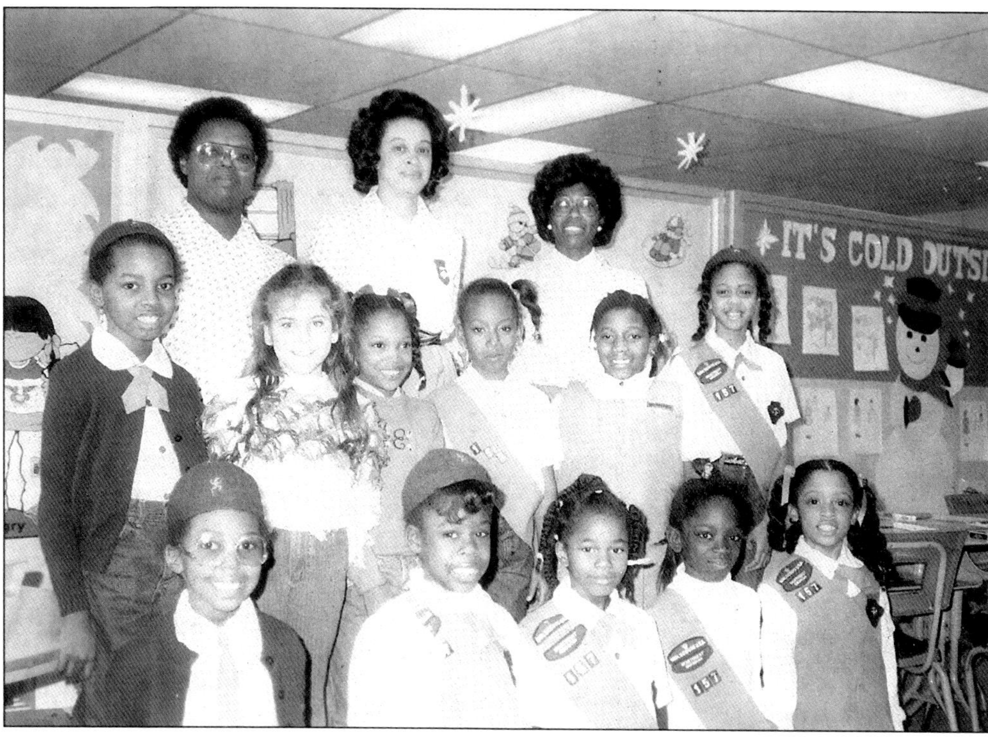

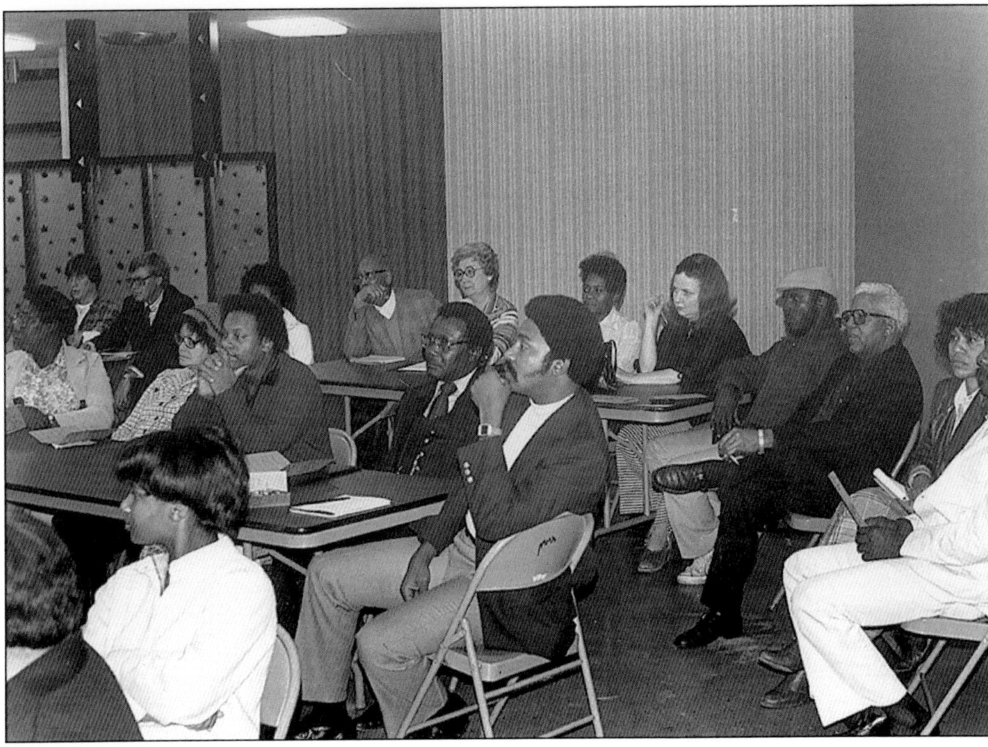

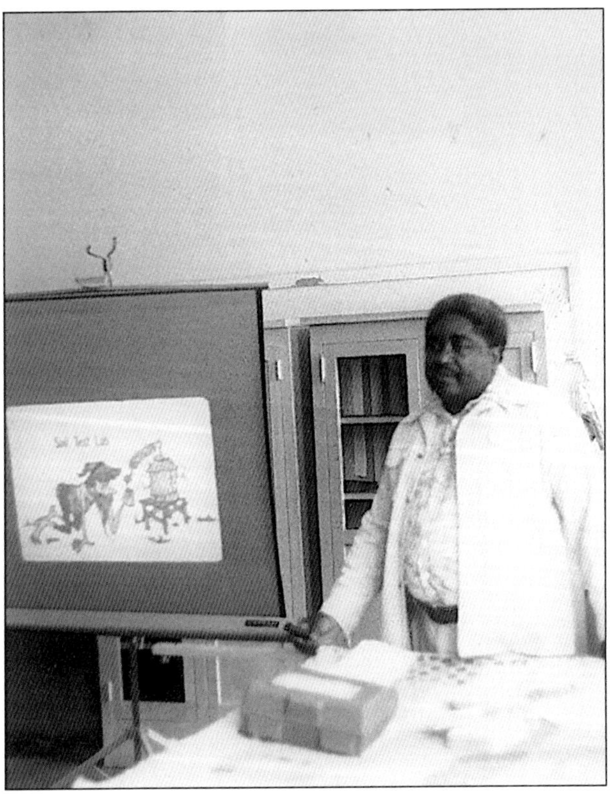

Participants of a leadership workshop sponsored by the Agricultural Extension Service are shown in this *c.* 1970 photograph. (Courtesy George Marshall.)

George Marshall is shown giving a 4-H demonstration at Monroe Elementary School *c.* 1980. The 4-H Club was one of the few youth organizations available to youth in the black community for years. It is a voluntary youth organization sponsored by the Agricultural Extension Service and supervised by the county extension agent. As the county agent from 1954 to 1985, Marshall was responsible for programs and activities. (Courtesy George Marshall.)

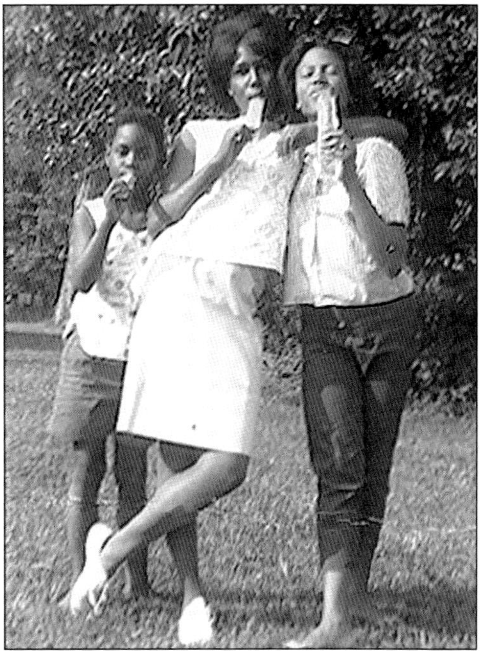

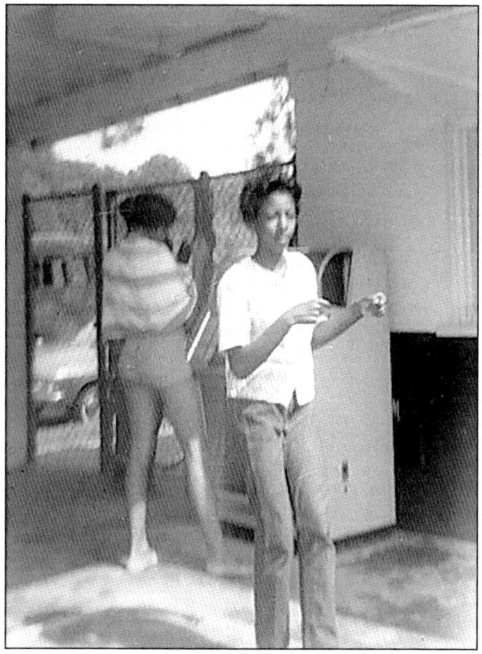

(*above, left*) Lynette, Maurice, and Mary Ann Hill enjoy a cool treat on a hot summer day in 1966 at their East Marble Street home. They are three of the seven offsprings of Charlie Albert and Leola Hill. (Courtesy Lynn Camp.) (*above, right*) Barbara Culbreath dances poolside to the music of a jukebox at Riverside Park in nearby Athens, *c.* 1965. The staff of the summer recreation program held at the Carver High School gym would bus the youths to Athens for swimming. There were no such recreational facilities for blacks in Monroe at the time. (Photograph by Lynn Camp.)

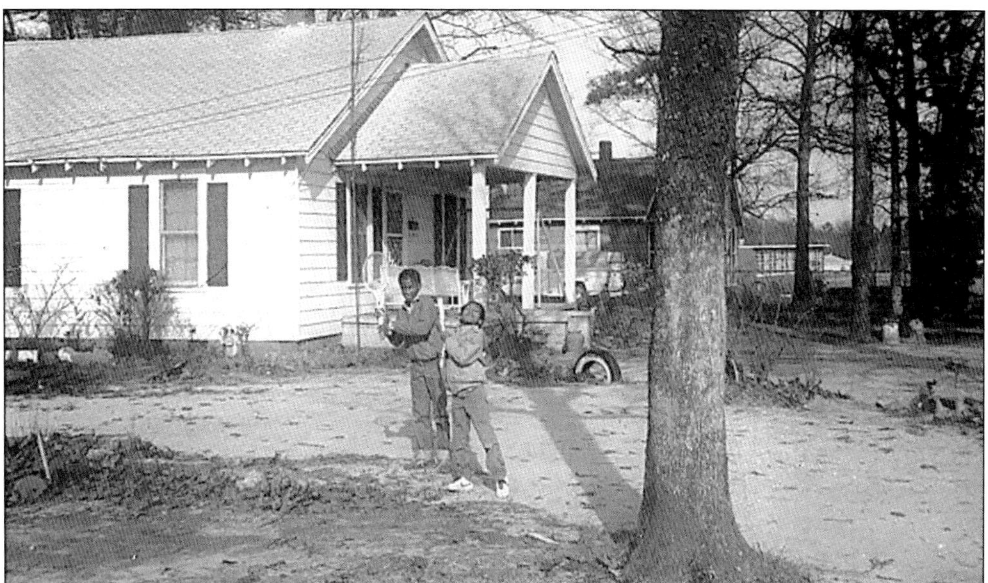

Craig Smith and Tarik Camp play in Tarik's grandmother's yard at 105 Sorrells Street as their parents did a generation earlier, *c.* 1982. (Courtesy Lynn Camp.)

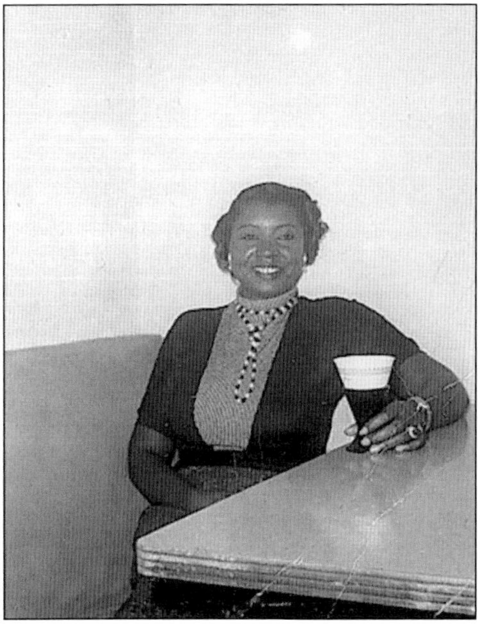

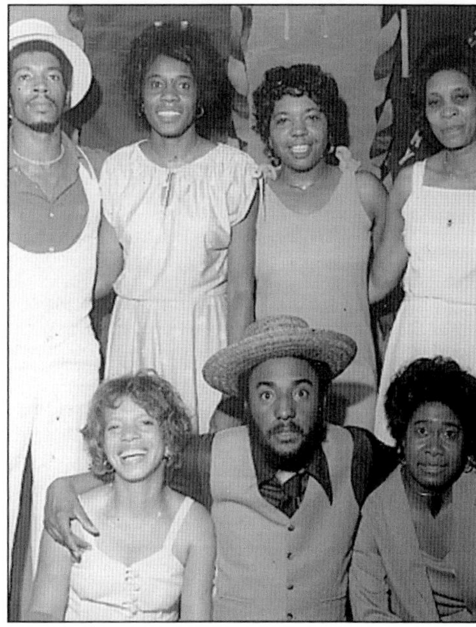

(*above, left*) Camilla Mattox is pictured having a "night out" at the American Legion Post #531, *c.* 1955. (Courtesy Camilla Maddox.) (*above, right*) This group of friends gathered for a photograph at the Social Advancement of Black Brothers Club (S.A.B.B. Club) *c.* 1970. From left to right are (front row) Millie Pascal, John Henry "Wienie" Maddox, and Mildred Tory; (back row) Willie C. Maddox, Mary Crawford, Claudia Mae Hillman, and Doyle Williams. John Henry Maddox (front center) operates Maddox Cab Co. as his parents did before him. (Courtesy Claudia Mae Hillman.)

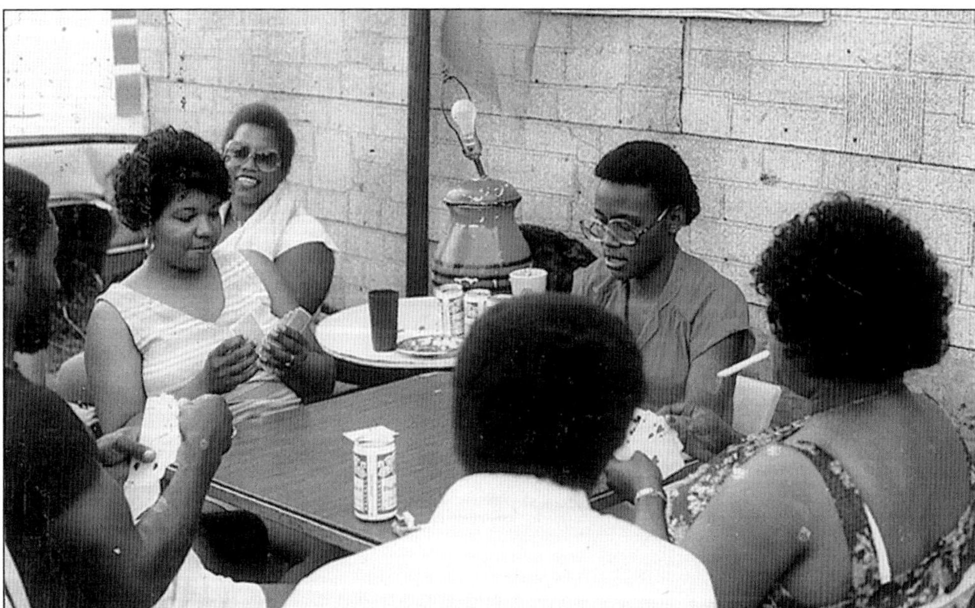

Enjoying a game of Bid Whiz are John Cooper, Claudia Hillman, Judy Baker, Carolyn Munford, and Mary Still, 1980s. This is a popular pastime. (Courtesy Claudia Mae Hillman.)

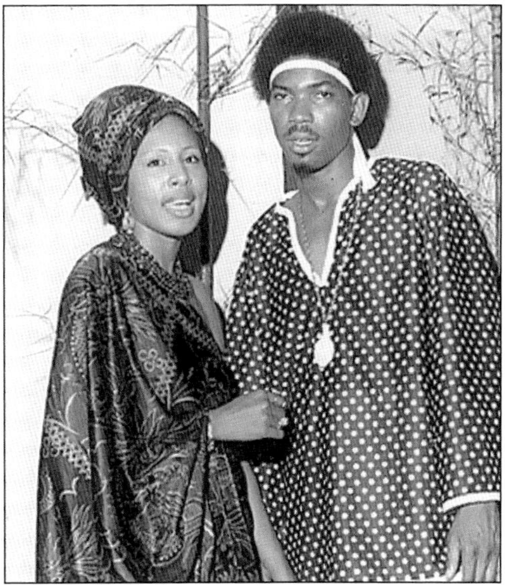
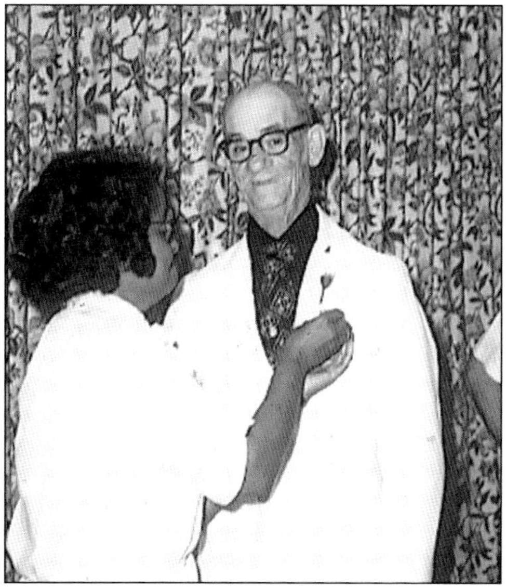

(*above, left*) Teressa and Errie Sorrells are shown at the Afro Ball *c.* 1974. Errie was a member of the Social Advancement of Black Brothers (S.A.B.B.). The organization operated a nightclub on Washington Street where they helped to bring quality entertainment to people of color in Walton County. These men also did various charitable projects in the county. (Courtesy Lynn Camp.) (*above, right*) Geneva Locklin pinned a flower on her husband, Orell Locklin, at a retirement dinner held in his honor. Mr. Locklin retired from General Telephone Co. after 18 years of service in 1978. Locklin was instrumental in getting buses for black Walton County children during the late 1950s. (Courtesy Geneva Locklin.)

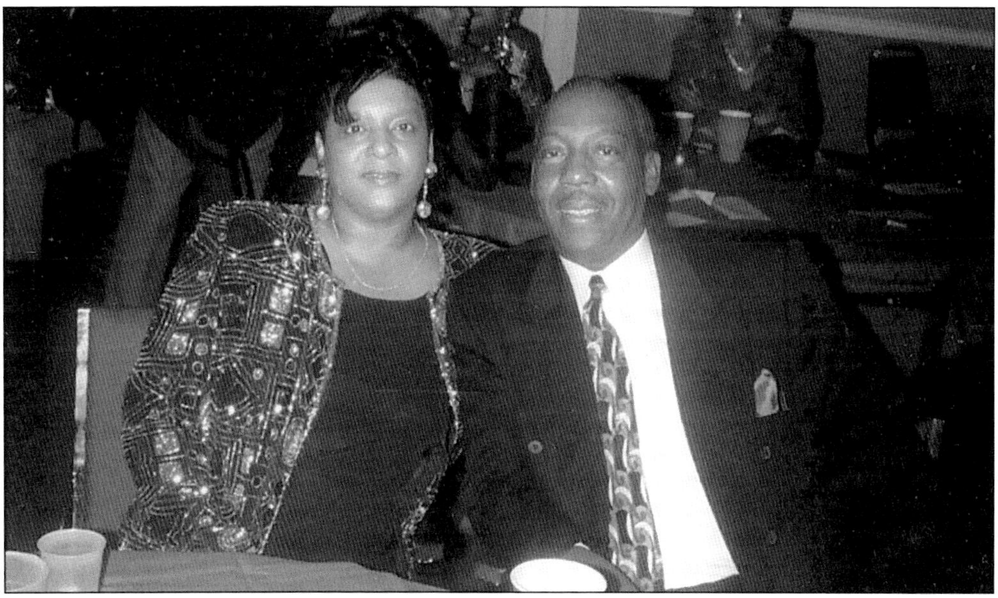

Barbara Knox is pictured with her husband William Knox Sr. at the 1996 Maroon and Gold Ball. Barbara is a pre-operative nurse at the Walton Medical Center and William retired as a forklift driver from General Motors after 31 years. William has also been in the National Guard for 29 years. (Photograph by Lynn Camp.)

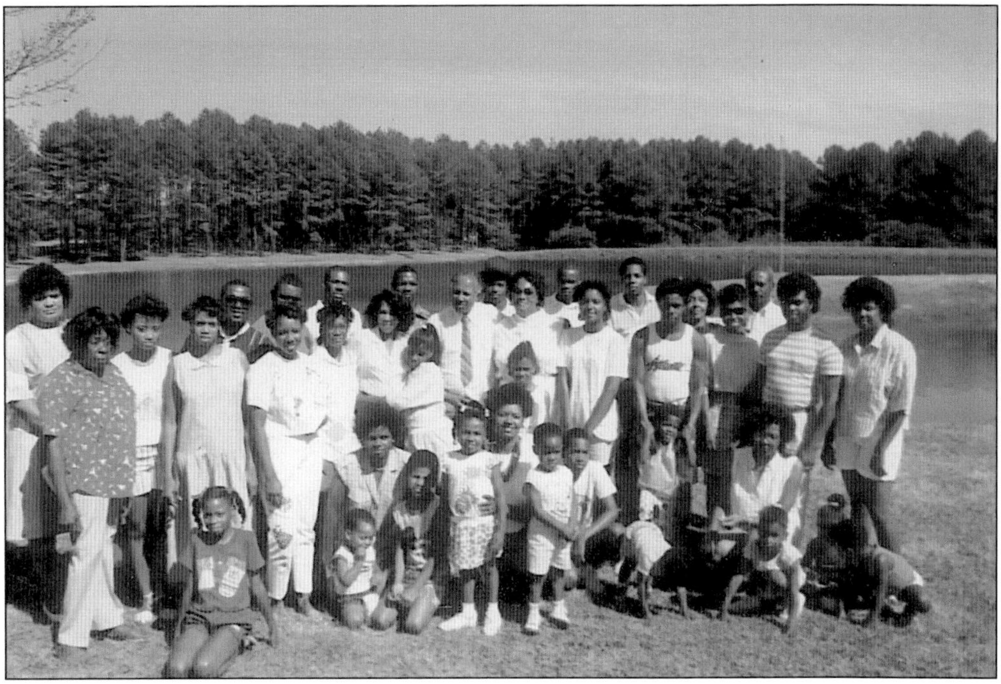

Five generations of the Vinsons pose during a family reunion. (Courtesy Patsy Vinson.)

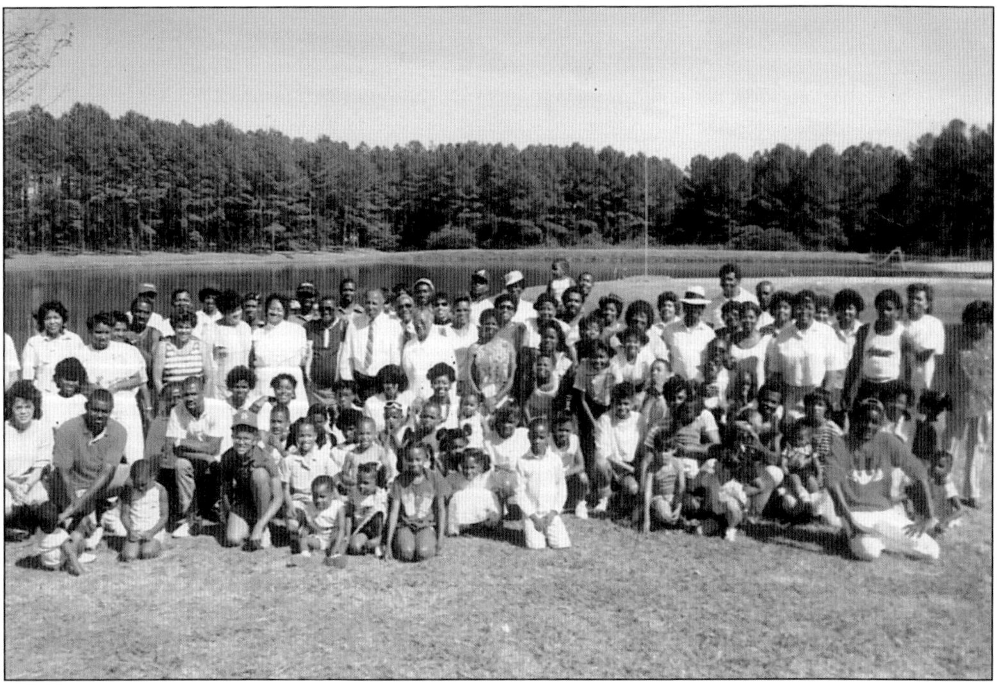

The Vinson Family Reunion has been held annually on the first Sunday in June since 1970. (Courtesy Patsy Vinson.)

Four

EDUCATION

BLACK SCHOOLS AND THEIR LEGACY

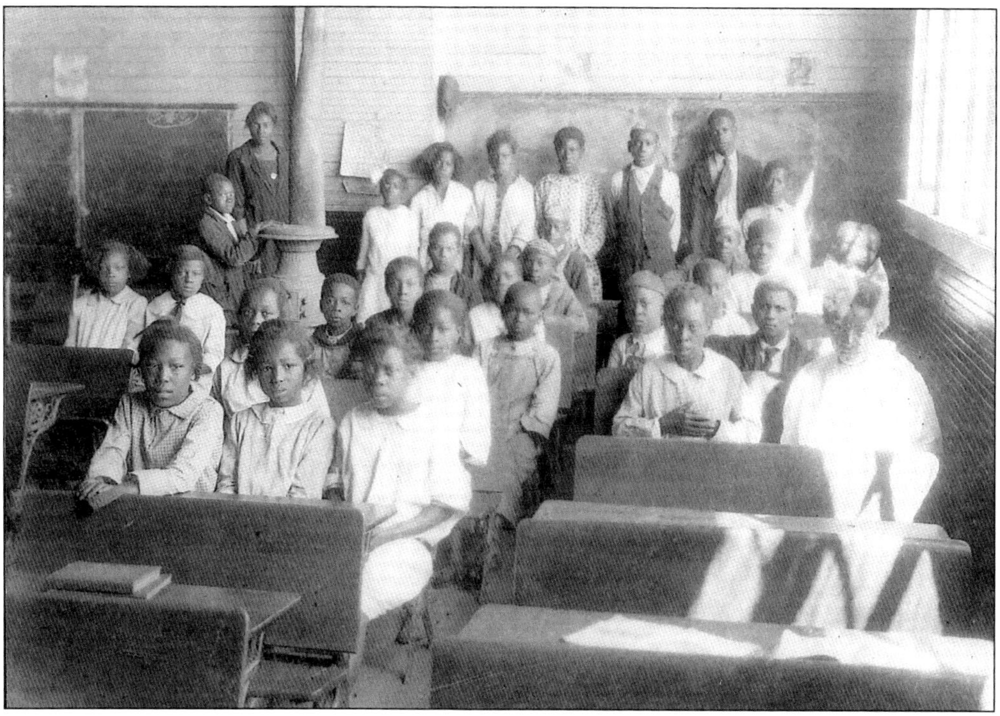

This photograph shows an early Walton County classroom. Walton County public schools for blacks students were established in 1906. The Northwestern Baptist Association, Madison Baptist Association, and local churches operated many of the early schools. Three Rosenwald schools were built in the county between 1912 and 1932. (The E.M. Carnes Collection; Courtesy Larry Witcher.)

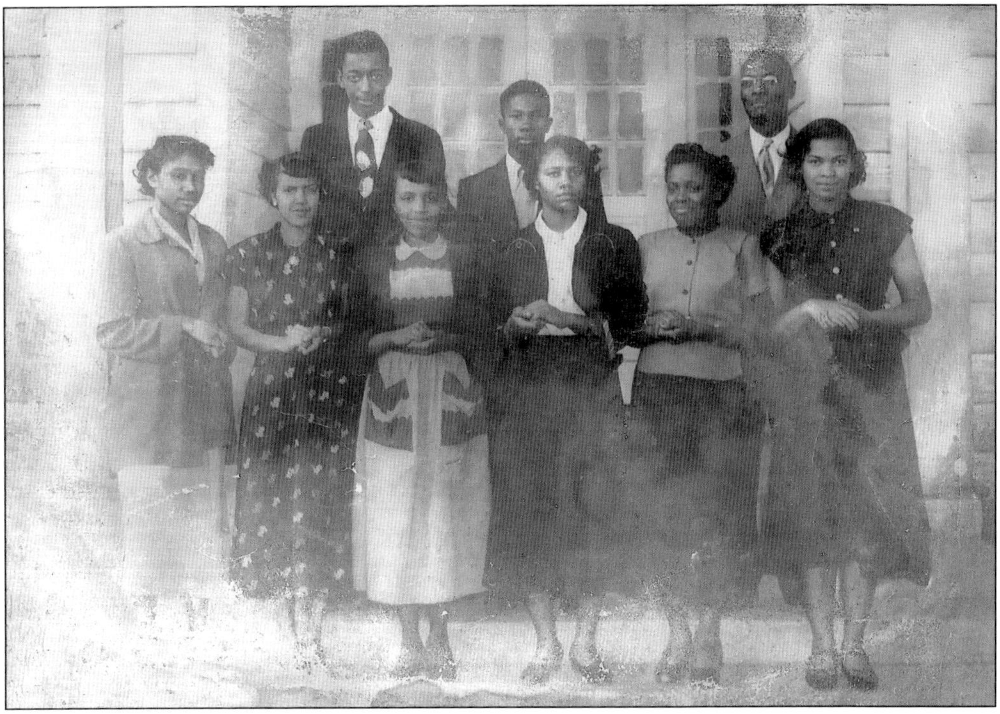

Members of Social Circle Training School's senior class of 1951 are pictured here. (Courtesy Sarah Knox Syphoe.)

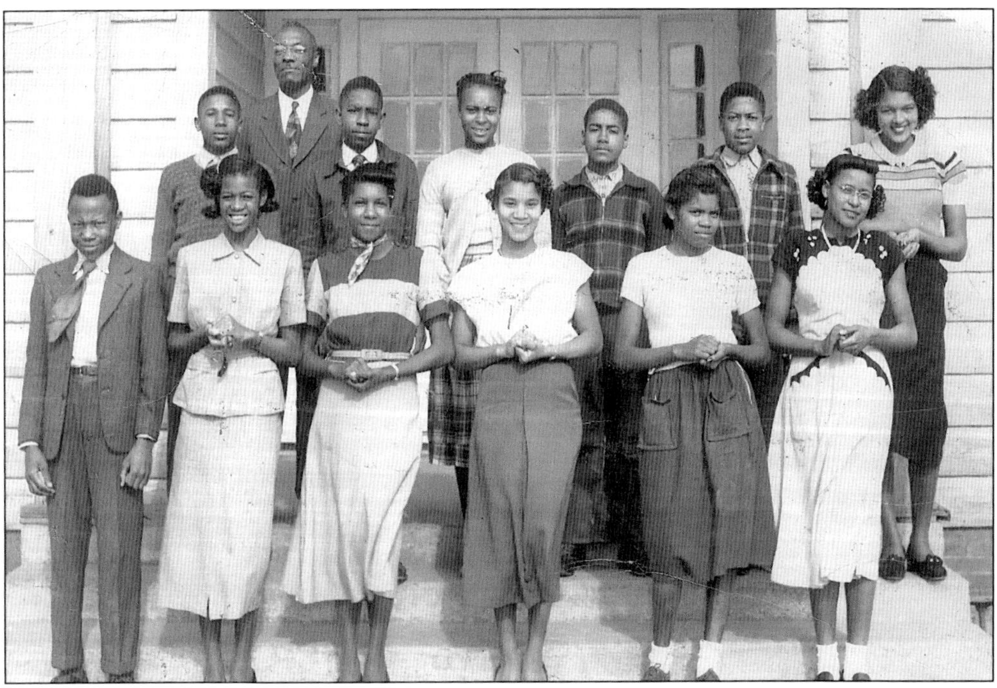

This is the ninth-grade class at Social Circle Training School in the 1940s. (Courtesy Sarah Knox Syphoe.)

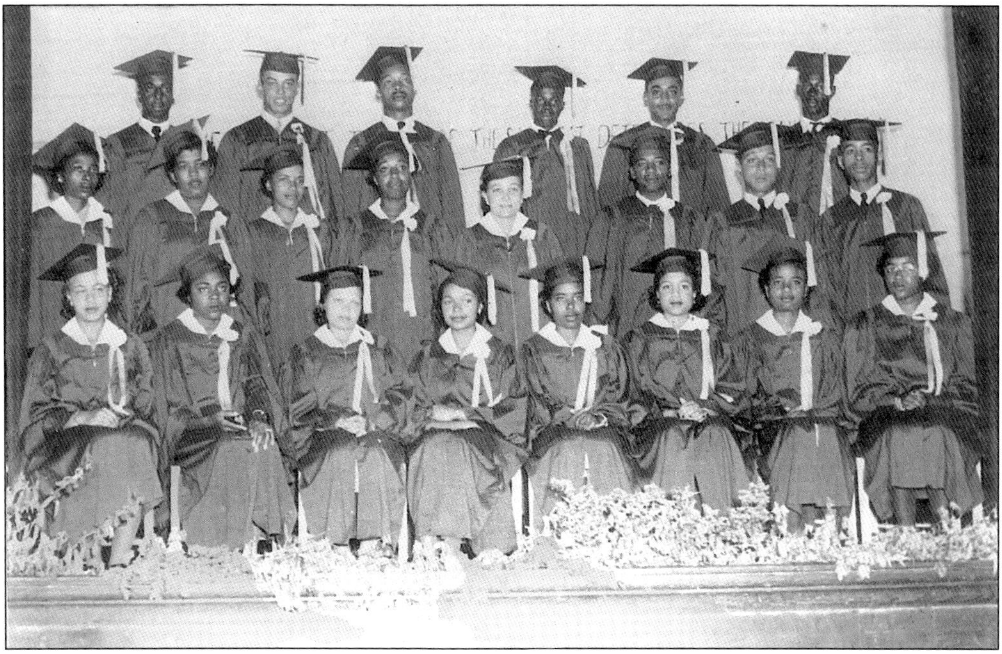

Members of the Monroe Colored High School Class of 1947 are pictured in their caps and gowns. The Monroe Colored High School was located on Oak Street in the building currently occupied by the Walton County Board of Education. (Courtesy Addie White.)

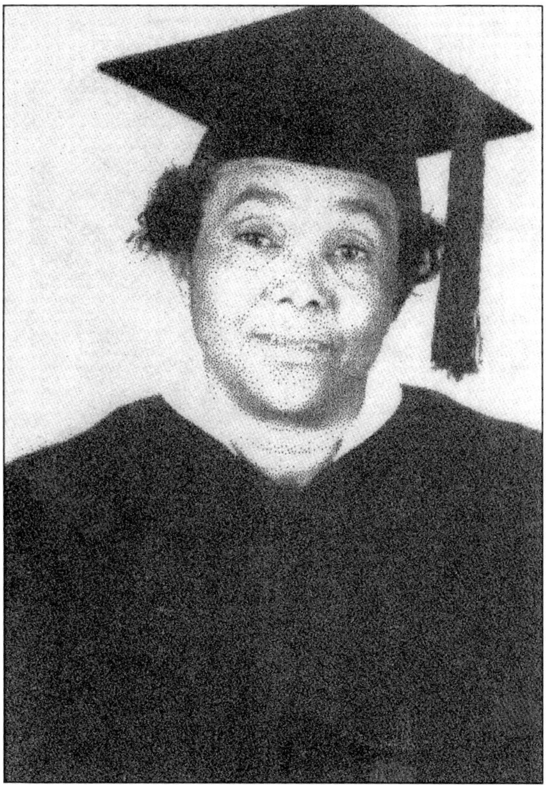

Ella M. Thompson Butler (1902–1967) was a Walton County native and the daughter of J. Marsh and Florence Smith Thompson, who taught school in Walton County for 46 years. Schools where Mrs. Butler taught and served as principal include Pleasant Hill, Spring Hill, O'Kelly's Chapel, Good Hope, Phillip's Grove, Mount Enon, Thompson, and Carver Elementary. Her life parable was entitled "The Wise Old Owl." It said, "There was an old owl who sat in an oak, the more he saw, the less he spoke, the less he spoke, the more he heard, now that's a wise old bird." (Courtesy Mollie Butler Lewis.)

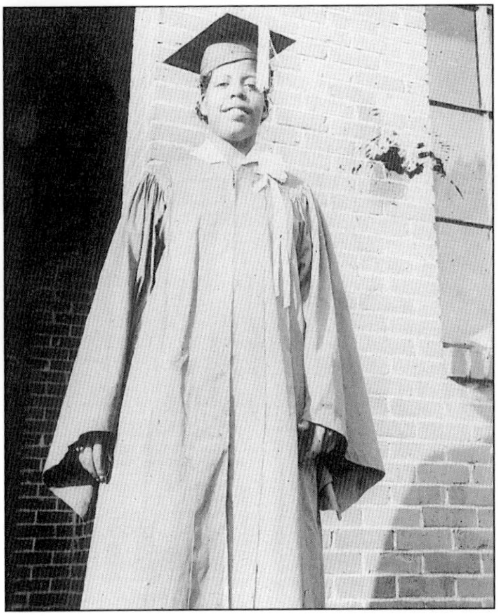

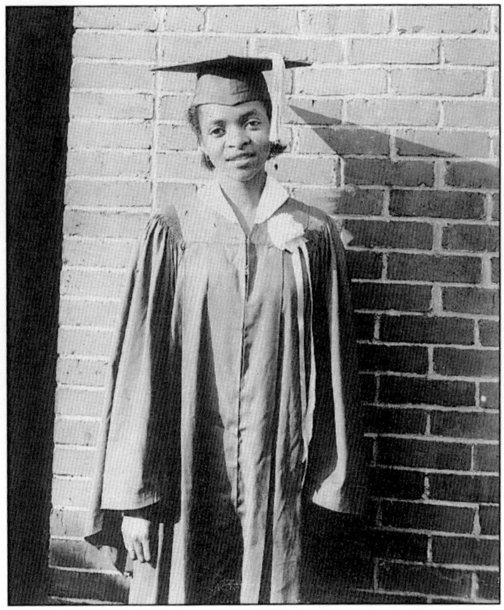

(*above, left*) Dorothy Carlton, a 1944 graduate of Monroe Colored High School, left Walton County after graduating to attend Clark College in Atlanta. (Courtesy Evelyn Bush.) (*above, right*) Evelyn Jackson was also a member of the class of 1944 at Monroe Colored High School—the first graduating class from the school. After completing high school, she attended Clark College in Atlanta. She became a teacher, overseer of the Jackson-Bush farm, and owner of the Jackson Funeral Home. (Courtesy Evelyn Bush.)

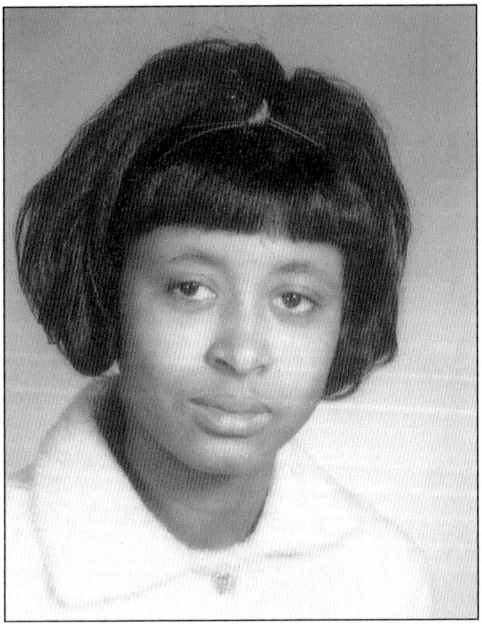

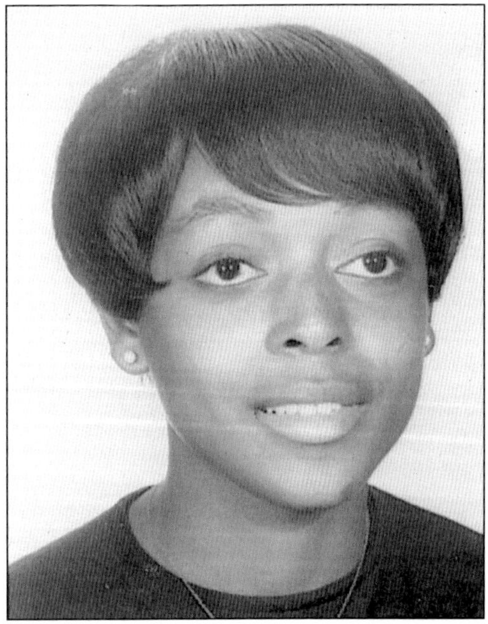

(*above, left*) Sandra Kay Locklin was Miss Carver Homecoming Queen and a 1966 graduate of Carver High School. (Courtesy Lynn Camp.) (*above, right*) Annette Ramey was Miss Carver Homecoming Queen, head majorette of the Marching Wildcat Band, and secretary of the senior class in 1969. (Courtesy Lynn Camp.)

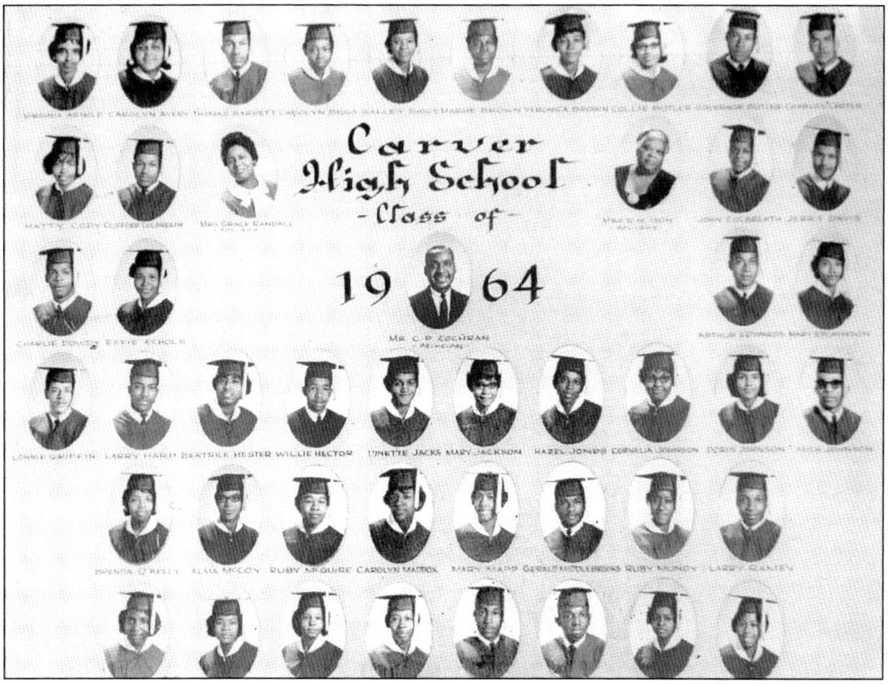

This is the 1964 graduating class of Carver High School. (Courtesy John Robinson, Assistant Superintendent, Walton County Schools.)

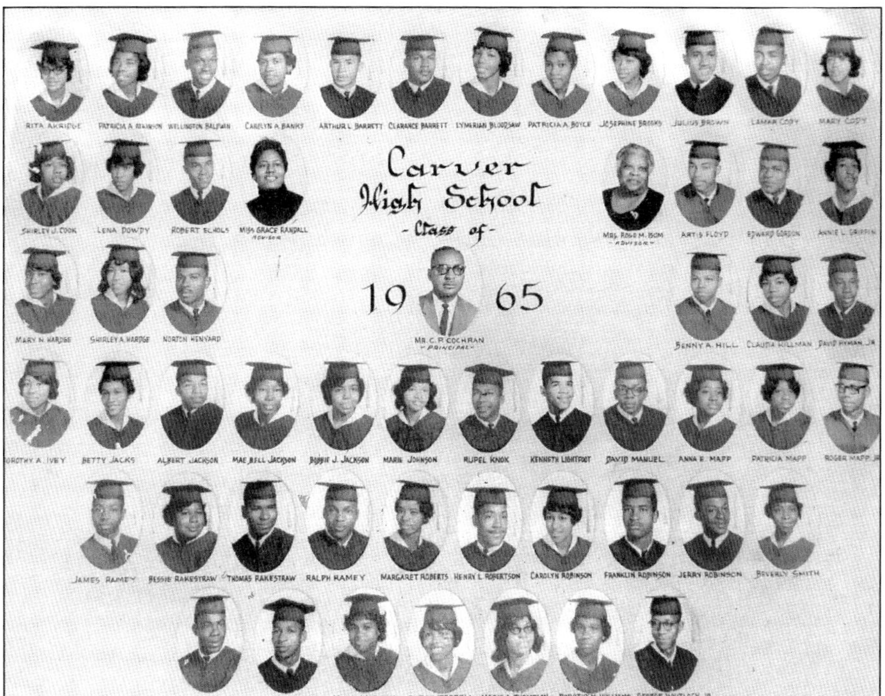

The Carver High School class of 1965 is pictured with principal and senior advisors. (Courtesy John Robinson, Assistant Superintendent, Walton County Schools.)

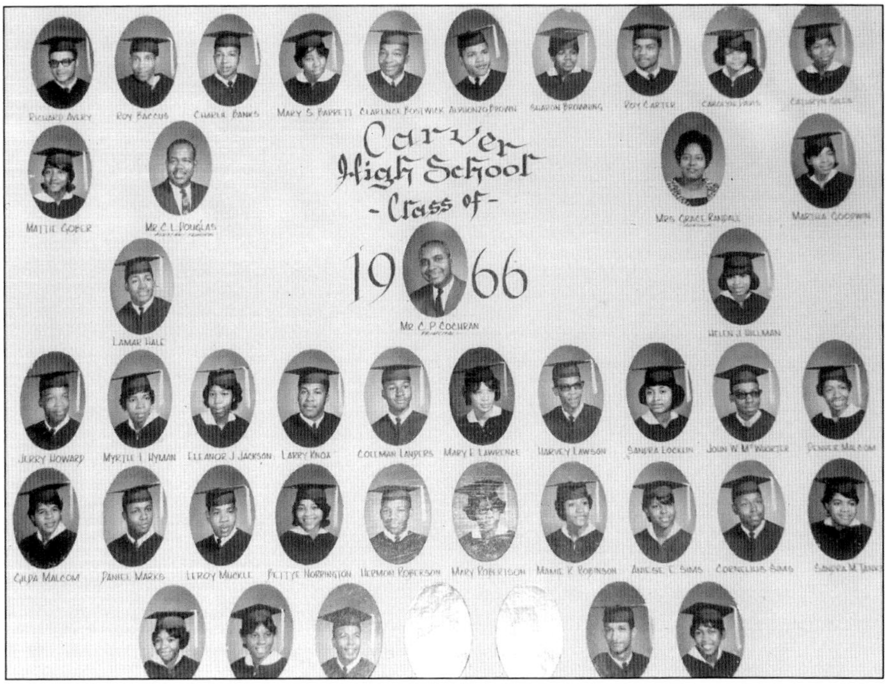

The Carver High School class of 1966 is shown with principal and senior advisors. (Courtesy John Robinson, Assistant Superintendent, Walton County Schools.)

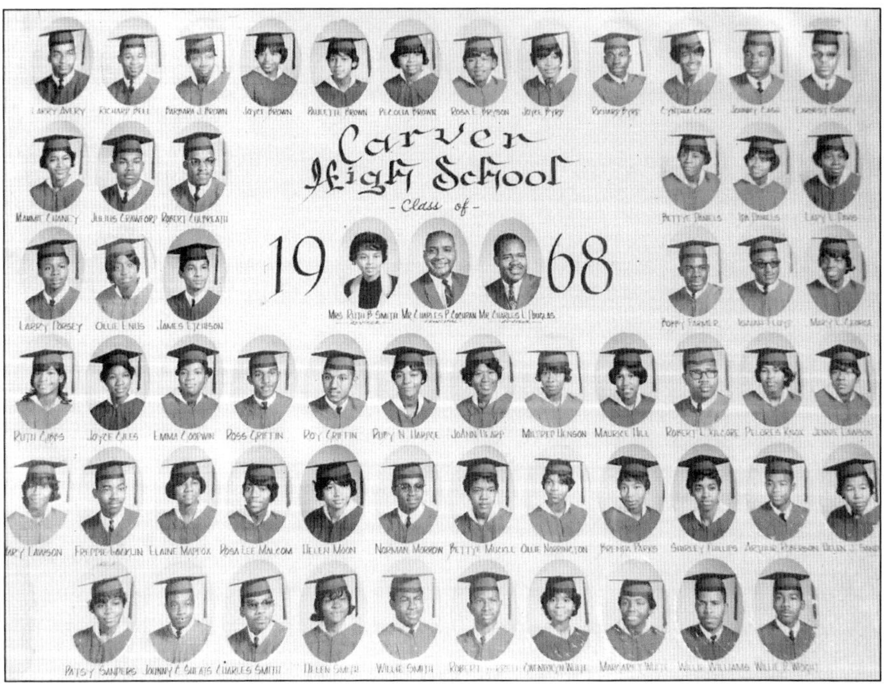

The Carver High School class of 1968 is pictured with principal and senior advisors. (Courtesy Timothy Kemp and John Robinson, Walton County Schools.)

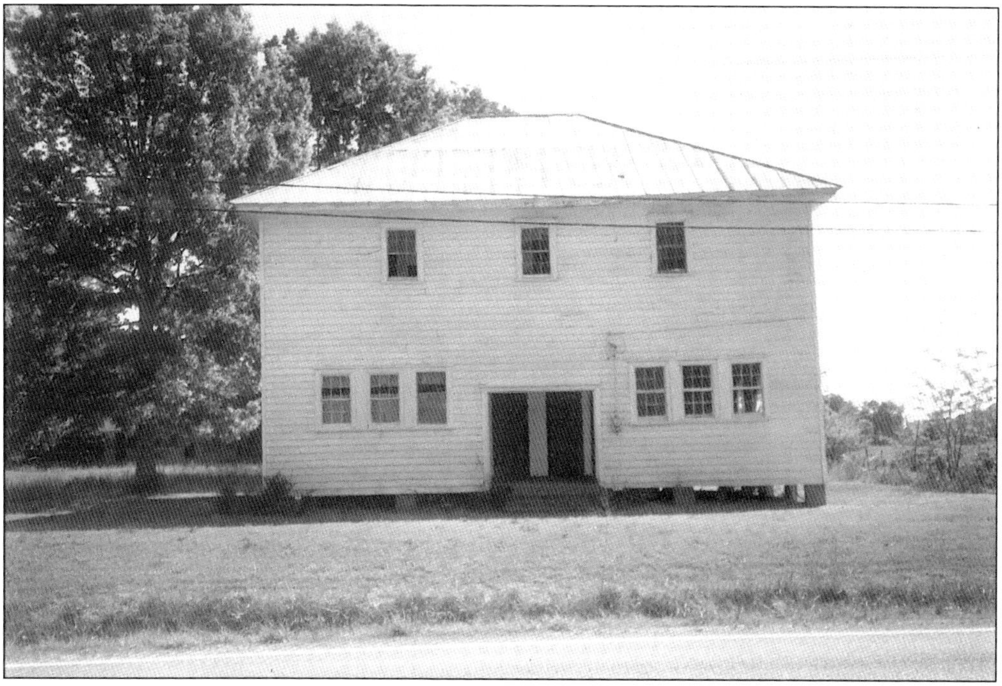

This building was the Good Hope School. It is now used as the Georgia Colored Men's Benevolent Association Lodge Hall. (Courtesy Emma Wiseman and Marilyn Williams.)

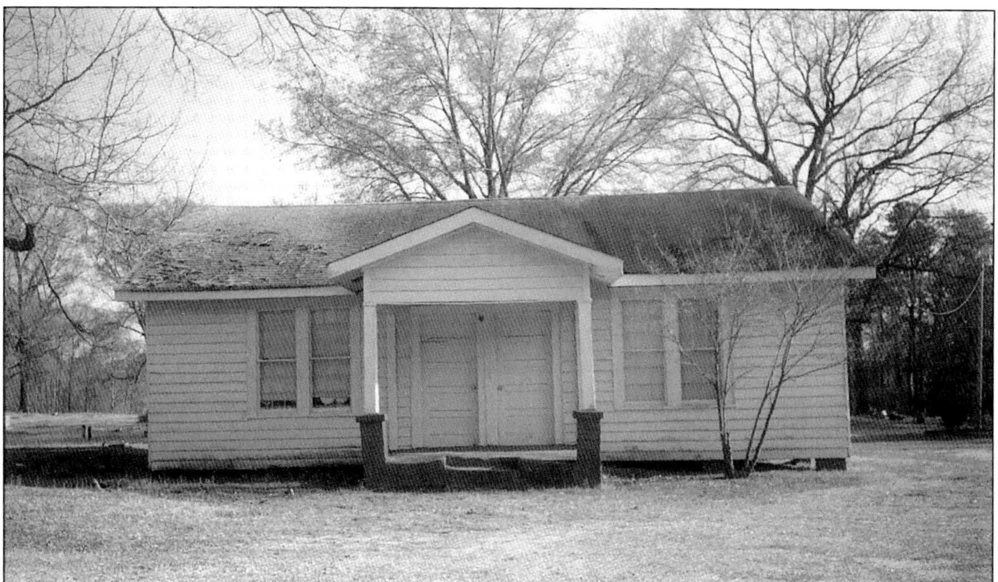

The Mount Enon School building is pictured here. Early schools included rural church schools and Rosenwald schools. There were three Rosenwald schools, which included Loganville School, Peters School, and Thompson School. Other rural schools were Spring Hill, Etchison School, Browns Hill, Good Hope, Bethany, Carters Hill, Dallas Chapel, and Ingram. Many of these schools were built by community members on land donated by black land owners. (Photograph by Lynn Camp.)

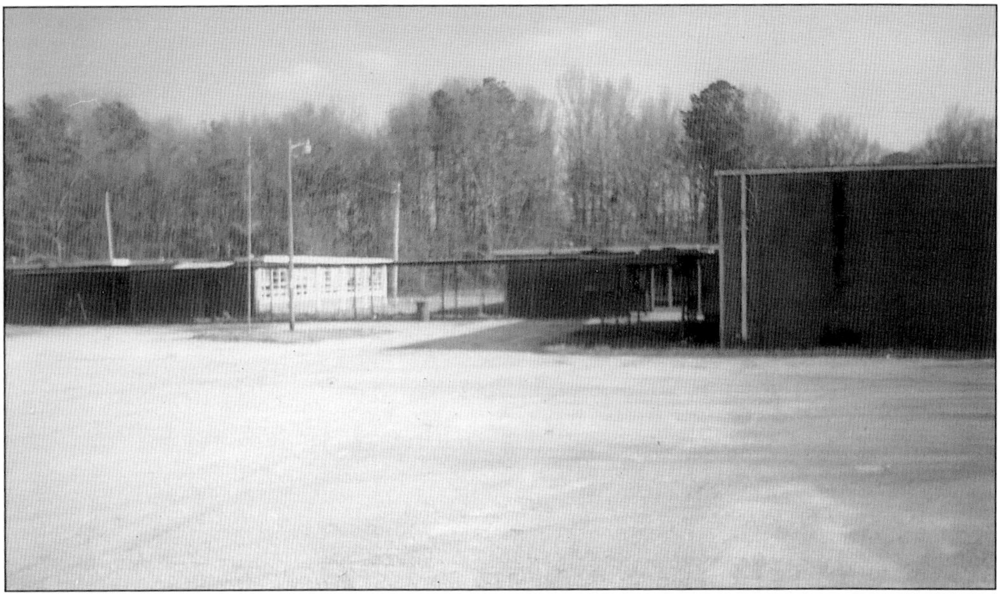

This is the Good Hope Peters School. African-American children in the Good Hope community were educated at this school for many years. (Courtesy Lynn Camp.)

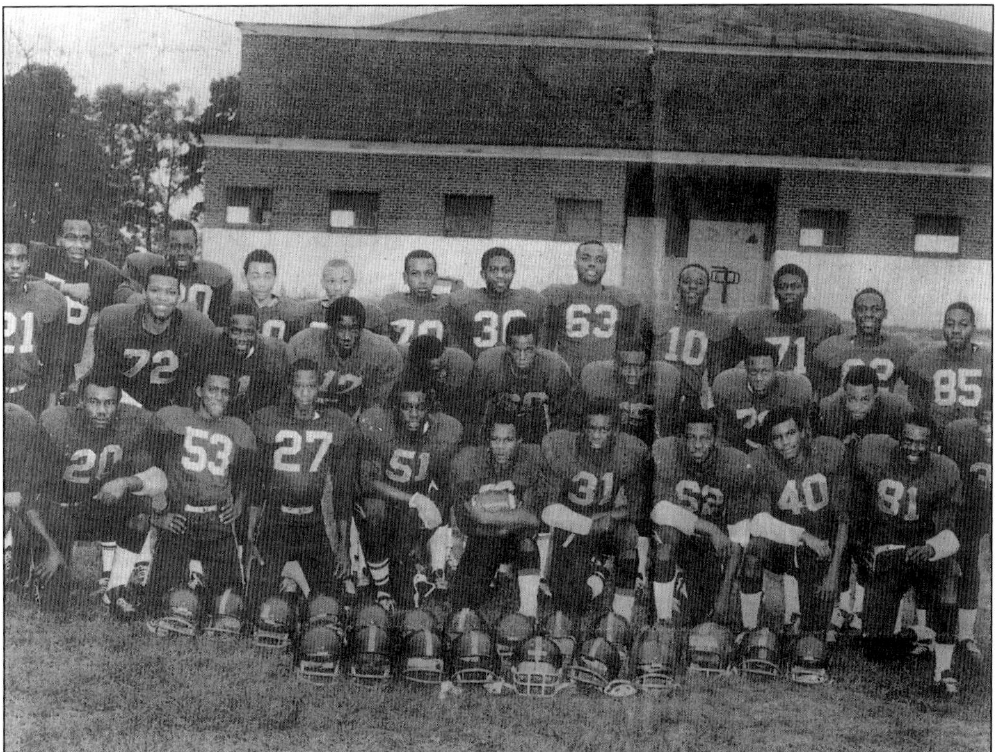

The state champions of the Georgia Interscholastic Association 1968 are shown in front of the Carver High School gym. This team captured the first state football championship in Walton County by defeating Risley High School of Brunswick 15-0. (Courtesy Lynn Camp.)

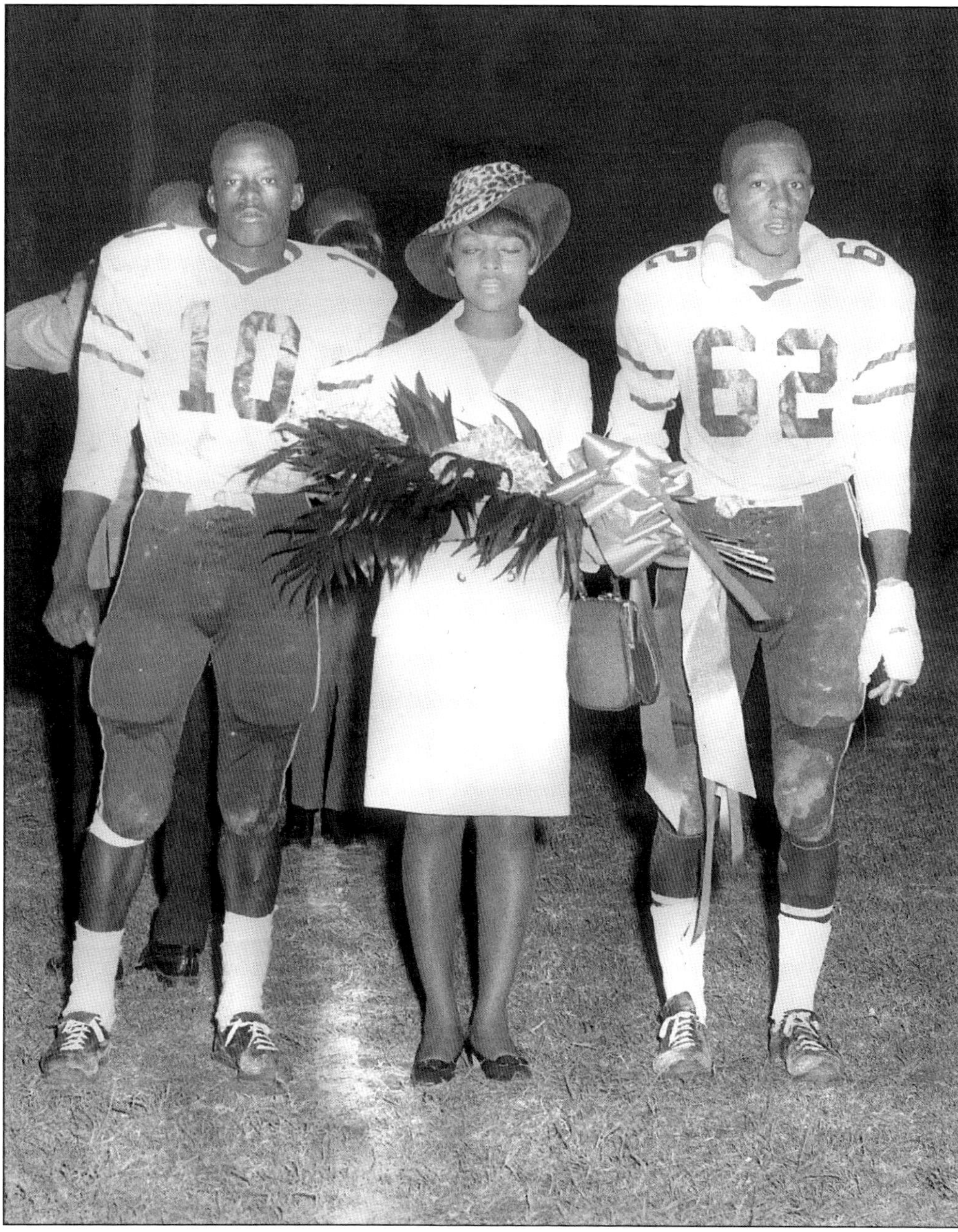

Pictured here are quarterback Harold Culbreath, homecoming queen Annette Ramey, and captain of the football team Tommie Lee Hillman Jr. at Carver High School's last homecoming game in 1968. (Courtesy Tommie Lee Hillman Jr.)

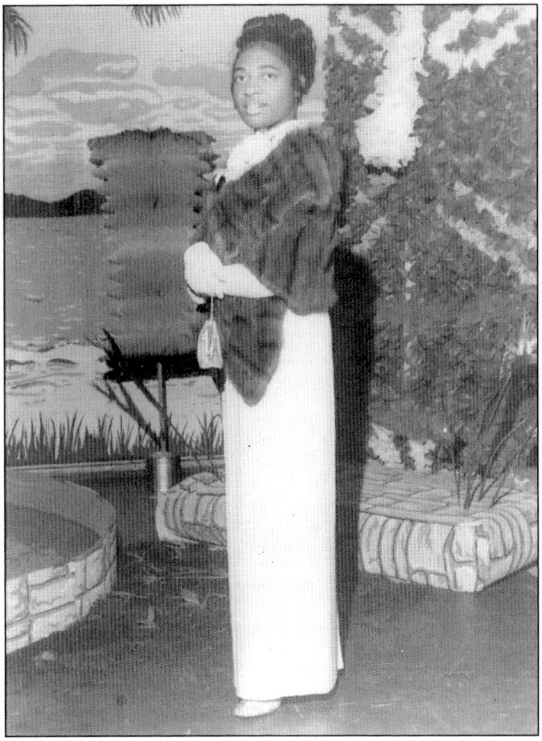

Ruby Lynn Robinson was at the senior prom in this 1969 photograph. Ruby Lynn was the editor of the only newsletter published at Carver High School. She was also editor-in-chief of the school's last yearbook. (Courtesy Lynn Camp.)

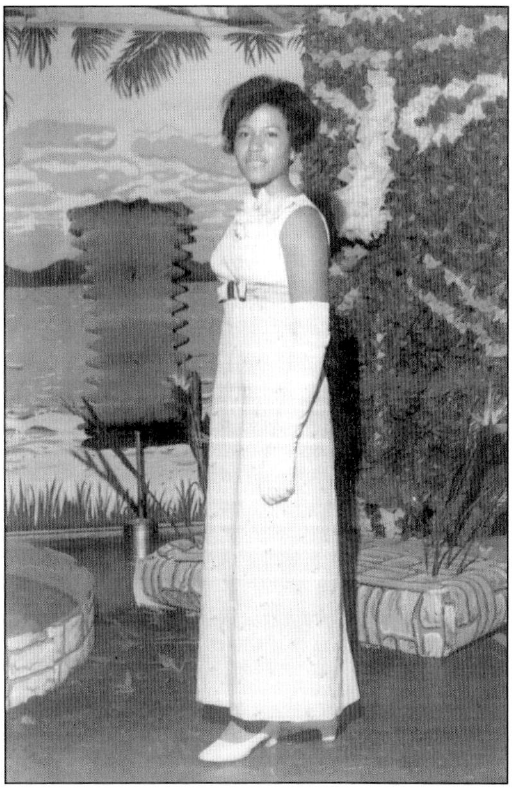

Mary Ann Hill was at the senior prom in this 1969 photograph. She was a talented vocalist, instrumentalist, majorette, and dancer in high school. Mary Ann was voted "most talented" in her 1969 graduating class at Carver High School. (Courtesy Lynn Camp.)

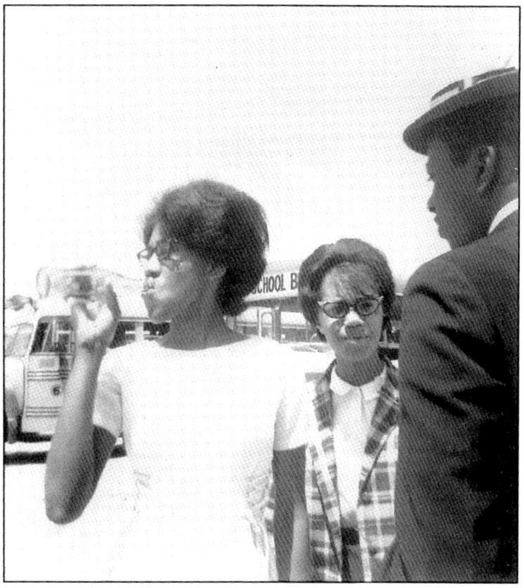 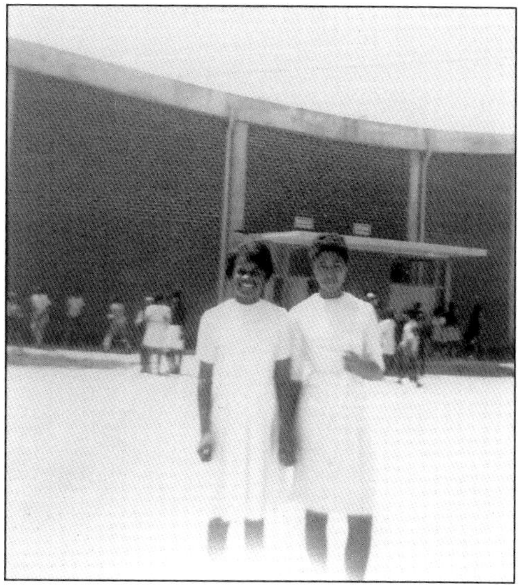

(*above, left*) Waiting to board the bus for home after a band trip in 1965 are, from left to right, Lena Dowdy, Rita Akridge, and David Manuel. Rita was one of the first blacks to hold an office job at the United States Department of Agriculture during the 1960s in Monroe. She is currently Rita Scott, Monroe councilwoman of the 5th district. (Photograph by Lynn Camp.) (*above, right*) Two members of Carver High School's concert band, Annette Williams and Linda Bloodsaw, posed while on a band trip *c.* 1965. Many excellent musicians were trained under the direction of Phillip N. Davis, band director at Carver High School from 1957 to 1966. (Photograph by Lynn Camp.)

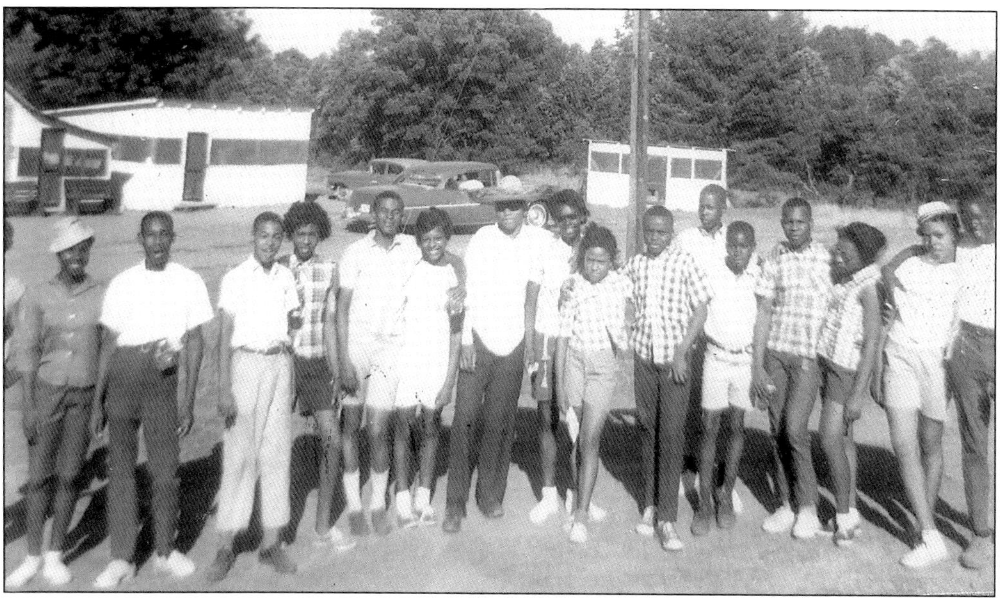

Seventh- and eighth-grade students on a school-closing trip to Jackson Lake are (from left to right) LaVerne Swaine, C.W. Knox, Tommie Maddox, Teressa Maddox, Charles Edward Bell, Barbara Ann Culbreath, Jimmy Etchison, Patsy Vinson, Mary Ann Hill, Leon Boyce, Ralph Booker, unidentified, Stanley Malcom, Ruby Lynn Robinson, Annette Ramey, and Harold Culbreath. (Courtesy Lynn Camp.)

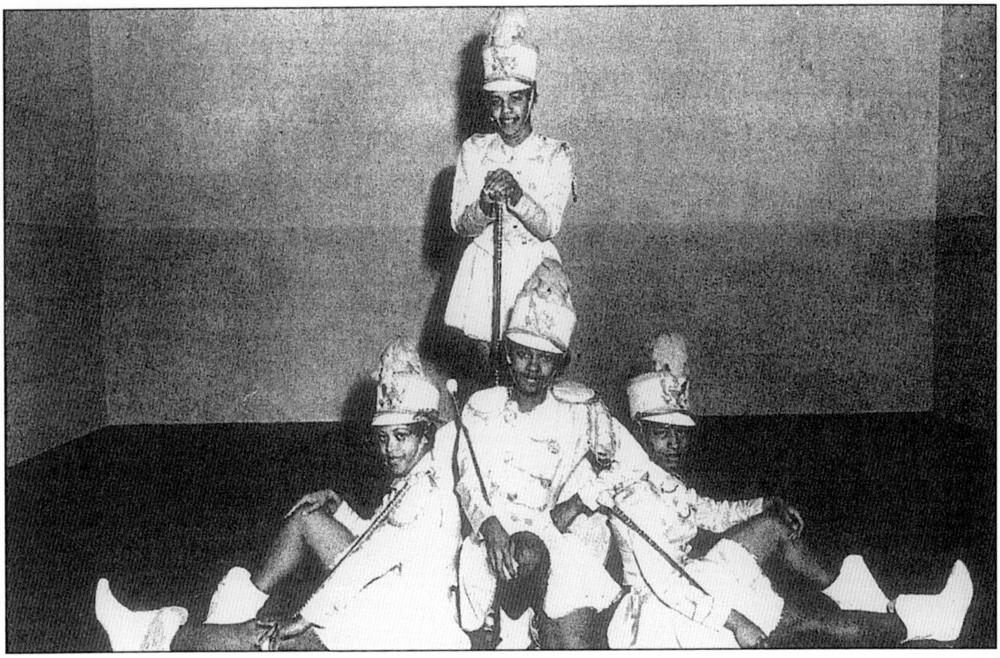

Here are majorettes of the Mighty Wildcat Marching Band of Carver High School in 1961. Alice Malcom is standing; and from left to right are Louise Brown, Maxine Henyard, and Shirley Starr. (Courtesy Lynn Camp.)

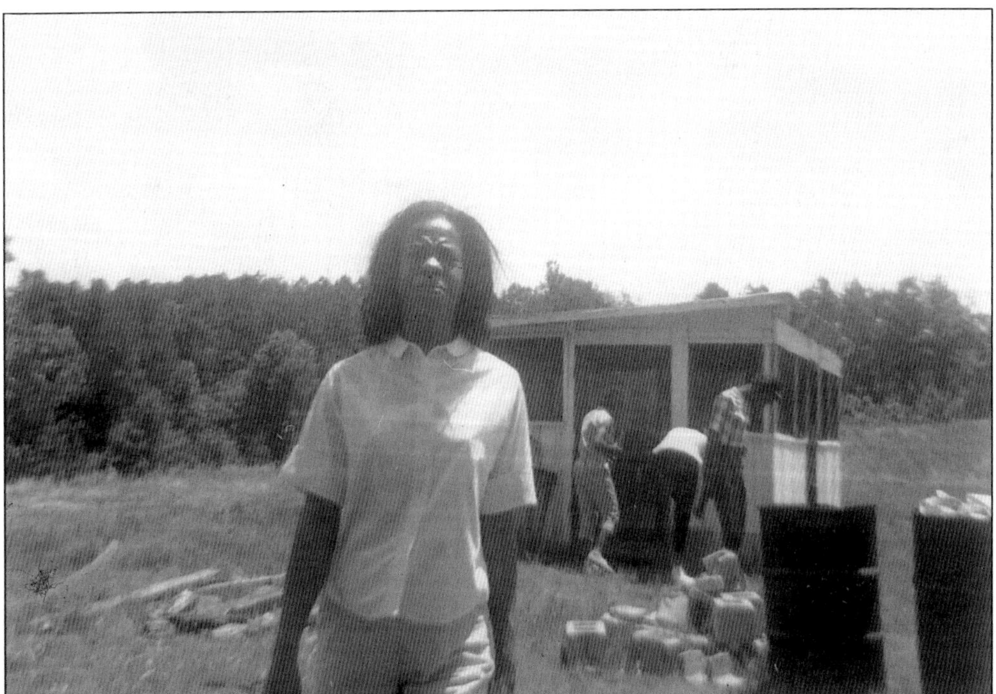

Willie Marshall, an eighth-grade teacher at Carver High School, chaperoned the students for the school closing trip to Jackson Lake. (Courtesy Lynn Camp.)

Members of the Monroe Colored High School class of 1944 are seen celebrating a reunion after 40 years. From left to right are Eleanor Franklin, Evelyn Bush, Junius "Junie Mae" Smith, and Sarah Braswell Starling. The class of 1944 was the first high school graduating class in the county. (Courtesy Evelyn Bush.)

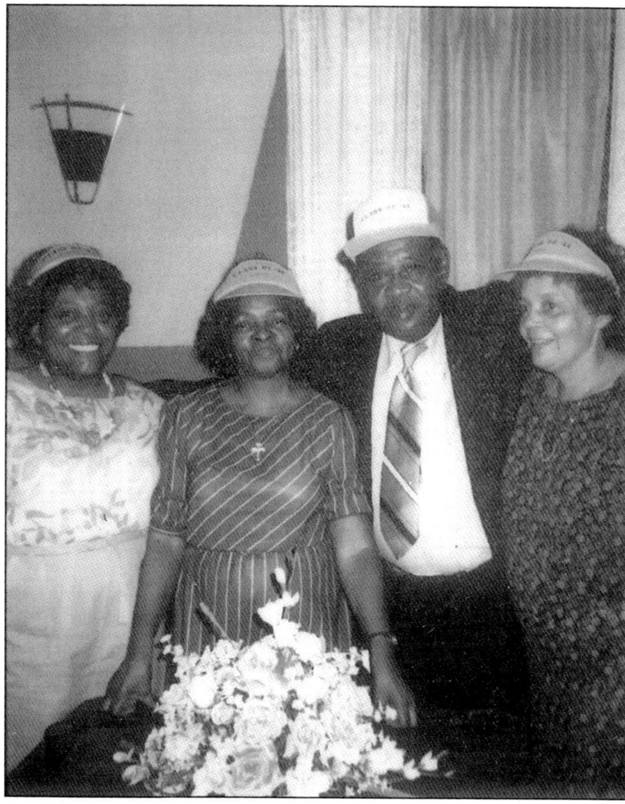

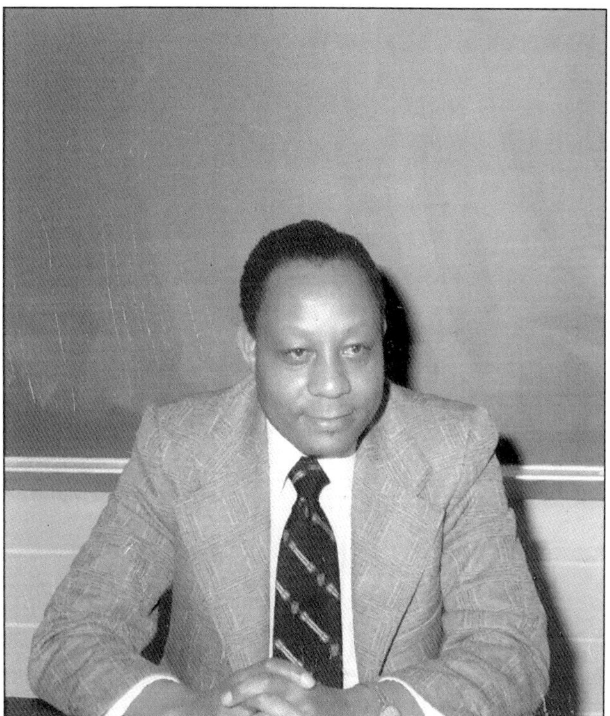

Dr. C.T. Wright, a 1960 graduate of Carver High School, obtained a B.S. from Fort Valley State College, an M.A. from Atlanta University, and Ph.D. from Boston University. He is currently president of the International Foundation for Education and Self-Help. A native of Social Circle, he received his early education in the public school system there. (Courtesy Dr. Willie Enus.)

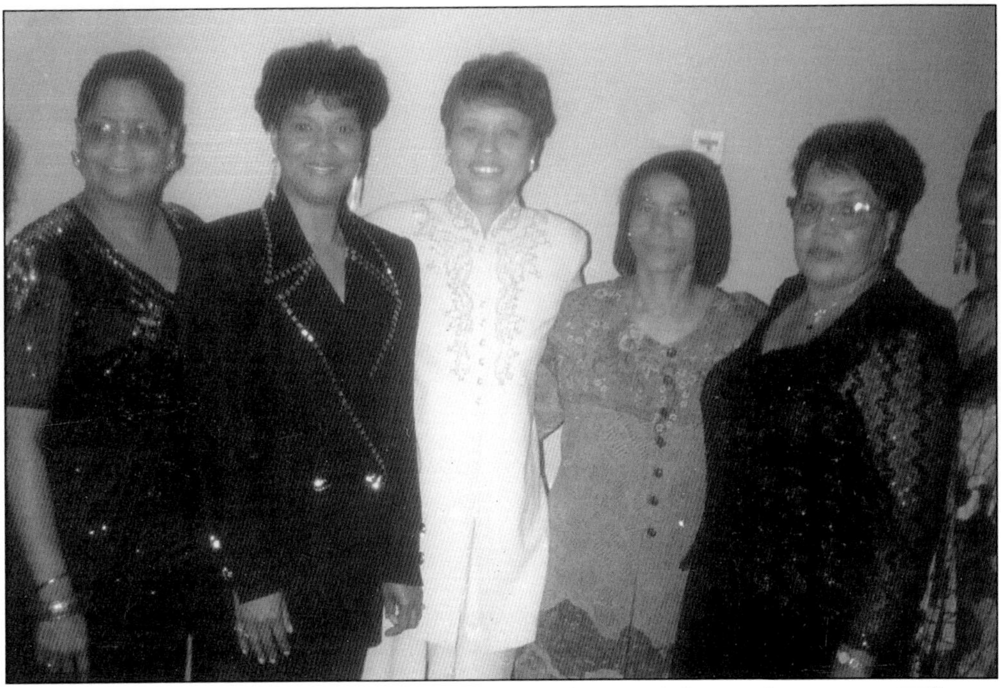

Friends unite at the Maroon and Gold Ball in 1996. From left to right are Lena Williams, Maxine Lucas, Ariel Sullivan, Shirley Griffin, and Alice Spurley. (Photograph by Lynn Camp.)

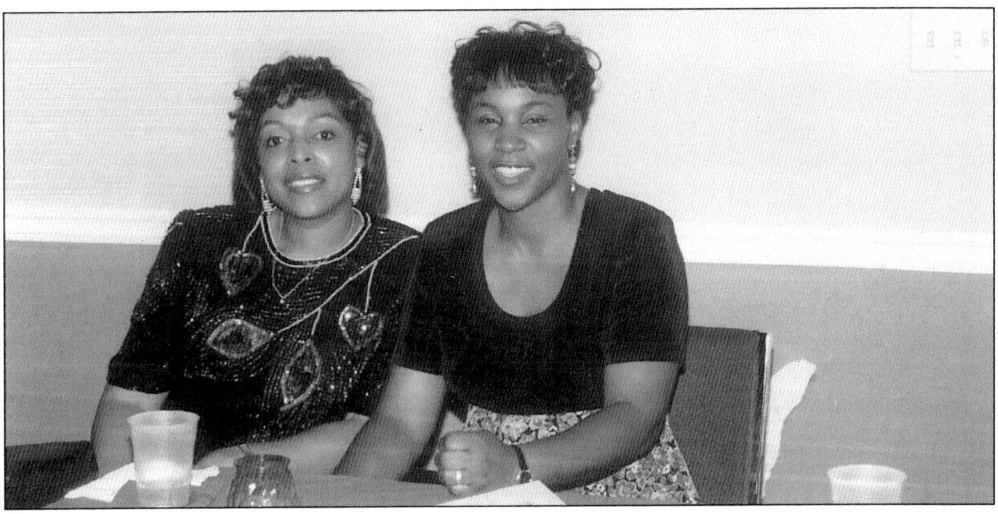

Dr. Annette R. Waller is pictured with LaVerne Dawkins at the Maroon and Gold Ball in 1996. Dr. Waller is the principal of Narvie J. Harris Traditional Theme School in Decatur, where students are under parental contract. The school opened in 1999 and under Dr. Waller's administration the school has attained scores in the 95th percentile and above on standardized testing in all grades. Dr. Waller received the 2003 Higher Year Achievement Award given by *Ross Report News*, recognizing outstanding leadership, discipline, and success. She is also a recent graduate of Leadership Dekalb, a non-profit organization whose mission is to cultivate the skills of the county's current and emerging leaders and to develop a more informed and educated network of citizens. (Photograph by Lynn Camp.)

Five

The Civil Rights Era

Remembering the Struggle

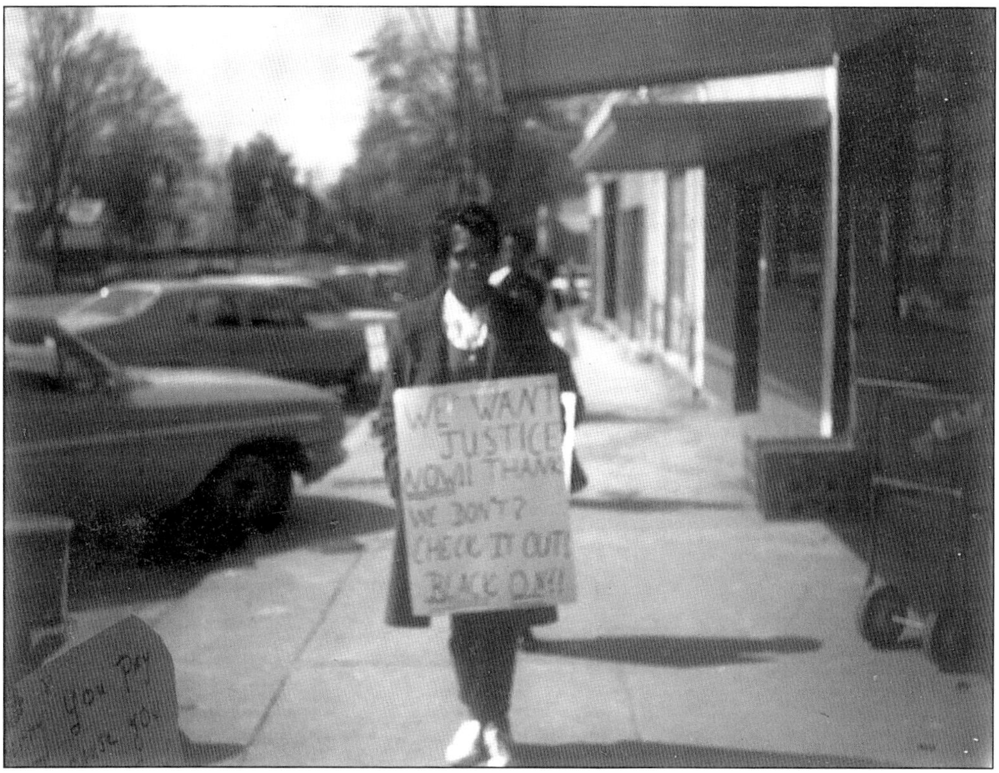

This unidentified protester is shown marching in downtown Social Circle in 1968. (Courtesy Robert Howard.)

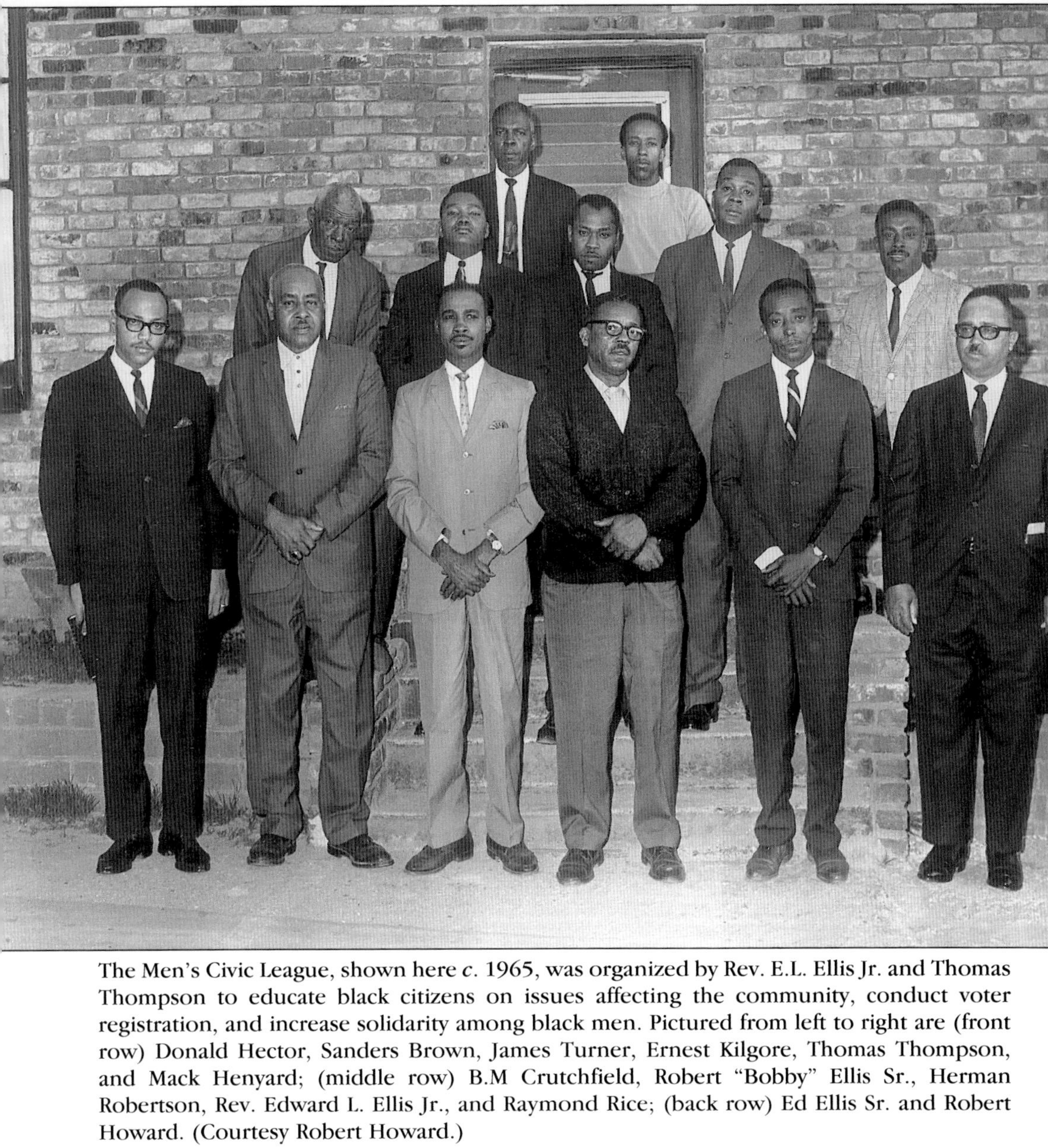

The Men's Civic League, shown here *c.* 1965, was organized by Rev. E.L. Ellis Jr. and Thomas Thompson to educate black citizens on issues affecting the community, conduct voter registration, and increase solidarity among black men. Pictured from left to right are (front row) Donald Hector, Sanders Brown, James Turner, Ernest Kilgore, Thomas Thompson, and Mack Henyard; (middle row) B.M Crutchfield, Robert "Bobby" Ellis Sr., Herman Robertson, Rev. Edward L. Ellis Jr., and Raymond Rice; (back row) Ed Ellis Sr. and Robert Howard. (Courtesy Robert Howard.)

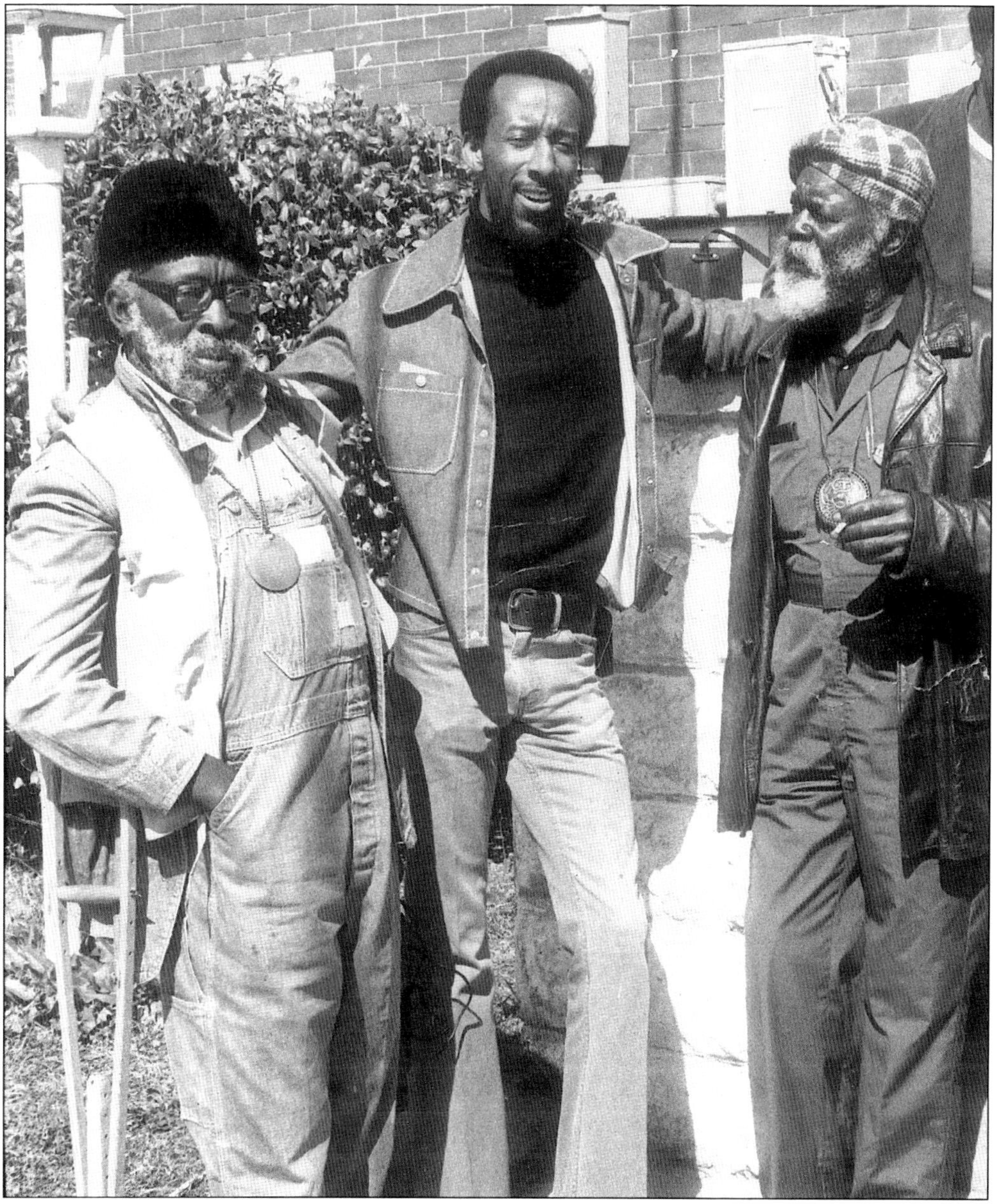

Robert "Bobby" Howard is pictured at center with other civil rights activists, Collins "Pop" Harris (right) and "Sunshine" (left), *c.* 1968. Howard became involved with activism as a teenager while riding with Dan Young to register voters. He was instrumental in establishing the Community Organization for Progress in Education (C.O.P.E.) and was chosen as its president. As president of that organization Bobby played a leading role in voter registration, integration of the school system, the organization of economic boycotts, and the fight for black political representation in local government. Bobby conducted his own unofficial investigation of the Moore's Ford Lynching over a period of 30 years. He currently serves on the board of directors of the A.P. Henderson Foundation and the Moore's Ford Memorial Committee. Bobby is well known in the Social Circle community and throughout Walton County as a "fighter of causes." (Courtesy Robert Howard.)

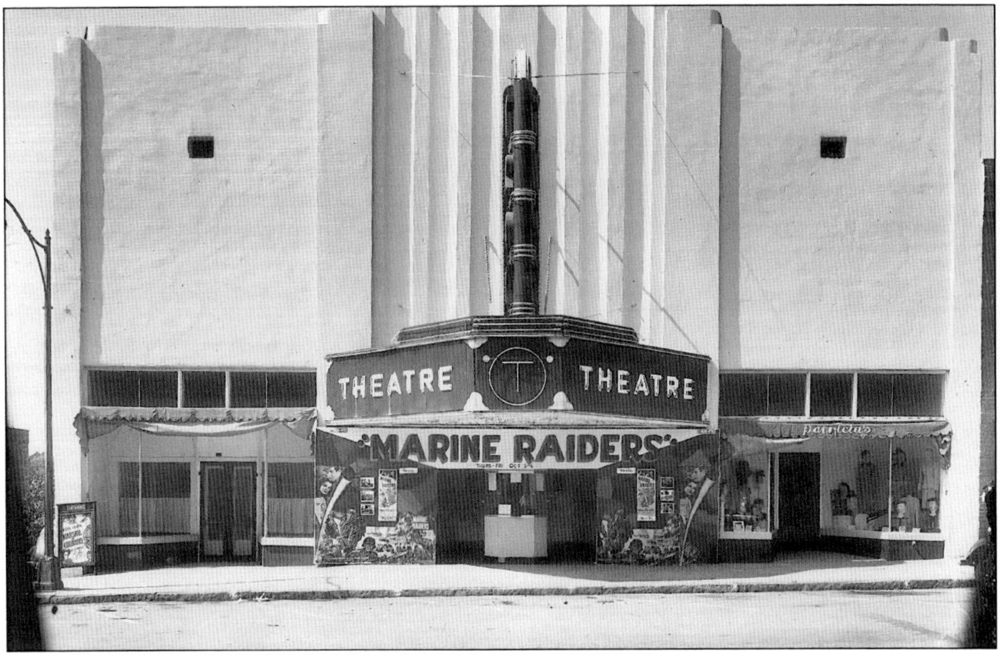

The Troy Theatre in downtown Monroe was a popular place to go. Black patrons climbed the fire escape to enjoy a "picture show" from the balcony. (From the E.M. Carnes Collection; Courtesy Larry Witcher.)

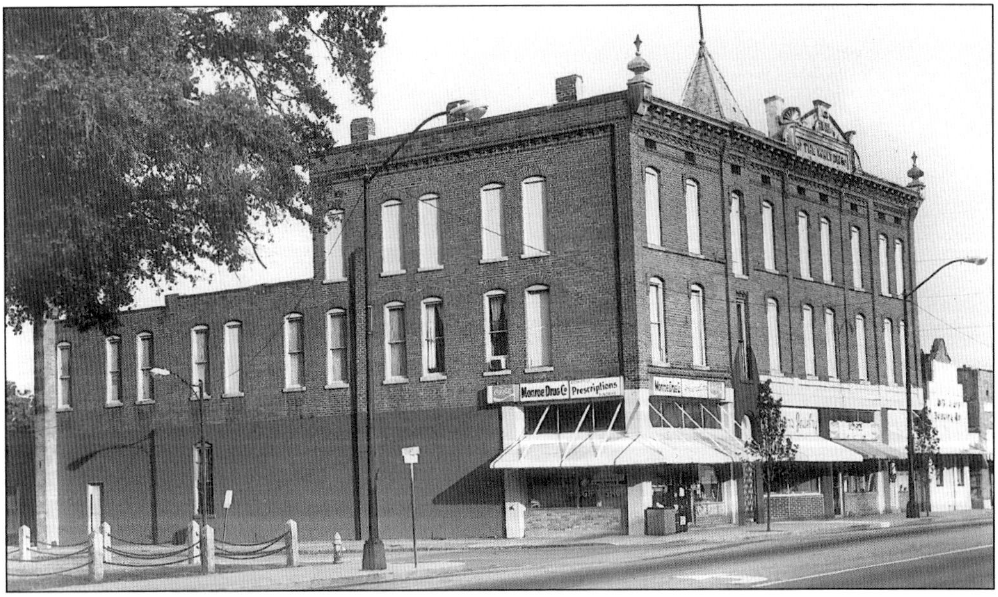

The Monroe Drug Store was housed in the Monroe Hotel building downtown. According to verbal lore, black teenage girls, who were babysitting white children, would gather on the corner here to chat while eating ice cream. Blacks were not allowed to make purchases while standing behind the counter or sit in the soda fountain area with other customers during the years of segregation. The soda fountain seating was discontinued after the Civil Rights Act was passed. (From the E.M. Carnes Collection; Courtesy Larry Witcher.)

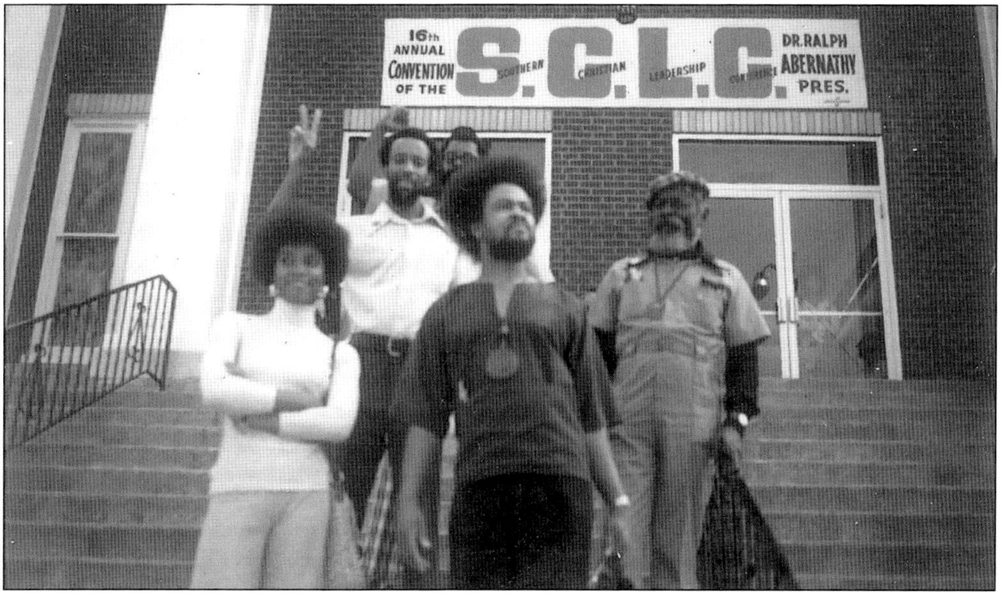

Tyrone Brooks (front center), currently a state representative, is pictured with Robert Howard (giving the peace sign), Collins "Pop" Harris (right), and other Walton County activists at the Southern Christian Leadership Conference in 1969. (Courtesy Robert Howard.)

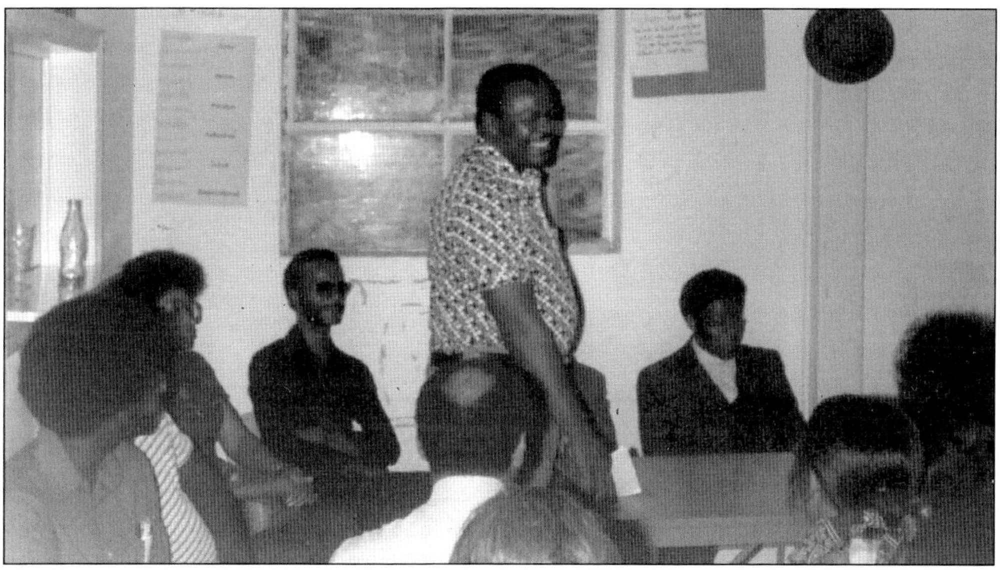

Edward Gordon (standing) addressed a group at a mass meeting at the First African Baptist Church in Monroe, *c.* 1964. Pictured to Gordon's right is Clinton Sorrells Sr., who was president of the youth chapter of the NAACP. Sorrells was arrested along with Shirley Arnold, Clara Bennett, and Willie George Reese for attempting to be served in Bolton's Restaurant in downtown Monroe. Their arrests led to a lawsuit resulting in the desegregation of downtown businesses. Mass meetings were held generally in churches to plan strategies for boycotts and protests. They featured freedom songs and various speakers. (Courtesy Geneva Locklin.)

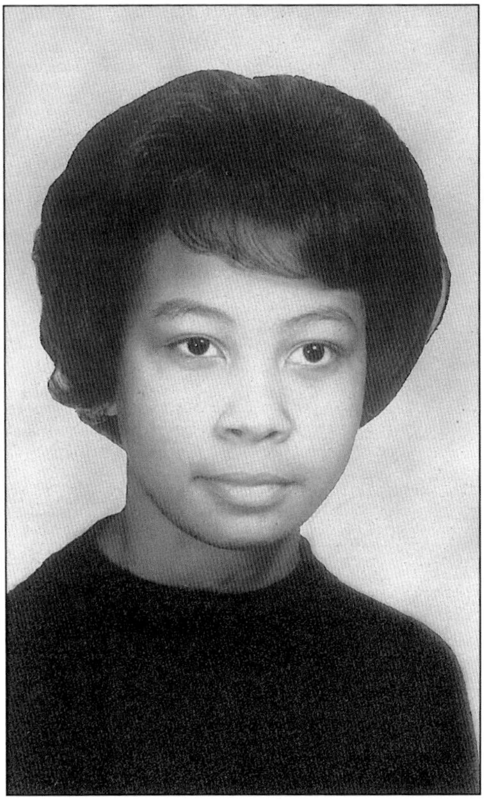

Dorcas Jernigan was a ninth-grade student (*c*. 1965) when she became one of the first black students to integrate the Walton County School system by attending Monroe Area High School. Dorcas said she remembers feeling that she deserved a better education than what the black schools were offering. So, when approached by a young Civil Rights activist from Atlanta about integrating the school system, she took the challenge. She recalls taking the I.Q. test and feeling she had to qualify. She also remembers the early days, as one of two black students, being filled with harassment. Even the teachers were not supportive of the black students. Dorcas was inspired by her grandparents, prominent farmers, Artee and Mollie Jackson Ethchison. The Etchisons owned approximately 600 acres of land and donated land for the Etchison School. Five of their seven daughters received post-secondary education and all of his six sons were skilled machinists and laborers. (Courtesy Dorcas Jernigan.)

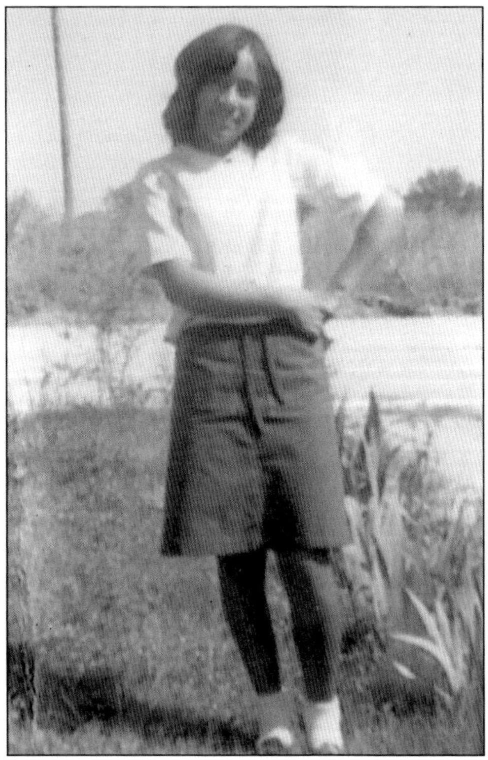

Sallie Robertson was a tenth-grade student (*c*. 1965) when she became one of the first black students to integrate the Walton County School system by attending Monroe Area High School. Odis Smith was the chairman of the local chapter of the NAACP at that time. He escorted Sallie and another young student into the school building. The school system did not comply with federal desegregation laws until 1969. (Courtesy Lynn Camp.)

Casteel Avery Jr. was the first black student to graduate from Monroe Area High School in 1966. He entered the school as a senior. He was faced with many challenges at the school, but he continued his studies and completed high school despite the harsh environment. (Courtesy Lynn Camp.)

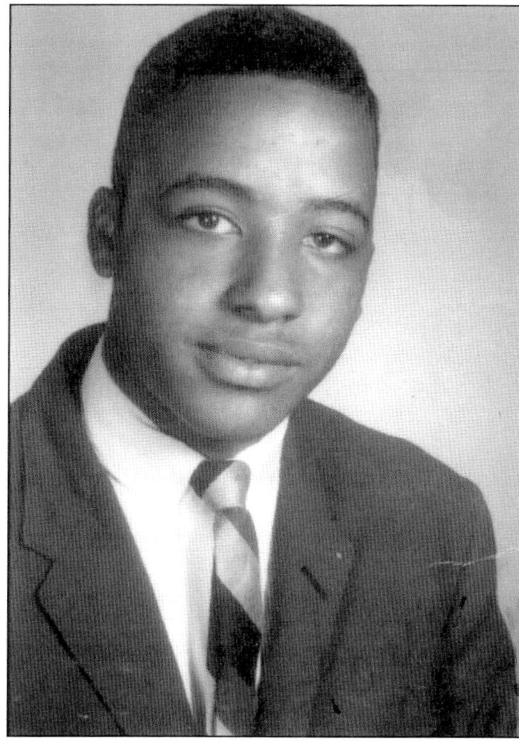

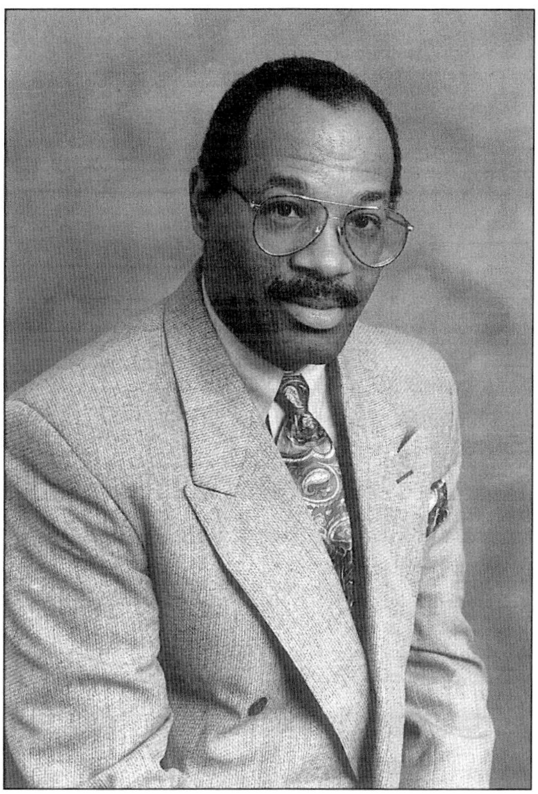

Billy Jones was president of the local Walton County chapters of the NAACP and Southern Christian Leadership Conference. He gave tremendous amounts of time and energy to educating blacks in Walton County about the importance of voting and the political process. He served as a member of the Monroe Housing Authority and as vice chairman of the Walton County school board. Jones was a Vietnam War veteran who served in the United States Army for 12 years. (Courtesy Linda Jones.)

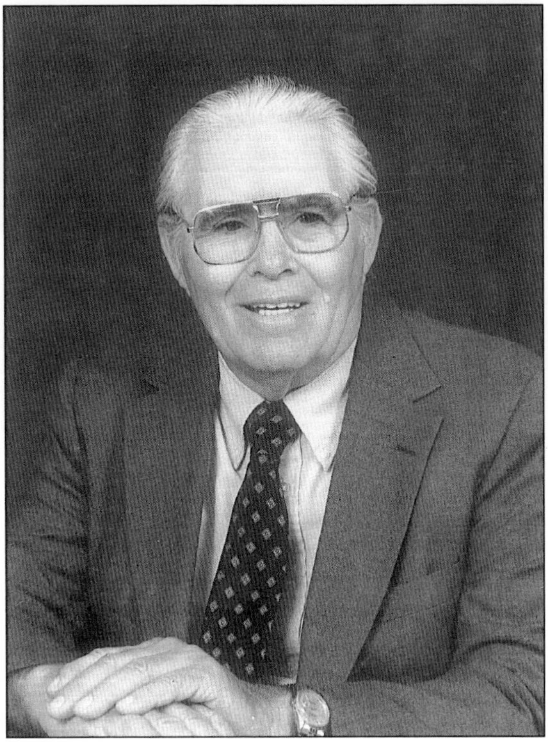

John J. Culbreath Sr.(1923–1998) served as the president of local chapters of the NAACP, Southern Christian Leadership Conference, and Black Citizens Council. He successfully advocated for the hiring of blacks as city and county government employees. Prior to the Civil Rights era Culbreath spoke out for the end of disparity in Walton County schools. He campaigned for voter registration and transported black citizens to the voting polls until his death. (Courtesy Debra Taylor.)

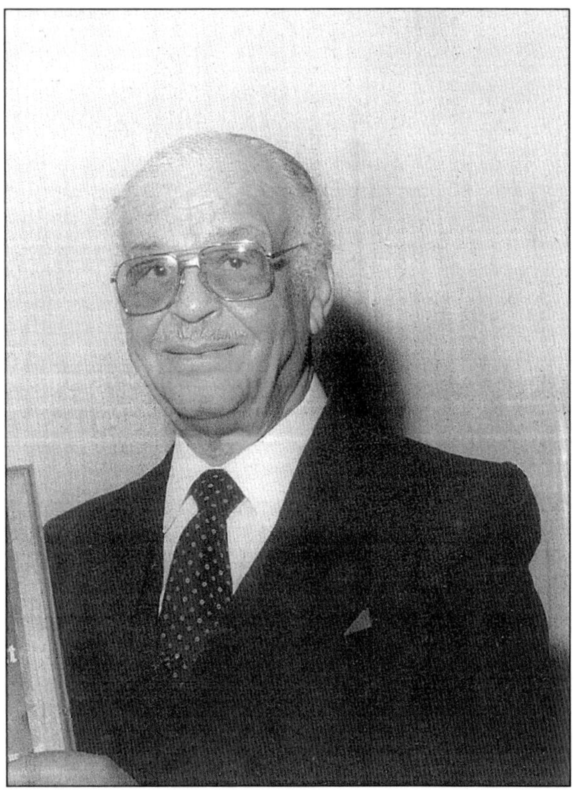

Daniel (Dan) W. Young Sr. (1904–1988) is considered by some to be "the father of the Civil Rights movement in Walton County." His name became synonymous with the movement when he begin to use his own funds to bond protesters out of jail. He provided his business as meeting place when it was too risky to meet in churches. An active member of the NAACP, Young went door-to-door registering Walton County black citizens to vote and provided transportation to the polls—sometimes in his hearse. Even before the 1960s, Young advocated higher pay for teachers, buses, and improved facilities for Walton County Schools. (Courtesy Ariel Young Sullivan.)

Six

Business and Economy

Owning Our Own

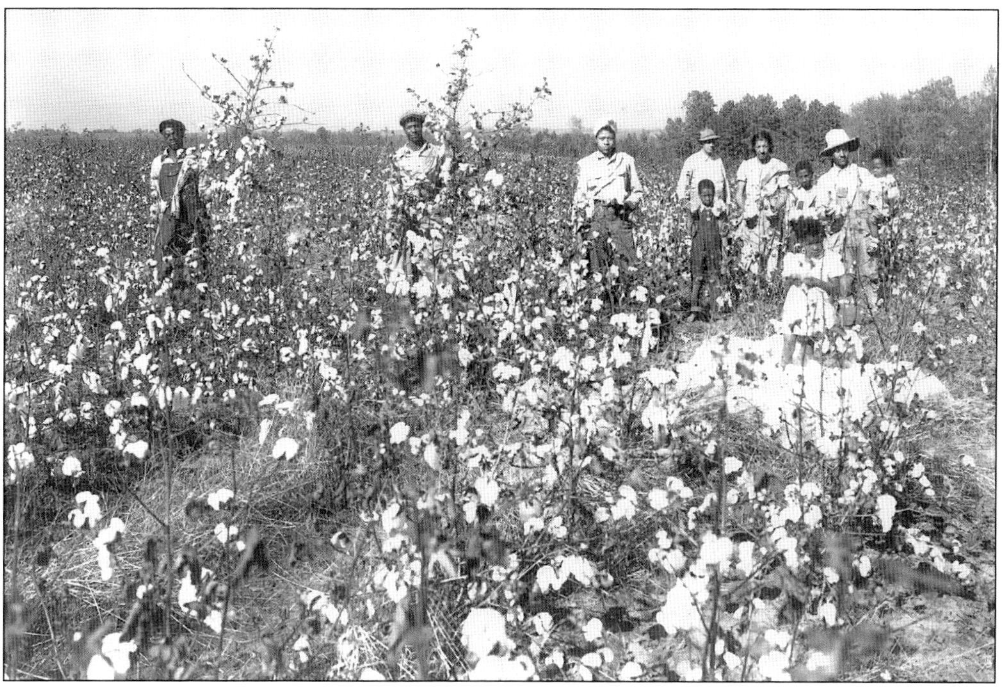

Mrs. Idora Battle is pictured with her family in her cotton field. Mrs. Battle was known in the county for being able to manage a farm and grow exceptional crops. In 1964 she received a certificate of honor for producing 775 pounds of lint cotton per acre on 5 acres, making her a member of the Georgia Money Maker Cotton Club. Mrs. Battle later became the first sales clerk to work in Millyer Aycock Department Store in downtown Monroe. (From the E.M. Carnes Collection; Courtesy Larry Witcher.)

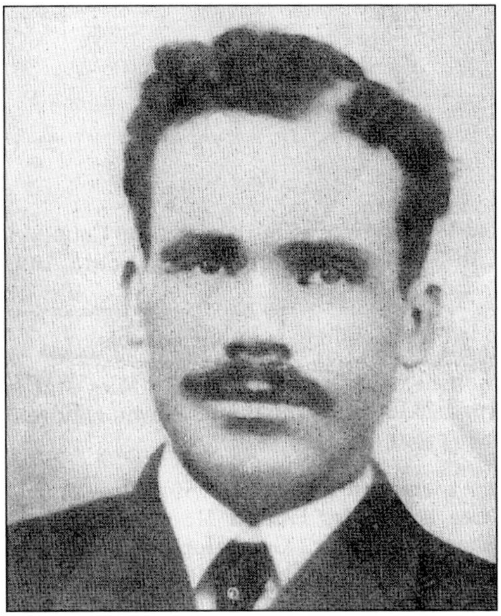

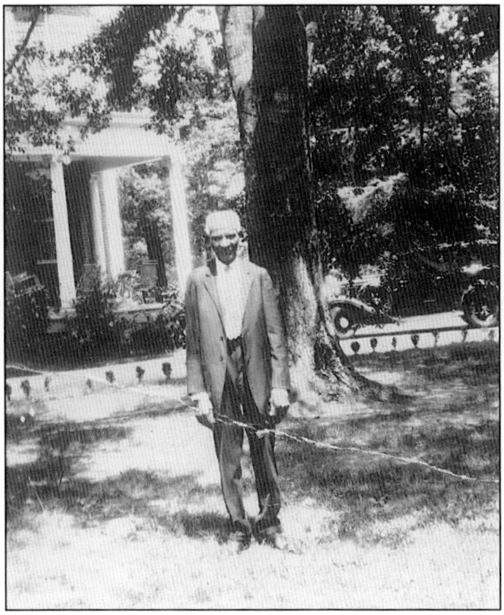

(*above, left*) Albert W. Martin (1879–1971), commonly called "Ab Martin," was one of the most prominent black farmers of his time, accumulating more than 500 acres of farmland, which included eight homes. According to family members, he once owned the land in downtown Monroe where Young Funeral Home is located. (Courtesy Herman Robertson and Anita Brown.) (*above, right*) Phinazy is shown in front of the McDaniel-Tichenor House in the 1930s. Emily Tichenor refers to Phinazy Snow in her garden journal. Here he had just finished planting box woods. (Courtesy the McDaniel-Tichenor House.)

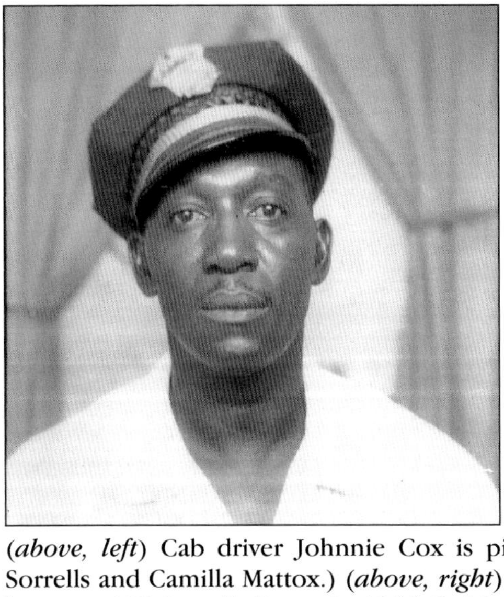

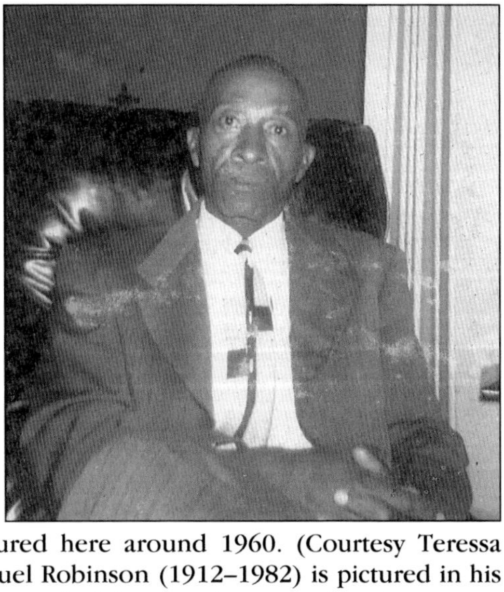

(*above, left*) Cab driver Johnnie Cox is pictured here around 1960. (Courtesy Teressa Sorrells and Camilla Mattox.) (*above, right*) Huel Robinson (1912–1982) is pictured in his home at 105 Sorrells Street in 1964. Robinson worked for the city sanitation department until he retired in 1974. Prior to purchasing a home and moving to Monroe in 1956, Robinson owned and worked a 129-acre farm in nearby Bostwick. The farm was sold when farming was no longer profitable and the family moved "to town." He was the father of co-author Lynn Robinson Camp. (Courtesy of Tessie Robinson.)

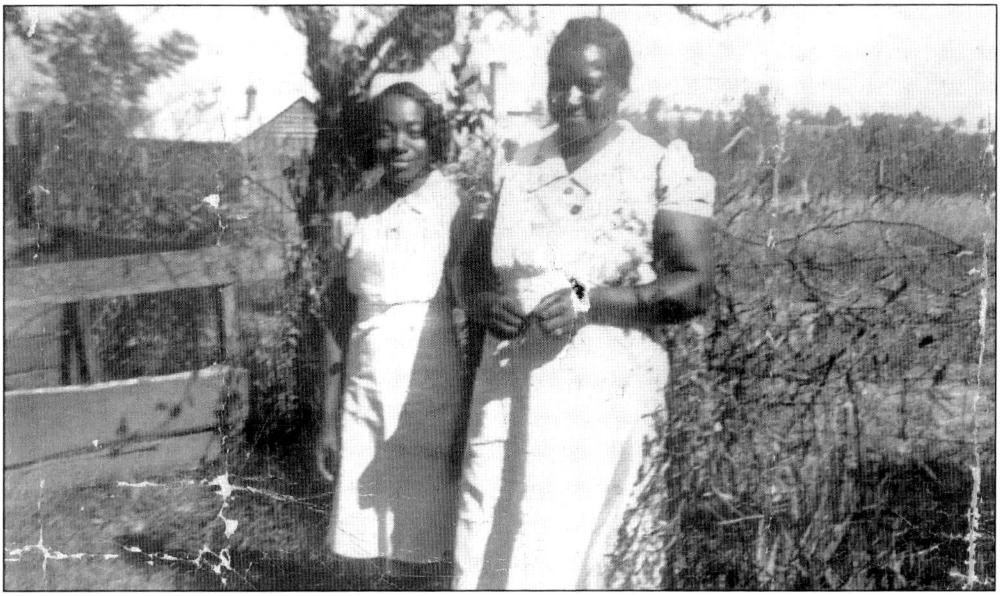

For many years, black women supported their families by working in the homes of whites as maids, cooks, and babysitters. Tessie Robinson (mother of co-author Lynn Robinson Camp) is pictured with an unidentified co-worker in the yard of their employer in this 1946 photograph. Tessie moved to Walton County with her husband, Huel Robinson, in 1936, and they began sharecropping that year. (Courtesy Tessie Robinson.)

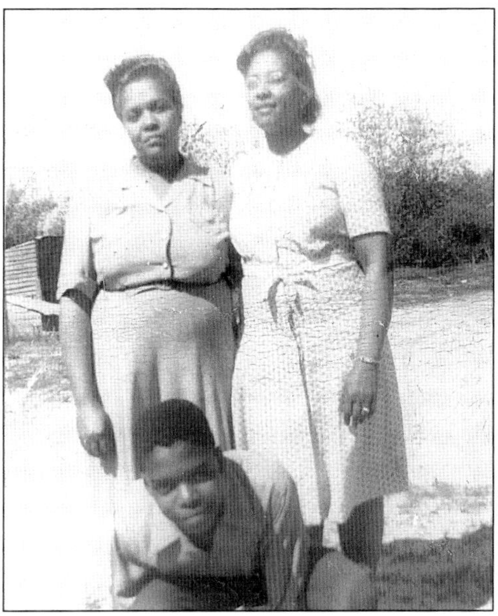

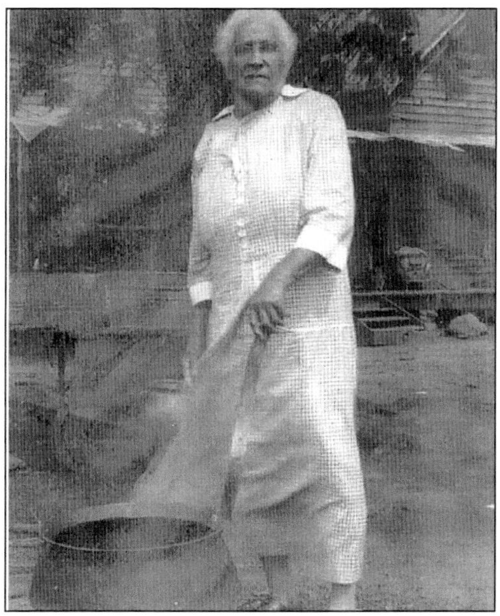

(*above, left*) Grace Jackson was owner and operator of Jackson Funeral Home located on Spring Street and later on Davis Street following the death of her father and business owner William "Cap" Jackson. Jackson's daughter, Evelyn Bush, currently owns and operates the Jackson Funeral Home on Gratis Road. (Courtesy Evelyn Bush.) (*above, right*) Lillie Bell Simmons is making soap in a wash pot *c.* 1939. The Simmons Family sharecropped on a farm in the Campton area. (Courtesy Catherine Jones.)

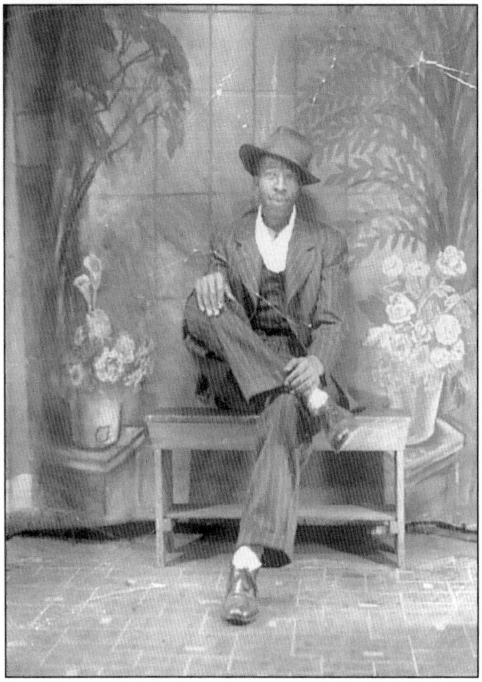

Frank Few, a railroad worker, is shown in this 1930s photograph. (Courtesy Claudia Mae Hillman.)

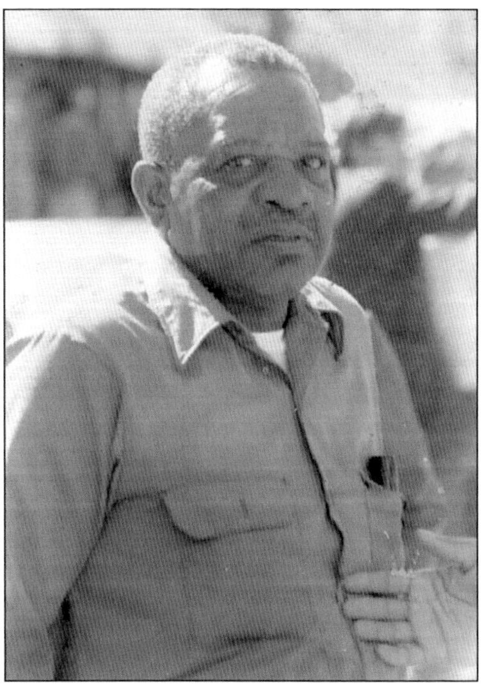

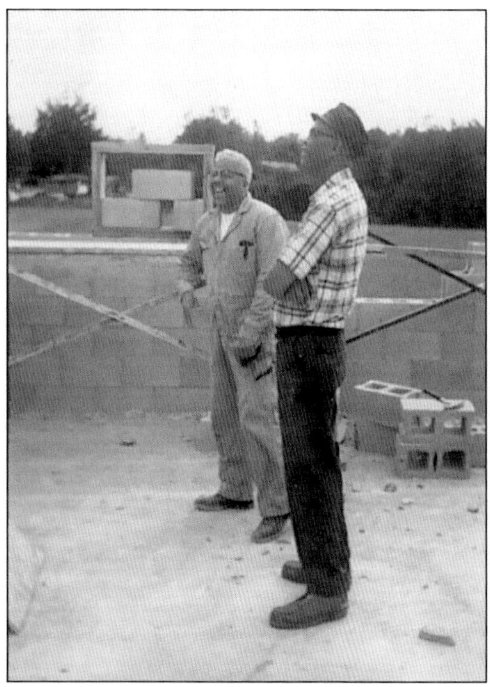

(*above, left*) Tommie Lee Hillman Sr. was a self-employed plumber for 35 years. (Courtesy of Claudia Mae Hillman.) (*above, right*) J.R. Morrow and Frank Caudle are shown on the construction site of the Masonic Lodge Hall *c.* 1974. Morrow operated a barber shop on Washington Street. Caudle was principal of Social Circle Colored School in 1943–1944 and county extension agent from 1945 to 1961. (Courtesy George Marshall.)

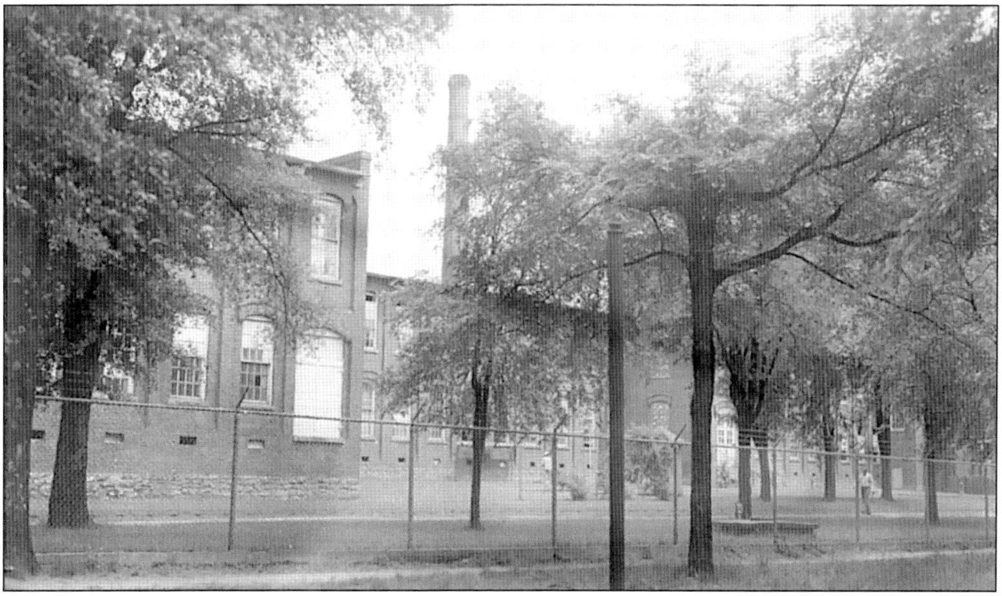

The Monroe Mill is shown here in the 1900s. Around 1964 many blacks sought employment as domestic workers, construction workers, and in the poultry and cotton mill since it was no longer profitable to farm. During the early days black women were employed as sweepers and cleaners while black men loaded cotton and kept yards clean at the cotton mill. (Courtesy Stephen Felker Jr., Avondale Mills, Inc.)

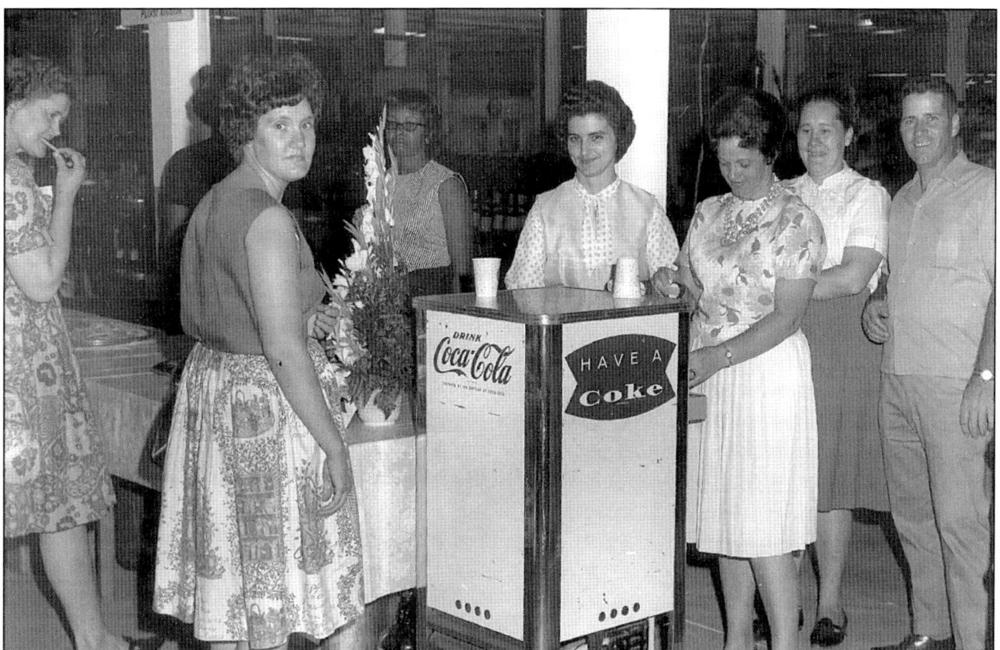

Cora Bell Cook is pictured fifth from right (behind flower arrangement) at an open house in 1965. Mary Cook, Cora Bell's mother, worked at the mill for 28 years. Cora Bell worked at the mill for 33 years, retiring in 1989. (Courtesy Stephen Felker Jr., Avondale Mills, Inc.)

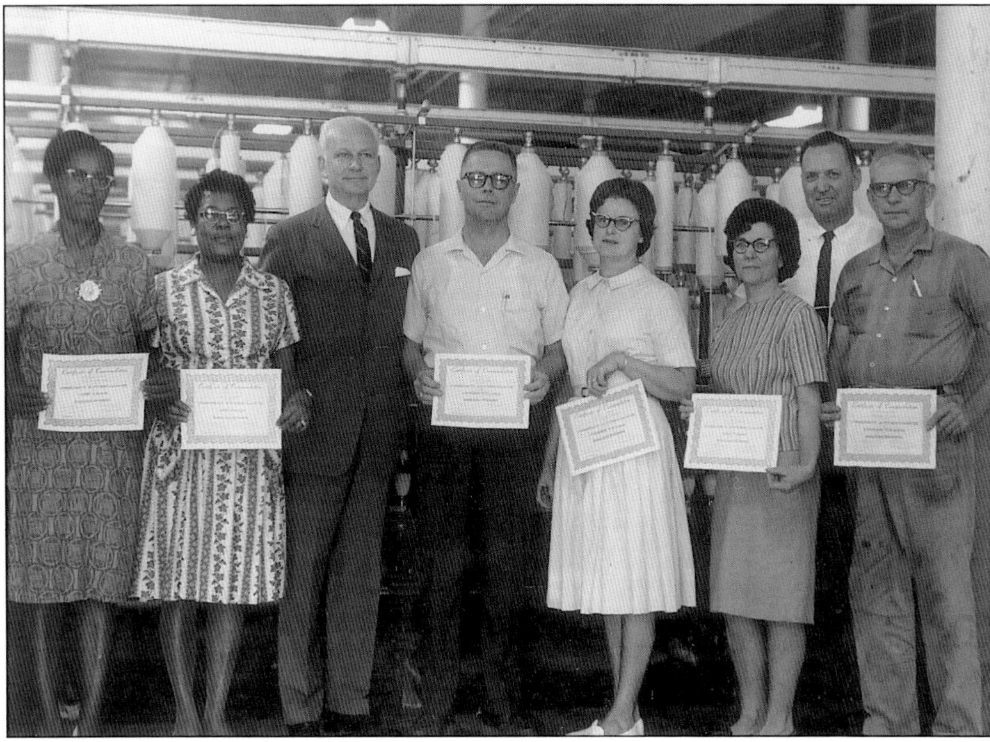

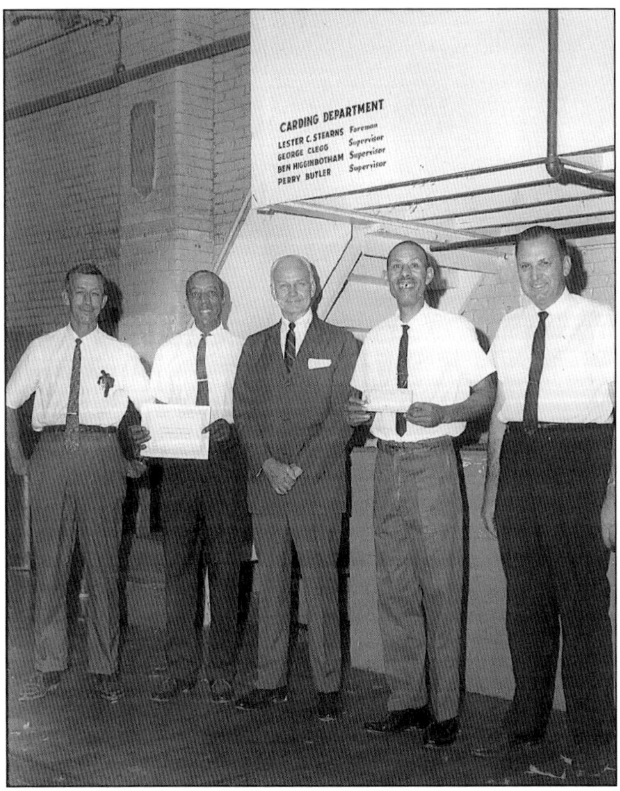

Female mill employees receive attendance certificates in this 1965 photograph. Sallie M. Brown and Daisy Gober have completed one year of service. (Courtesy Stephen Felker Jr., Avondale Mills, Inc.)

Mill employees receive attendance certificates in the 1960s. From left to right are Dan Hilton, Junius McKinley Smith, George Felker III (president), Willie Henry Brown, and foreman Lester Stearns. Junius Smith began working at the mill in 1945. Prior to that he worked for the Work Progress Administration (WPA) in its night school program, was teacher-principal of Thompson school, and served in the United States Army for four years. (Courtesy Stephen Felker Jr., Avondale Mills, Inc.)

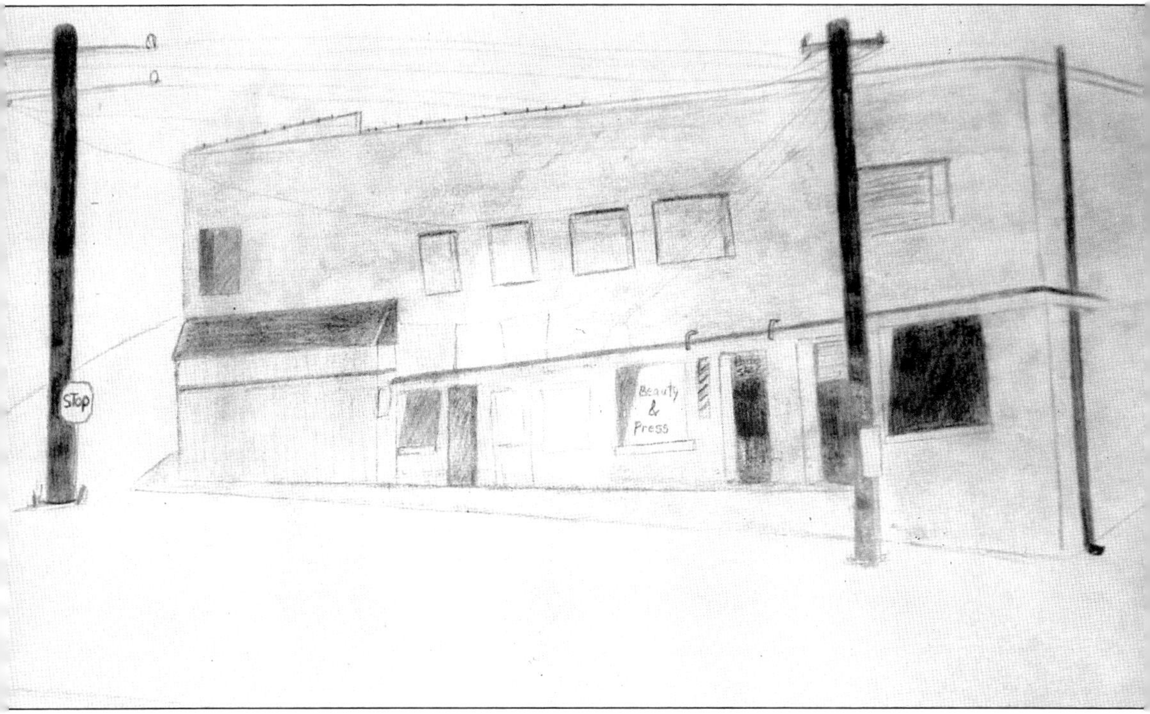

This building was part of the business complex on Washington Street, known as "The Corner." It housed social clubs over the years, including the Elks Club, the Upper Room, and the Social Advancement of Black Brothers (S.A.B.B. club). These clubs were centers of social activity in the black community. (Drawing by Teressa Sorrells.)

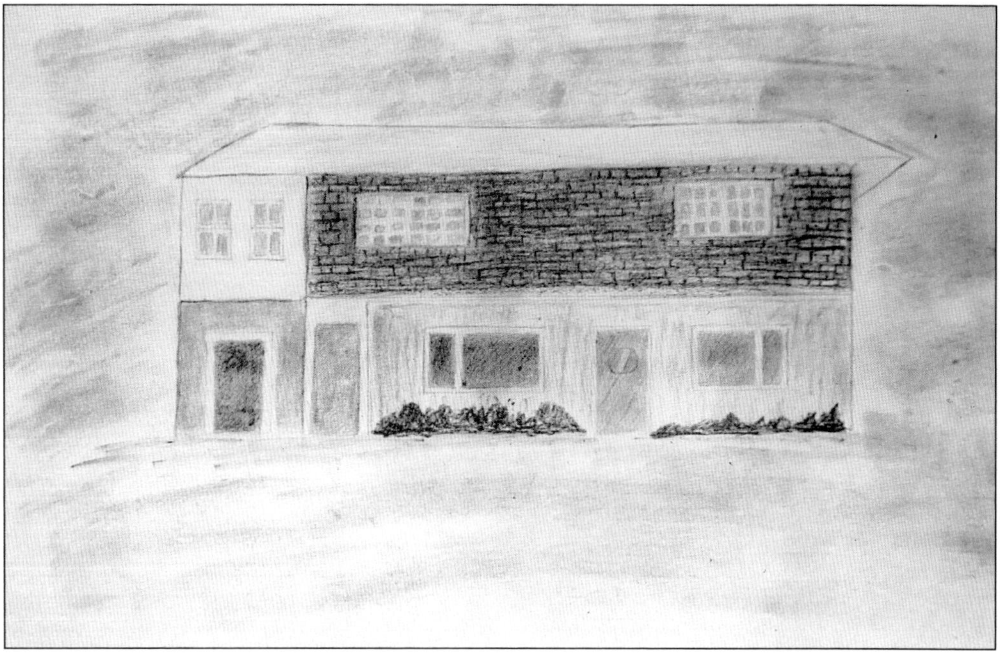

The last building at the end of the business complex housed an apartment upstairs, a laundry mat on one side, and a café (restaurant) on the other. Amy and Oscar (Bo) Briggery operated the café during the 1950s and 1960s. (Drawing by Teressa Sorrells.)

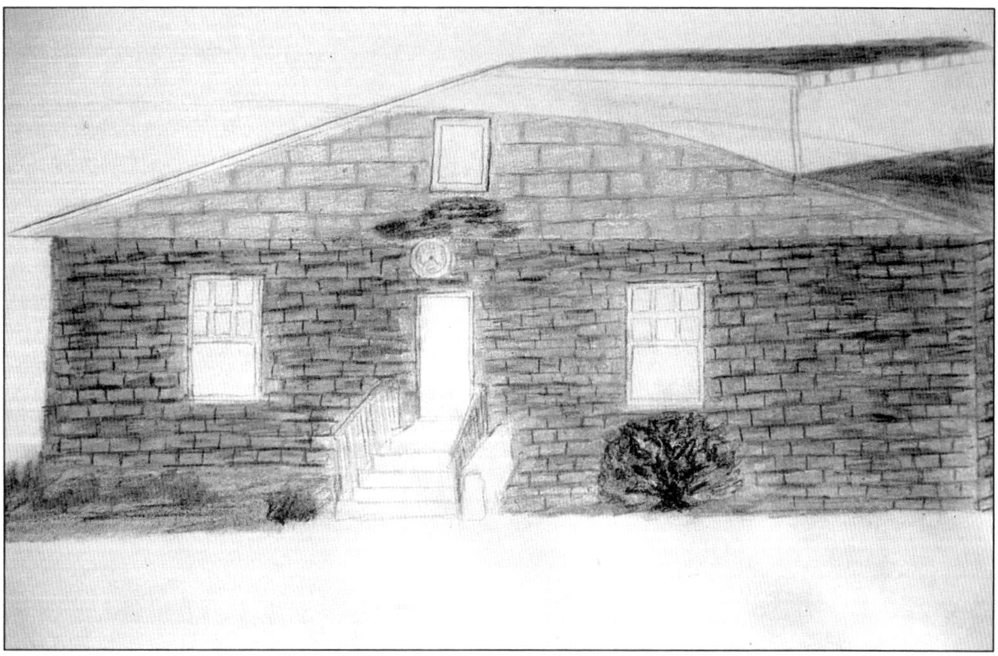

Young Funeral Home was established by Daniel W. Young Sr. in 1938 on Washington Street. He opened the business complex in the early 1950s; it consisted of a club, restaurants, dry cleaners, a barber and beauty shop, poolroom, and laundromat. The funeral home is now operated by Young's daughter, Ariel Young Sullivan. (Drawing by Teressa Sorrells.)

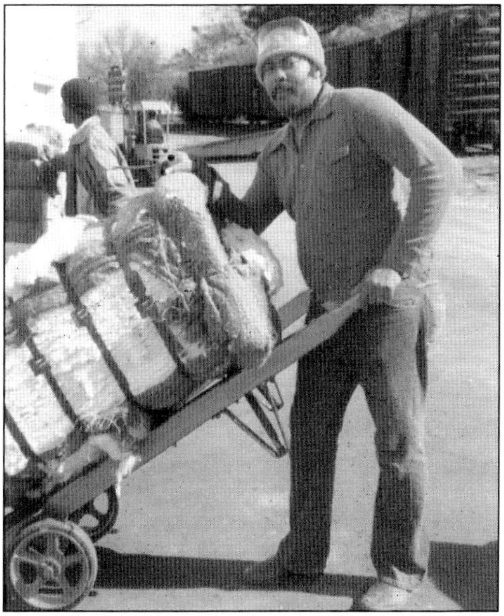
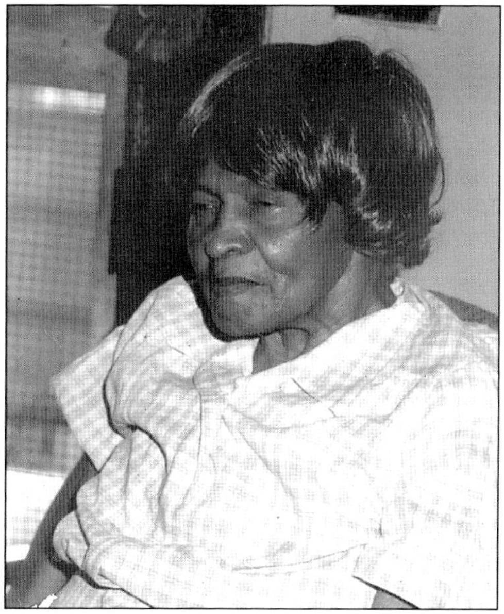

(*above, left*) This unidentified man is loading cotton in the 1970s. (Courtesy Stephen Felker Jr., Avondale Mills Inc.) (*above, right*) Mattie Lou Martin was the wife of Ab Martin and had 11 children. She helped her husband on the farm and cared for the home and children. (Courtesy Herman Robertson.)

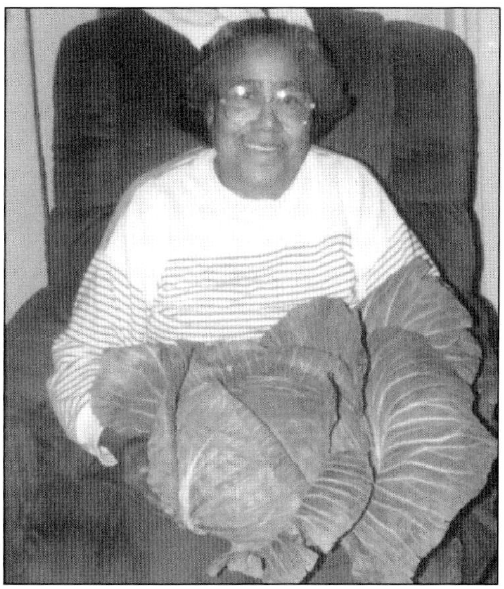
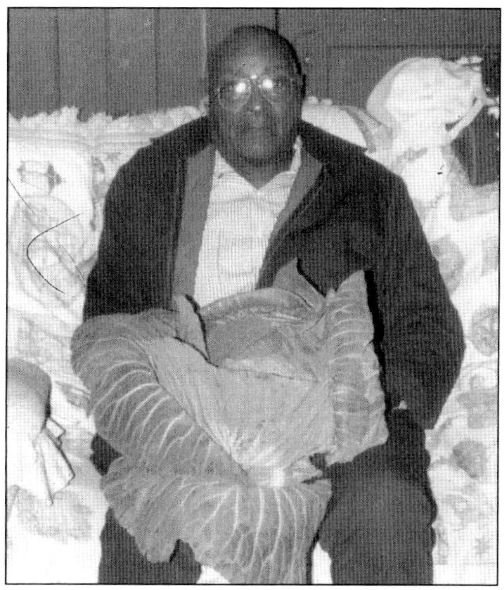

(*above, left*) Hazel Butler, pictured in the 1980s, is shown holding a large cabbage from the family garden. She and her husband began farming when they married in 1944. During the early years Butler followed the farming tradition he learned from his father and plowed with a mule. The Butlers farm was once one of the largest black-owned farms in the county. They farmed 350 acres between 1969 and the early 1980s. (*above, right*) Governor Butler Sr. is shown in this 1980s photograph displaying a large cabbage from the garden he and his wife Hazel grew. The Butlers were well known for their garden of wonderful vegetables. (Both photographs courtesy Hazel and Governor Butler Sr.)

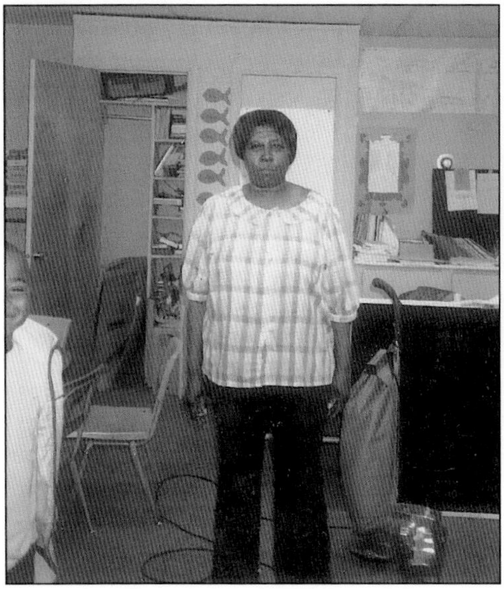

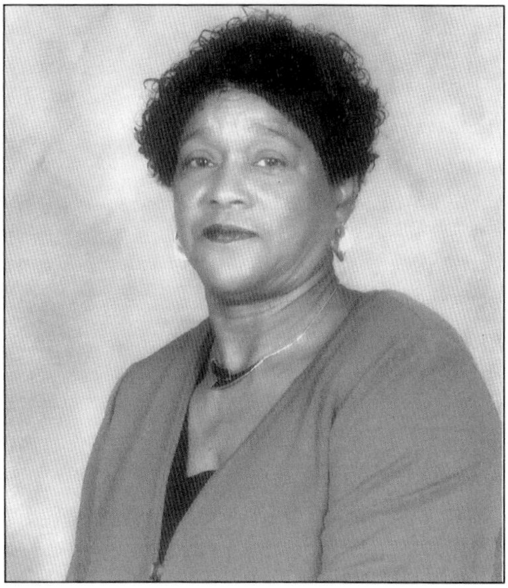

(*above, left*) Claudia Hillman, seen *c*. 1980, worked at Monroe Primary School for 18 years. (Courtesy Claudia Mae Hillman.) (*above, right*) Mollie Butler Lewis opened Mollie's Learning Center, Inc. in 1973 after an extensive career as an educator in both public and private schools. The learning center is recognized today in the community as a leader in quality early childhood education. In addition to operating the learning center, Mrs. Lewis has served on numerous panels, boards, and committees in her church and the community. (Courtesy Mollie Butler Lewis.)

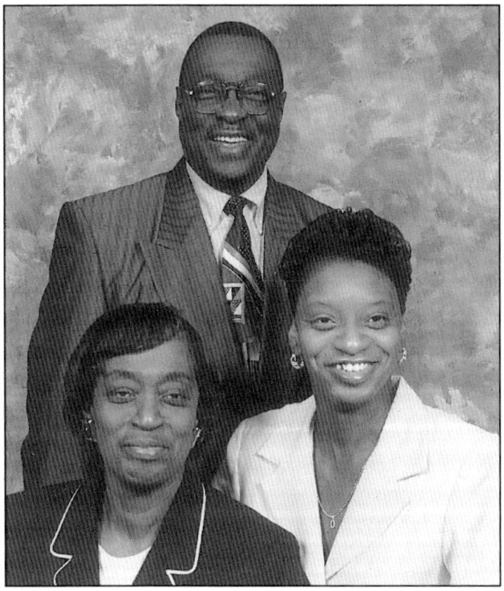

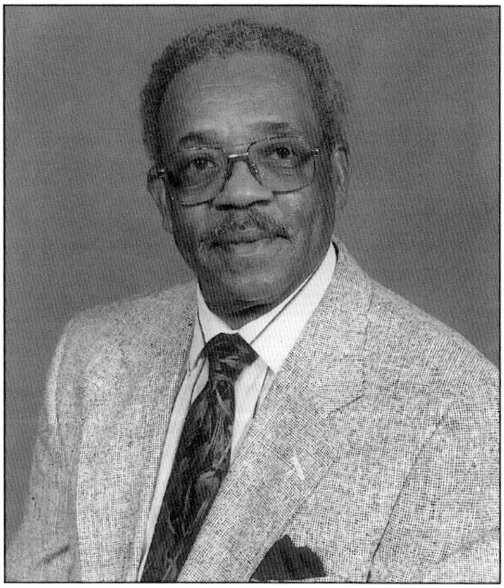

(*above, left*) Ollie E. James, owner and operator of James Personal Care Home in Social Circle, is pictured with her brother, Dr. Willie Enus, and daughter, Dr. Olivet James. (Courtesy Dr. Willie Enus.) (*above, right*) Ernest Kilgore, a professional drycleaner and respected businessman between the late 1950s and 1970s, opened Kilgore Cleaners on Washington Street in 1958. He opened a second store on Gratis Road and operated the businesses until 1979. (Courtesy Ethel Kilgore.)

Seven

SERVING OUR COMMUNITY AND COUNTRY

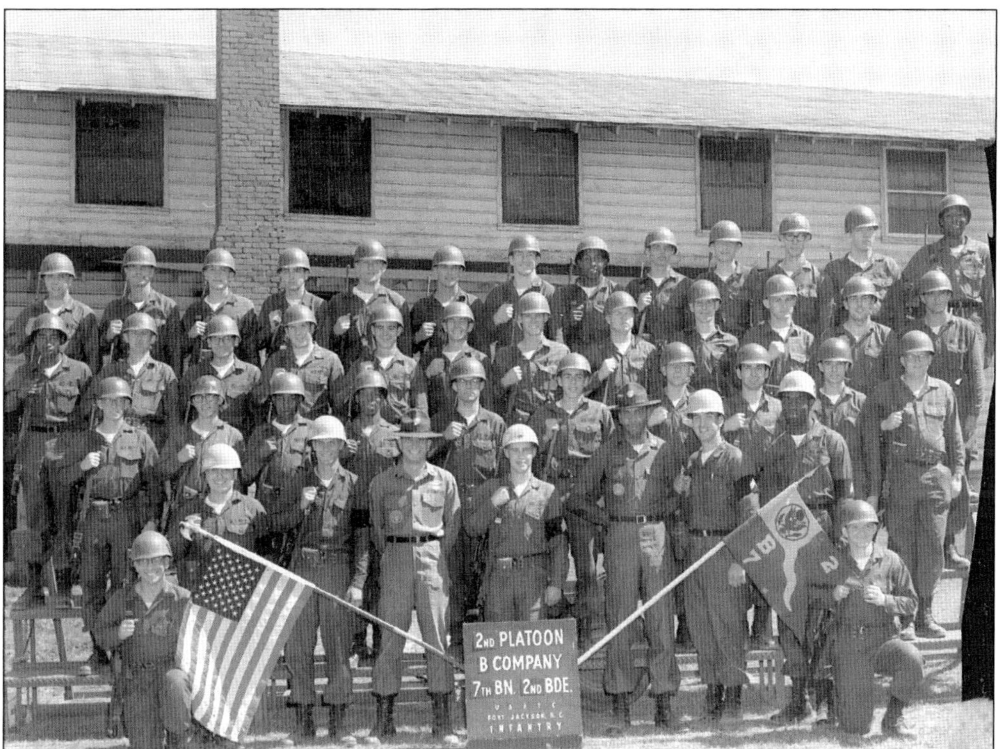

Tommie Lee Hillman Jr. is pictured sixth from the right on the top row in this photograph. Hillman, who was captain of the Carver High School state championship football team in 1969, joined the military soon after high school. (Courtesy Claudia Mae Hillman.)

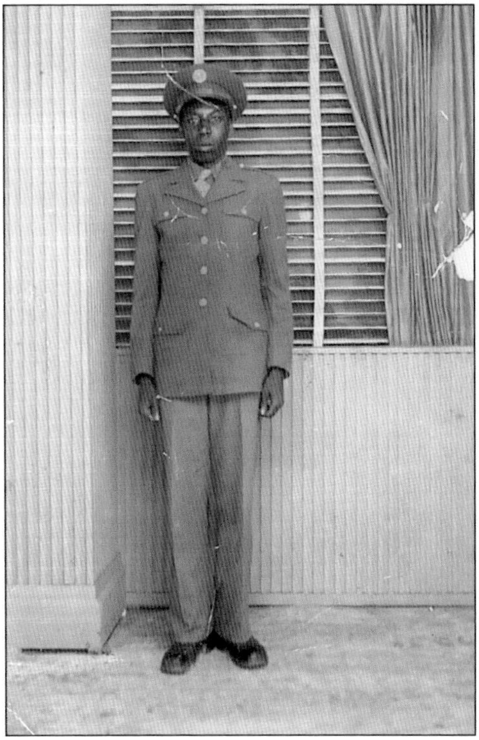

EuGene "Bo" Witcher was a proud member of the United States Air Force during World War II. (Courtesy Teressa Sorrells and Camilla Mattox.)

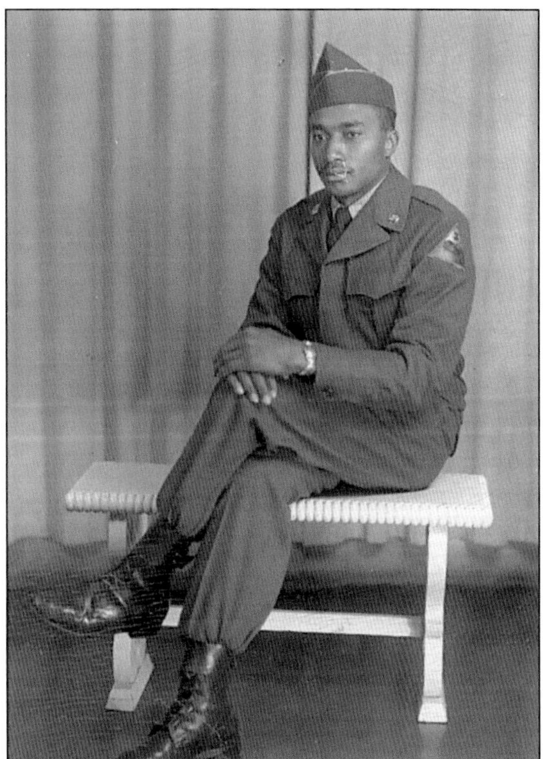

Robert Heard served in the military during World War II. (Courtesy Teressa Sorrells and Camilla Mattox.)

This is an unidentified Walton County sailor. (Courtesy Willie Smith.)

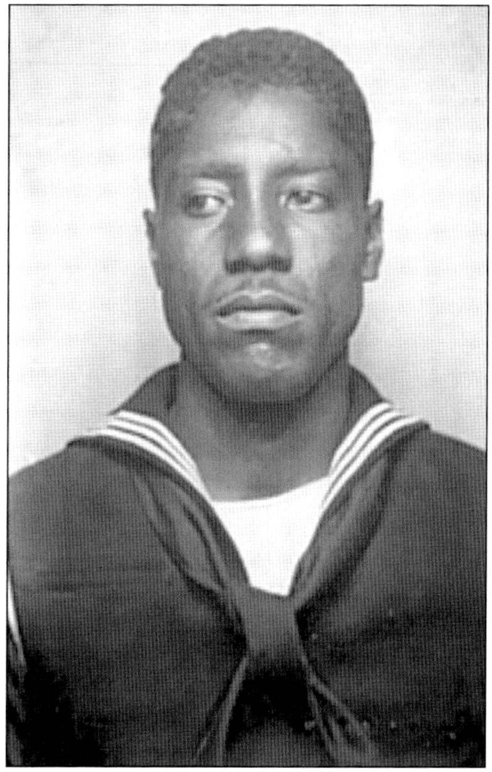

(*below, left*) Clarence Mapp served in the United States Army during World War II. (Courtesy Robbie Mapp Vaughn.) (*below, right*) Roosevelt Cooper served in the military. (Courtesy Mary Lee Jordan.)

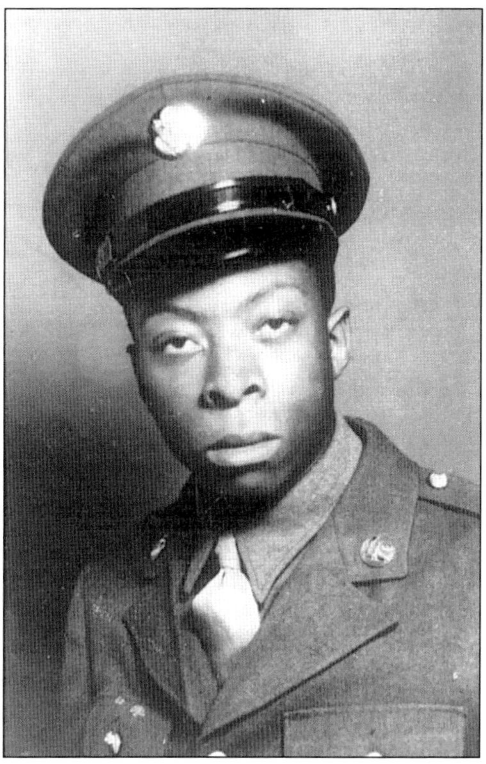

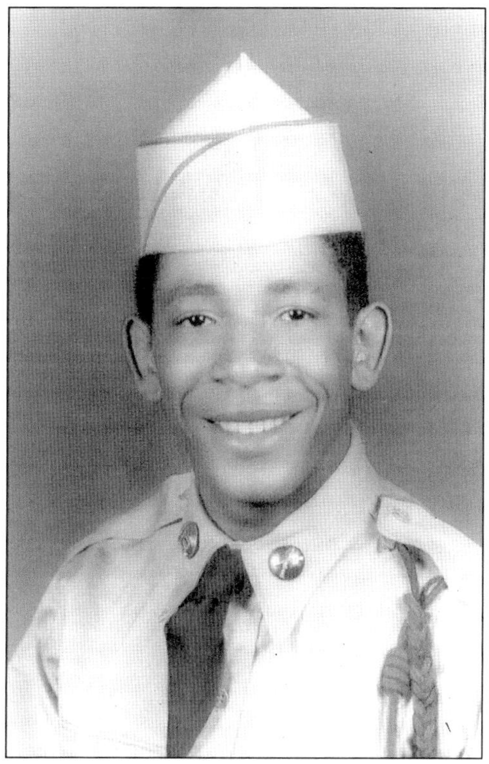

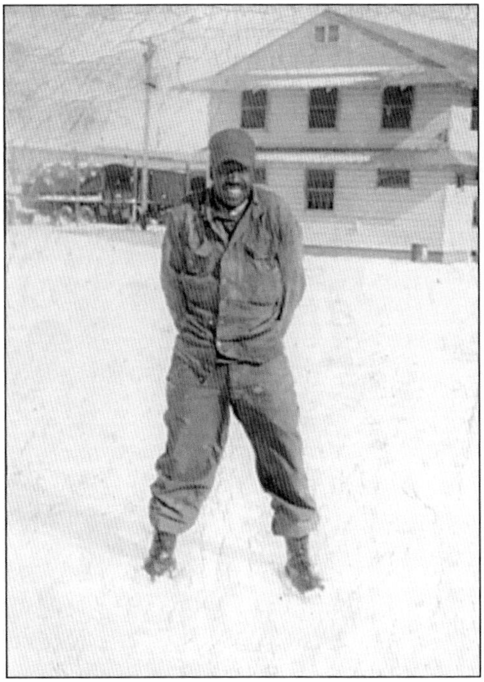

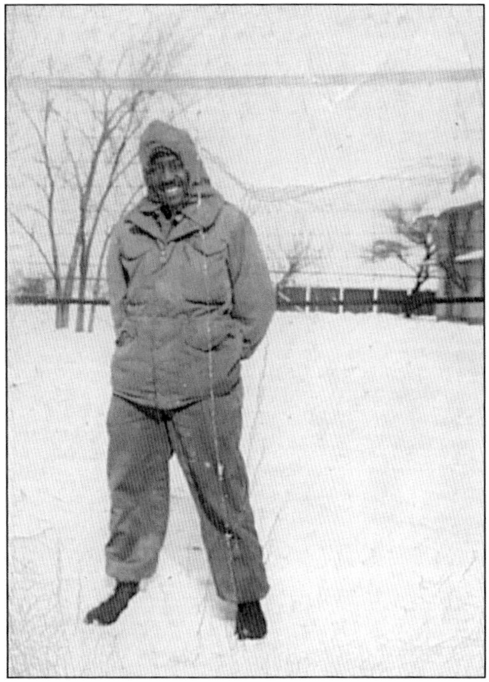

Here are two unidentified Walton County soldiers who served during World War II. (Courtesy Camilla Mattox.)

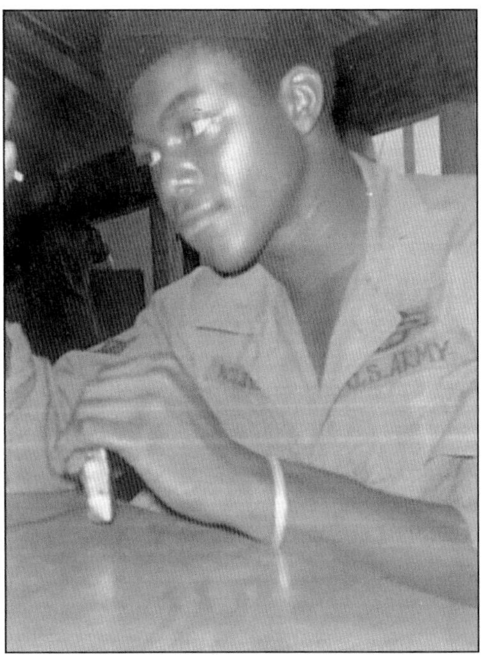

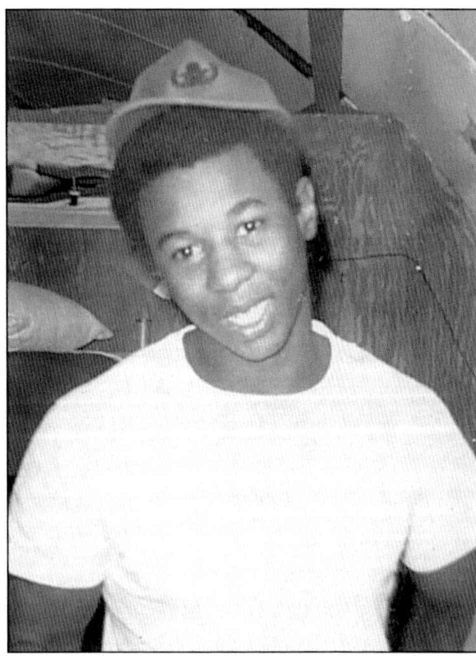

(*above, left*) This photograph of Mark Willingham was taken in Vietnam while he was stationed there in 1969. (Courtesy Lynn Camp.) (*above, right*) Richard E. (Ricky) Bell was a member of the United States Air Force stationed in Vietnam in this 1969 photograph. (Courtesy Lynn Camp.)

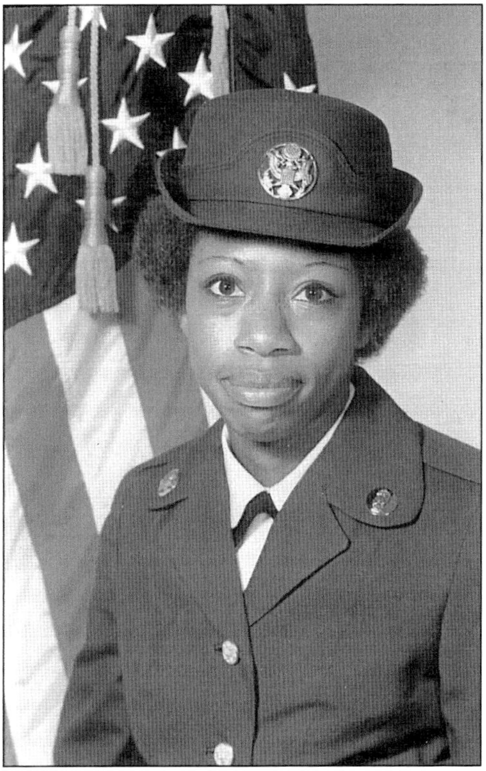

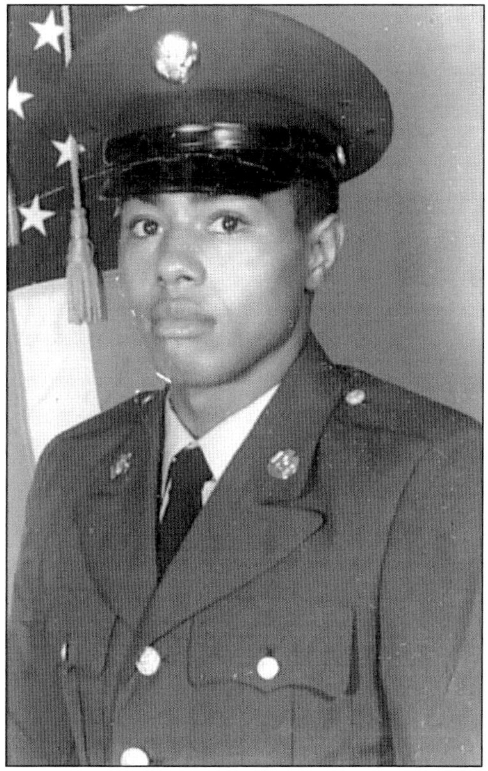

(*above, left*) Pvt. Second Class Catherine Mapp was the first woman to join the National Guard's 178th Military Police Company, *c.* 1970. (Courtesy Robbie Mapp Vaughn.) (*above, right*) Gregory Maddox served in the United States Army in the 1970s. (Courtesy Sarah Maddox.)

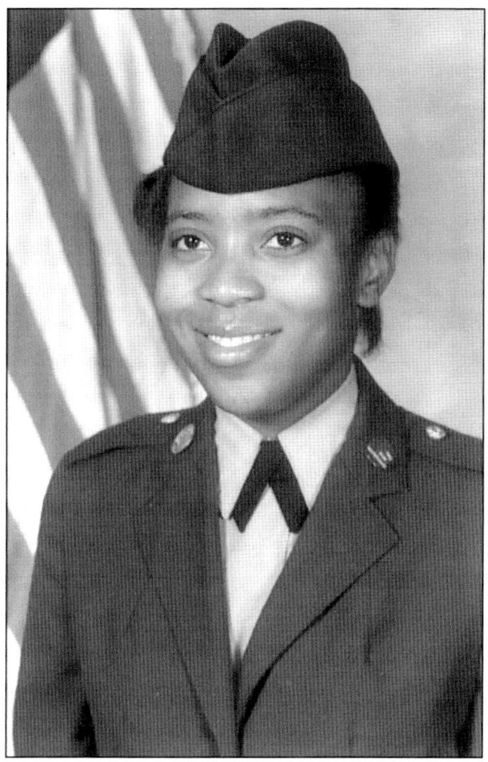

Pvt. Teresa Whitlock is shown while serving in the United States Army in 1989. (Courtesy Tessie Robinson.)

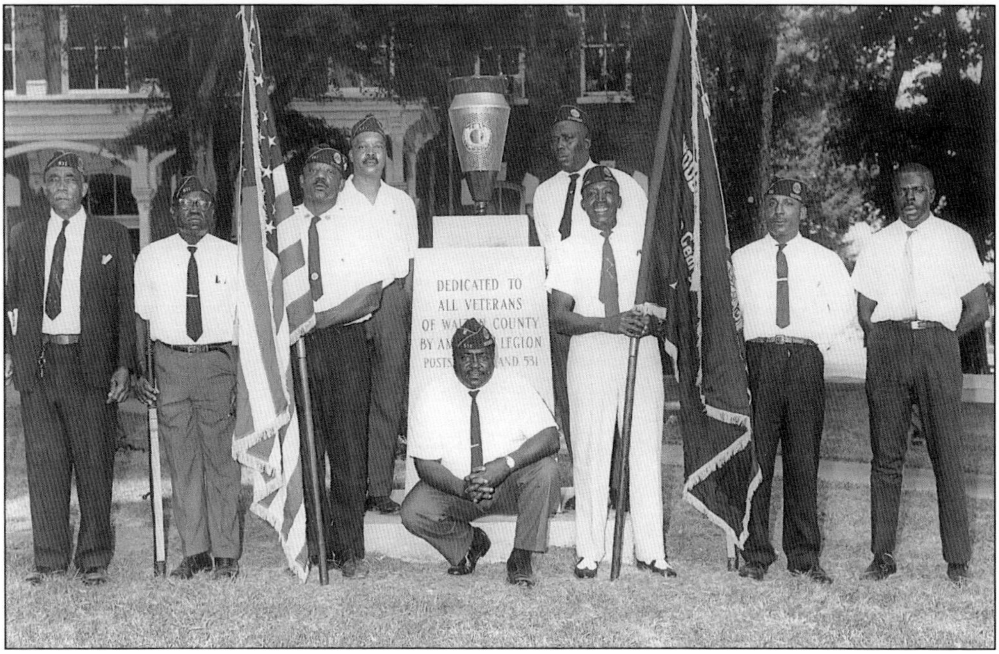

Members of the American Legion Post 531 pose in front of the Monroe courthouse after participating in the Dedication of the Eternal Flame in 1970. From left to right are Buddy Colquitt, Mack Manuel, Sam Moon, Livingston O'Kelley, Cmdr. Georgia Marshall (kneeling), Avery Atkinson, Edward Locklin, Edward Williams, and Clinton Foster. (Courtesy George Marshall.)

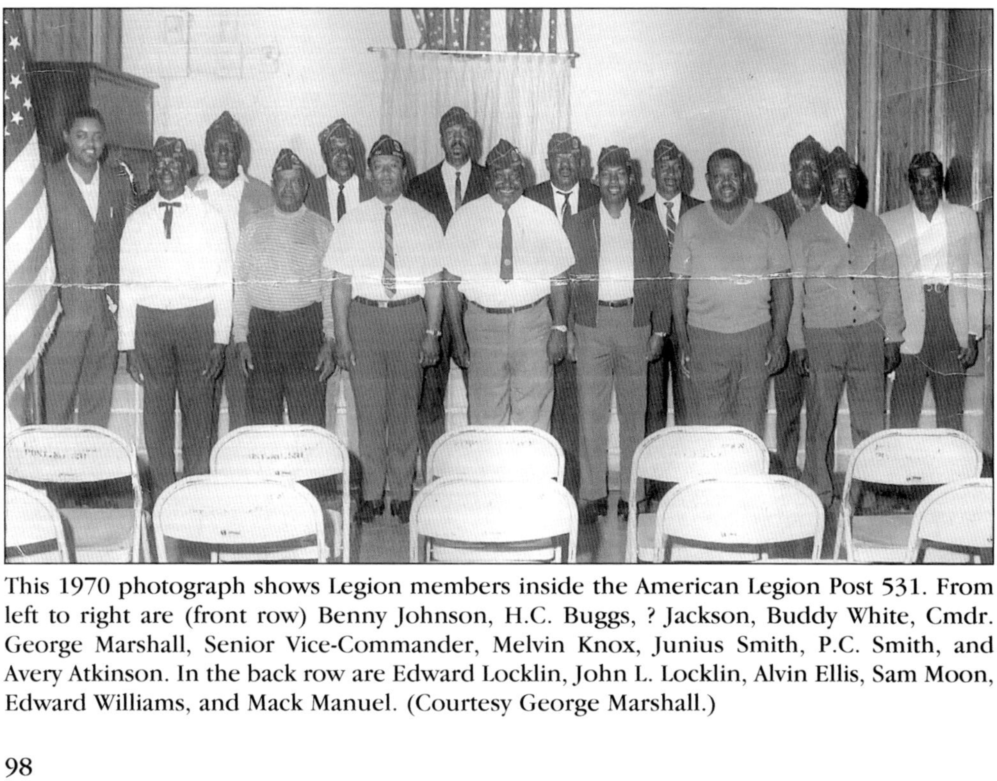

This 1970 photograph shows Legion members inside the American Legion Post 531. From left to right are (front row) Benny Johnson, H.C. Buggs, ? Jackson, Buddy White, Cmdr. George Marshall, Senior Vice-Commander, Melvin Knox, Junius Smith, P.C. Smith, and Avery Atkinson. In the back row are Edward Locklin, John L. Locklin, Alvin Ellis, Sam Moon, Edward Williams, and Mack Manuel. (Courtesy George Marshall.)

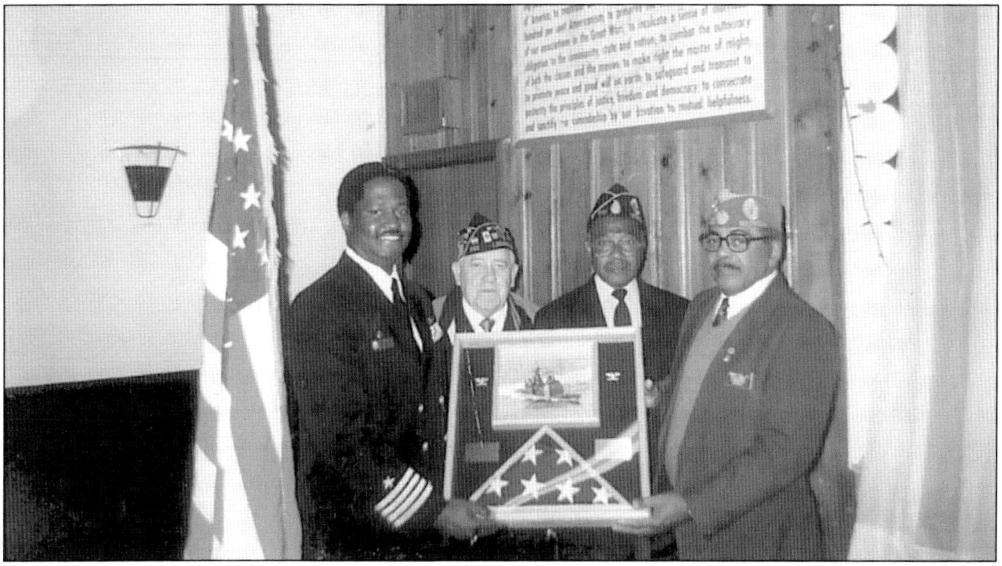

Coleman Landers was the guest speaker for a Veteran's Day program in 1992. Pictured with him are (from left to right) 10th District commander Jerry Childers, commander of American Legion Post 531 (1992–1994), Herman Robertson, and state commander of the Sons of the Legion, John Hill. (Courtesy Herman Robertson.)

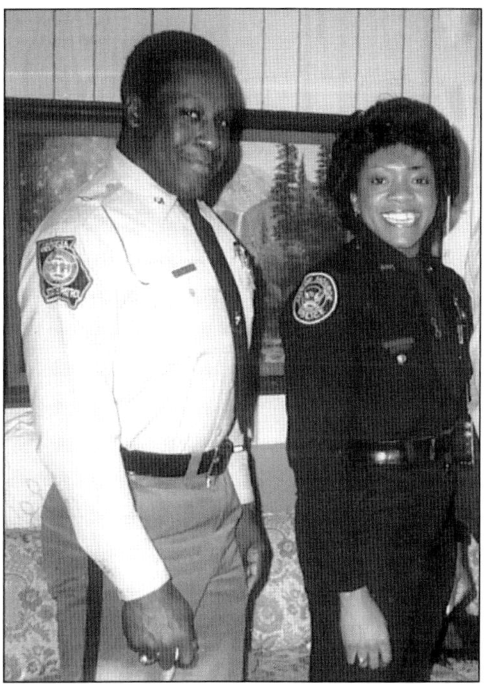

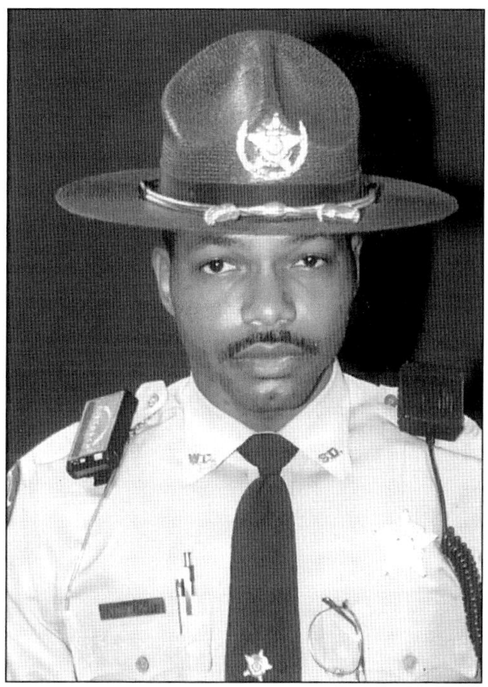

(*above, left*) Walton County law enforcement officers pose together. From left to right are James H. Vaughn of the Georgia State Patrol and Emily Hunter of the Monroe Police Department. (Courtesy Robbie Mapp Vaughn.) (*above, right*) Capt. Darren Vinson went to work at the Walton County sheriff's office as a detention officer in 1989 after serving three years in the U.S. Army. He was promoted to Captain in 2001. (Courtesy Patsy Vinson.)

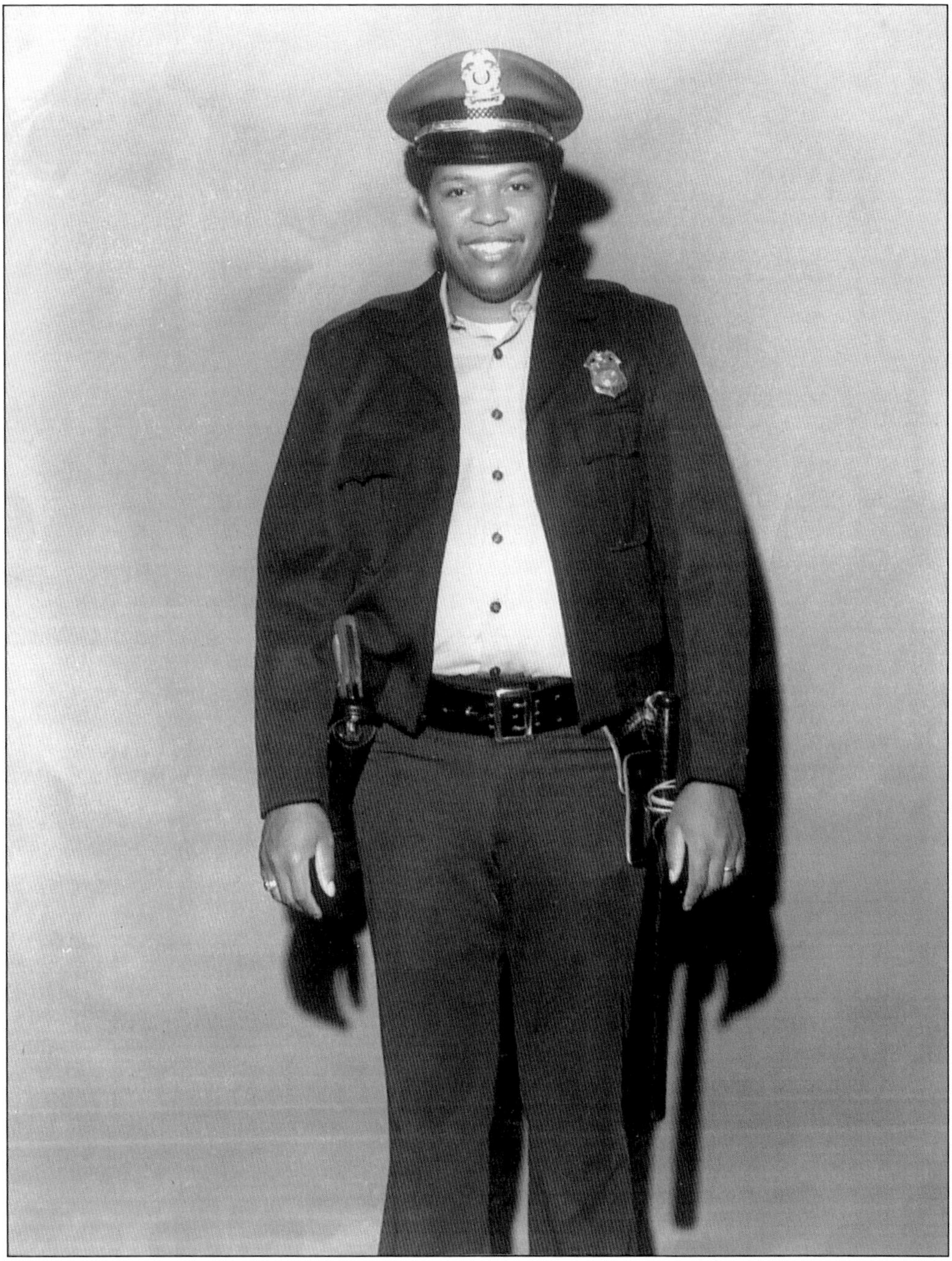

Lt. Michael E. Etchison Sr. joined the Monroe Police Department in 1969. He became the first black officer to be promoted to lieutenant and to be killed in the line of duty. (Courtesy Robbie Mapp Vaughn.)

Eight

Everyday People

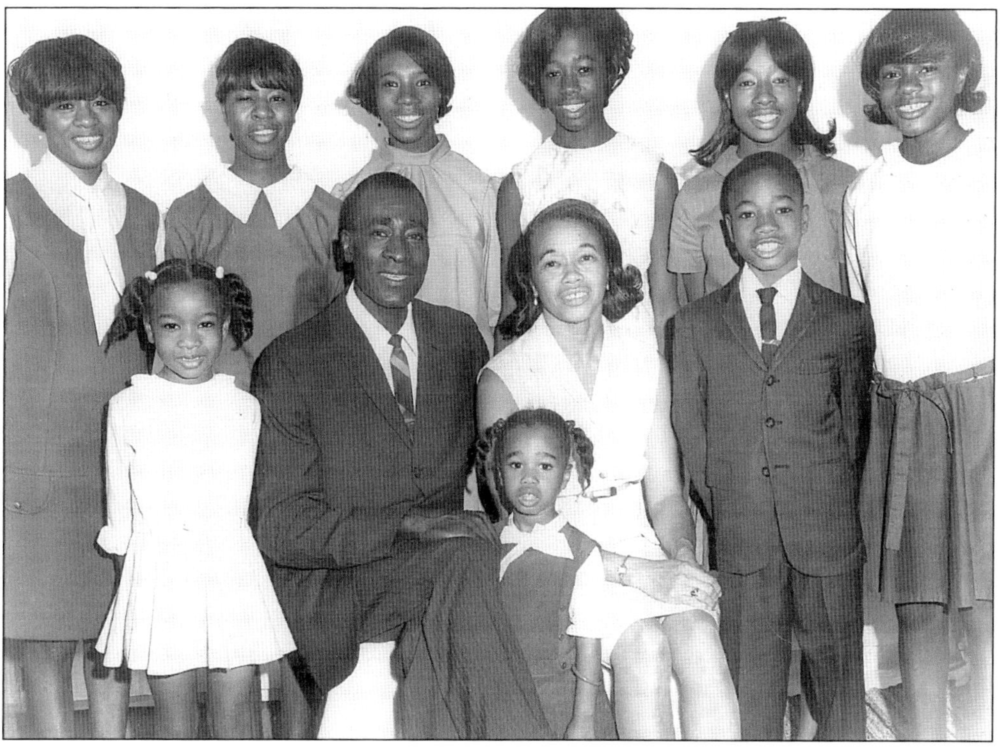

Clifton and Hattie Butler and family are shown in this 1969 family photograph. From left to right are (front row) Rita, Clifton (father), Hattie (mother), Sherry, and Clifford; (back row) Collie, Emma, Marilyn, Lorene, Eloise, and Yvonne. (Courtesy Emma Wiseman and Marilyn Williams.)

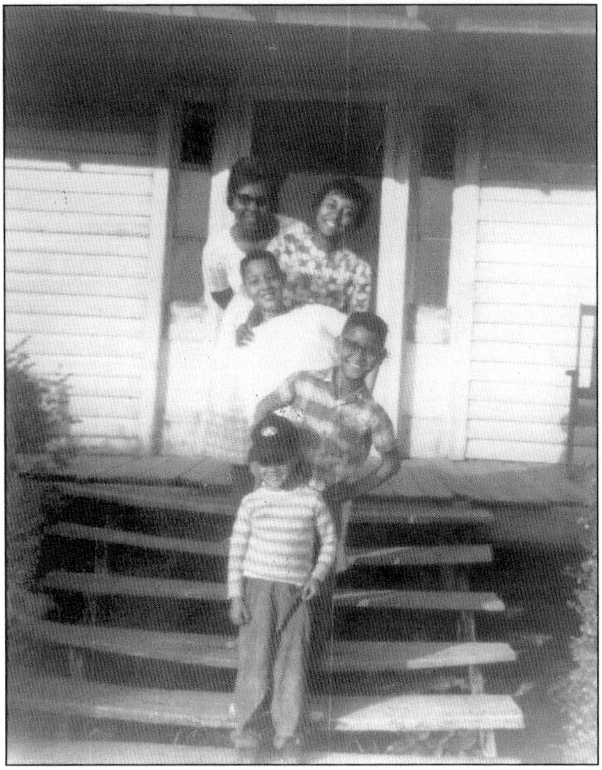

The Locklin children are pictured on the front steps of their home. In the front from top to bottom are Cornelia (Cherry) Johnson, Sandra Locklin, Joseph Locklin, Kenneth Locklin, and James Locklin. The latter four are the children of Orell and Geneva Locklin. (Courtesy Geneva Locklin.)

Shown here at a baby shower in 1973 are, from left to right, Helen Harris and Irene White. Mrs. White hosted the shower with her daughter Allene (not shown) at their home in Monroe. (Courtesy Lynn Camp.)

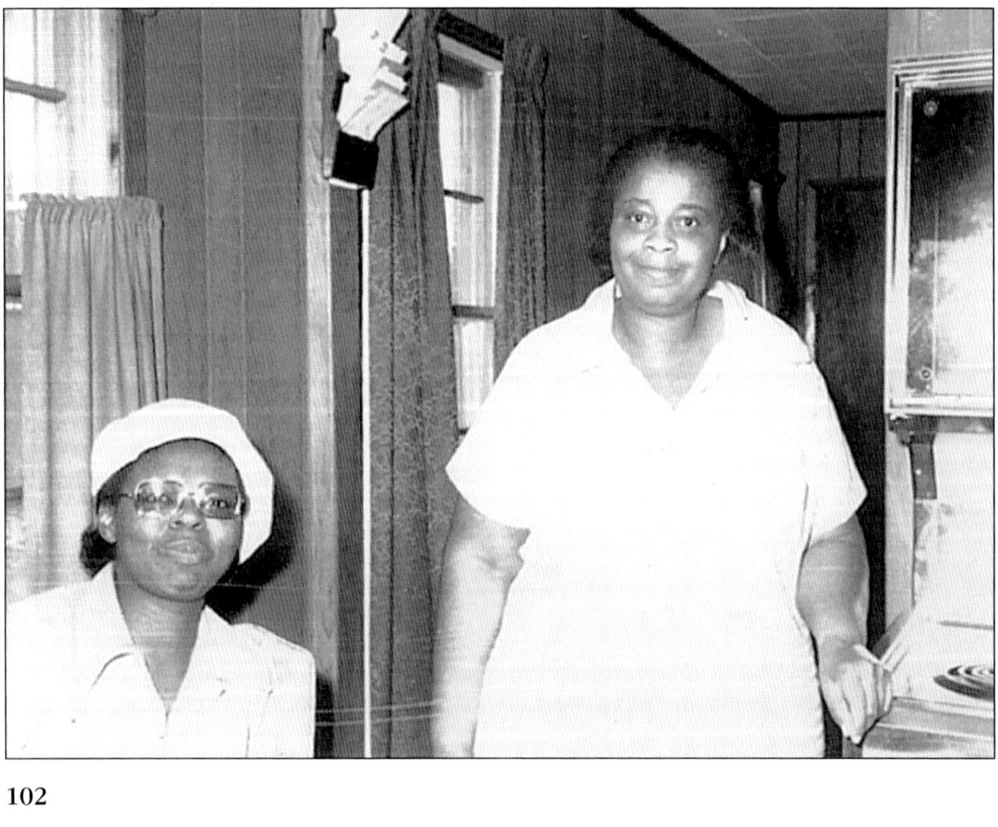

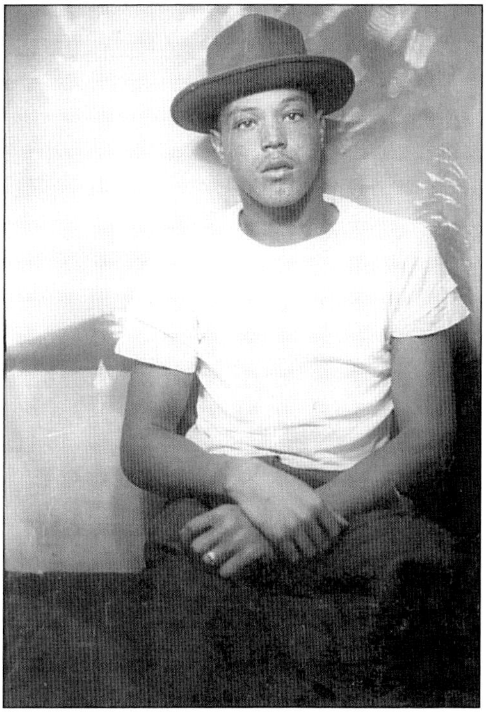

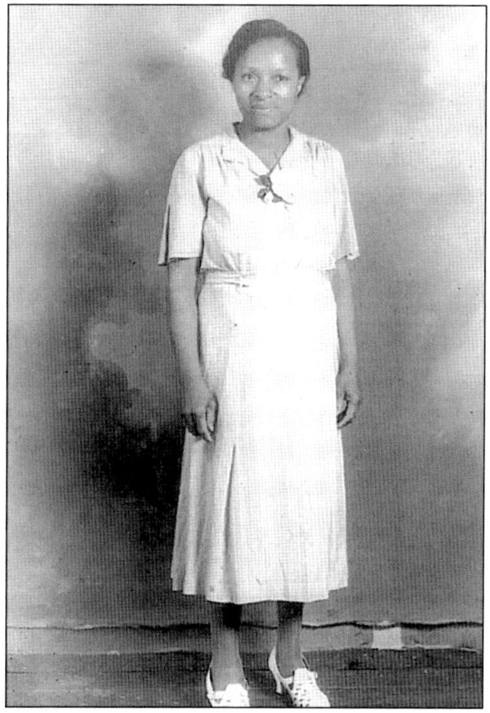

(*above, left*) George Reese was a resident of the Howardville Community (Midland Avenue) *c.* 1940. (Courtesy Betty Foster.) (*above, right*) Nettie Howard Reese was known in the community as a "spiritual healer." She lived at 600 Midland Ave in Howardville, *c.* 1940. (Courtesy Betty Foster.)

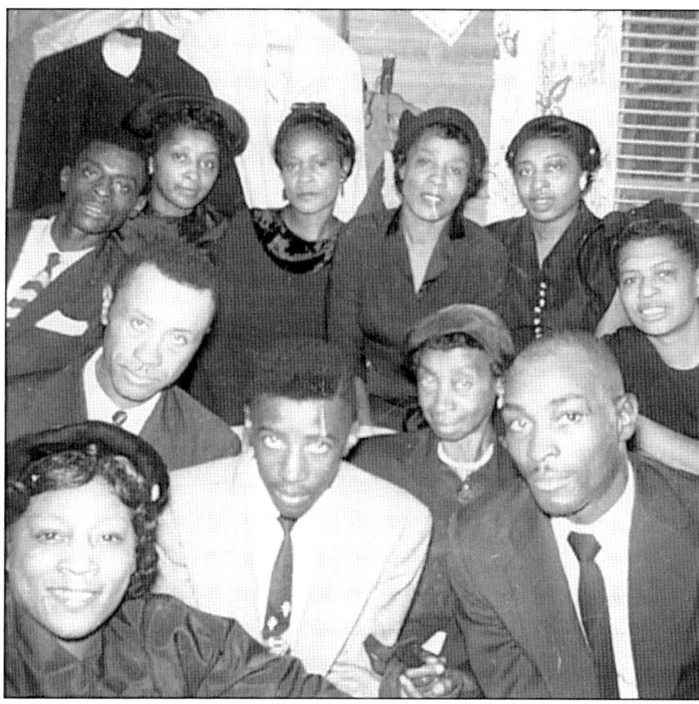

The Butler family surrounds their mother in her home after the funeral of their father in the 1950s. They are, from left to right, (front) Emma Smith, Roosevelt Smith, Caroline Butler, and Governor Butler Sr. In the second row are Ardinus Butler, Ethaniel Butler, Parile Morning, Julia Solomon, Mattie Lou Austin, Myrtle Lee Holloman, and Rachel Gibson. (Courtesy Tessie Robinson.)

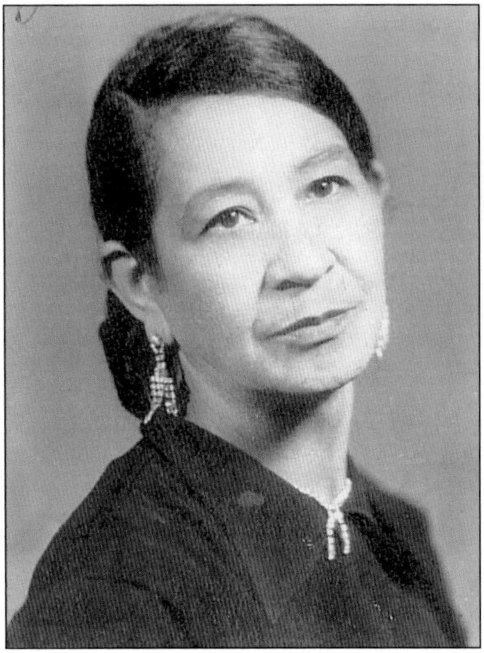

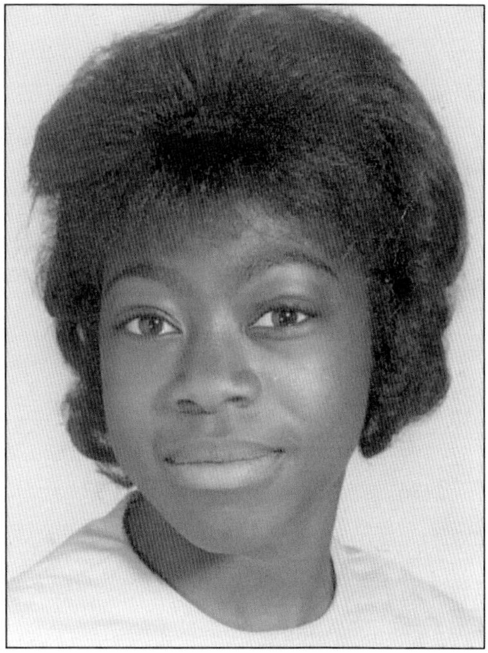

(*above, left*) Julia Daniel is dressed elegantly for this 1920s photograph. (Courtesy Betty Foster.) (*above, right*) Robbie Jewell Mapp was a seventh-grade student at Good Hope Peters School when this 1963 school picture was taken. (Courtesy Robbie Mapp Vaughn.)

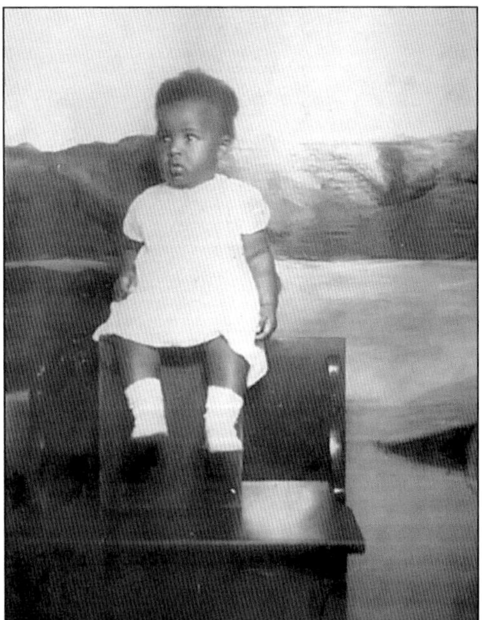

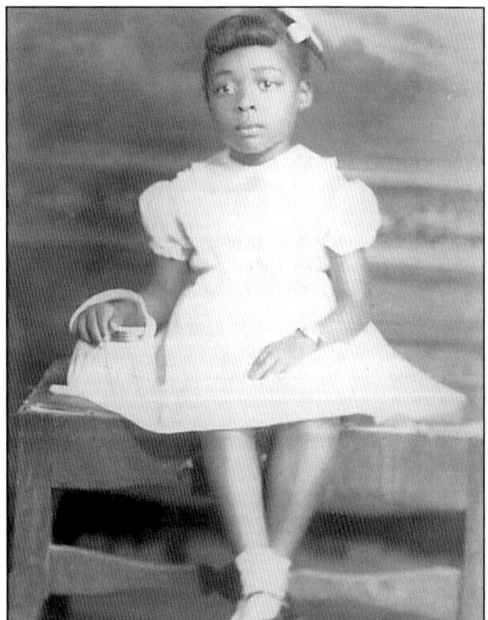

(*above, left*) Roosevelt Smith is seen in the typical dress for baby boys *c*. 1939. Roosevelt was raised by his grandmother, Caroline Butler. (Courtesy Tessie Robinson.) (*above, right*) Ruby Lynn Robinson is dressed typical of little girls during the 1950s. This photograph was taken in the studio of E.M. Carnes in 1956. (Courtesy Tessie Robinson.)

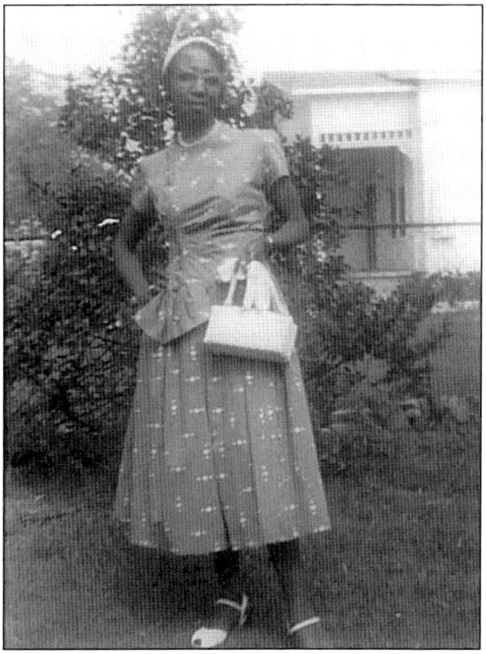

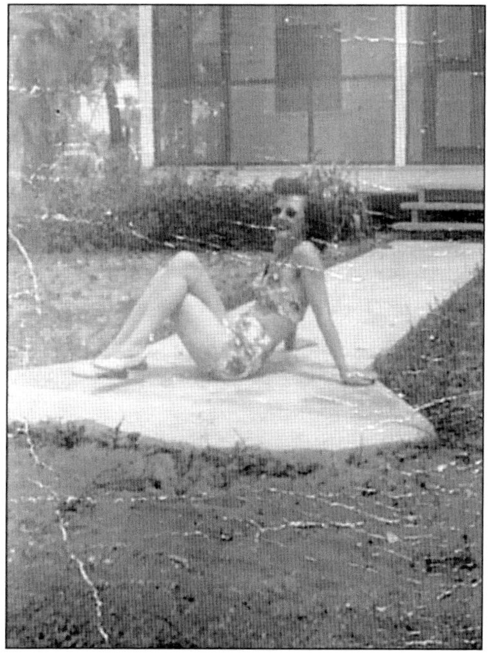

(*above, left*) This unidentified woman is dressed for church with handbag, hats, and gloves in this 1957 photograph. (Courtesy Betty Foster.) (*above, right*) Flora Bell Sheats sunbathes in front of her home *c*. 1960. (Courtesy Teressa Sorrells and Camilla Mattox.)

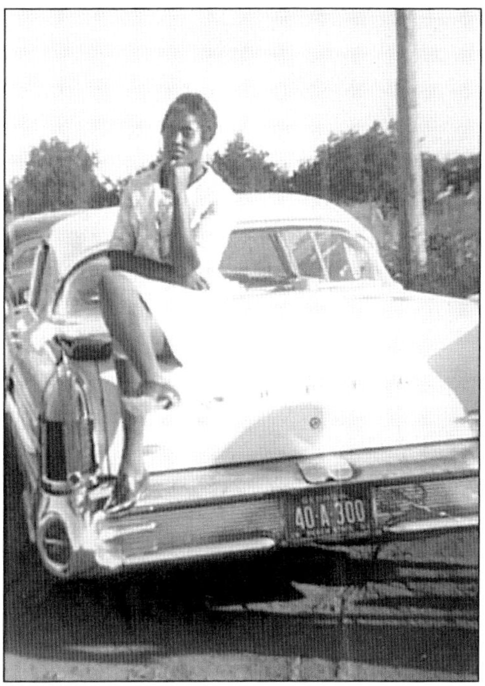

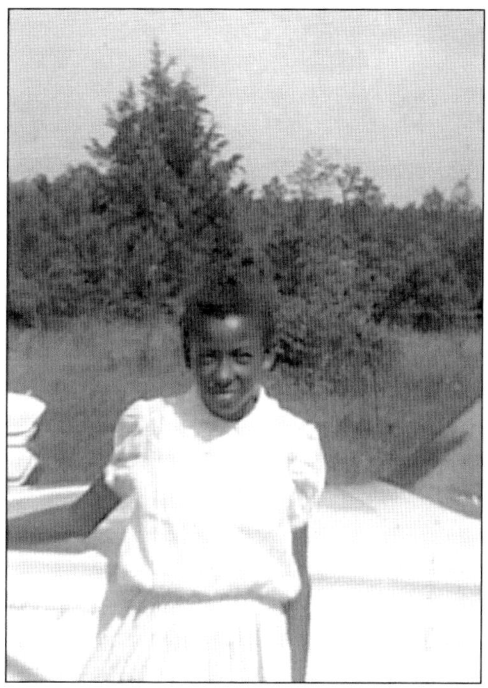

(*above, left*) Florida "Bee" Walton strikes a pose for this 1963 photograph. (Courtesy Teressa Sorrells and Camilla Mattox.) (*above, right*) Sheila White was 11 years old in this 1964 photograph. (Courtesy Lynn Camp.)

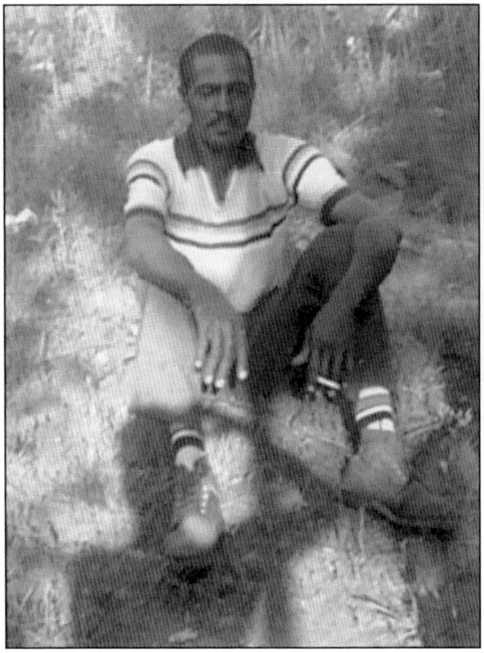

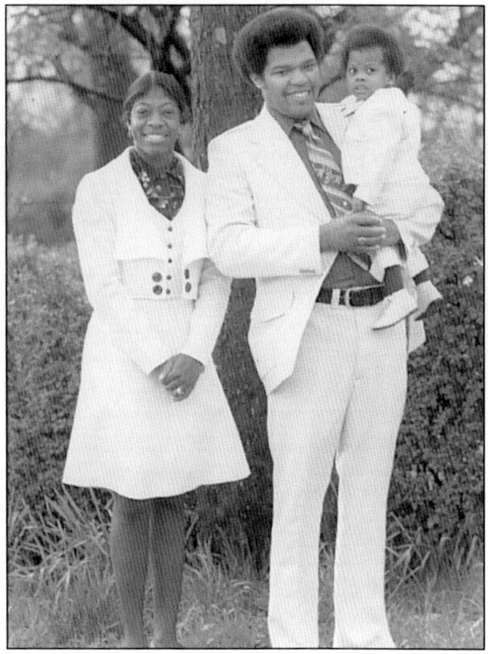

(*above, left*) Tommie Lee Maddox relaxes in his front yard in the 1970s. (Courtesy Sarah Maddox.) (*above, right*) Robbie, Michael, and Everette Etchison are shown in this 1974 family photograph. (Courtesy Robbie Mapp Vaughn.)

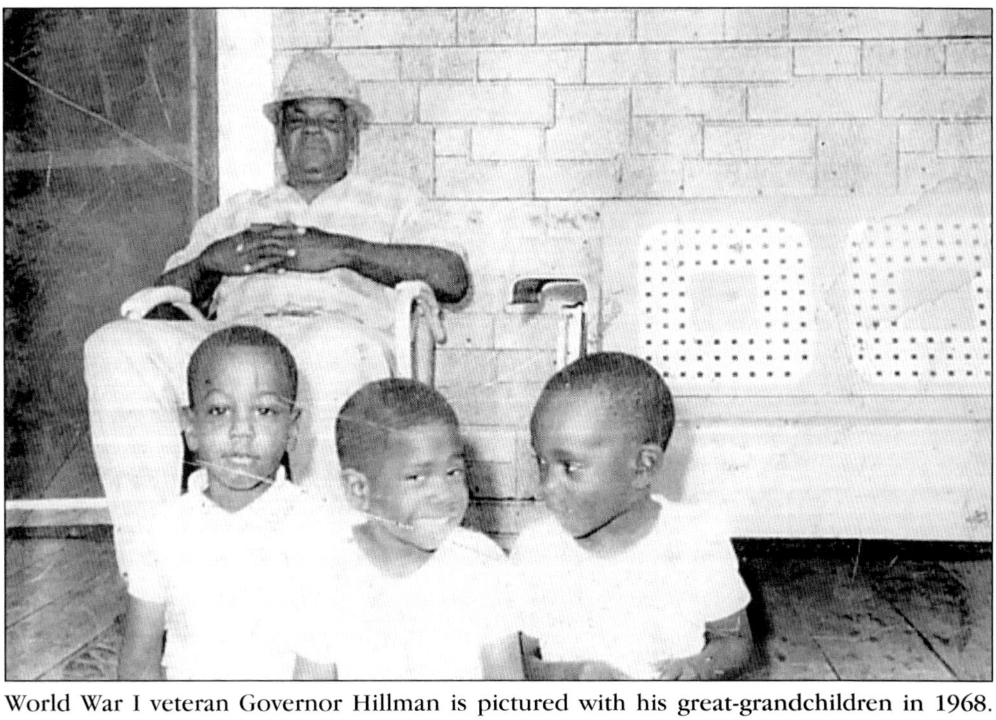

World War I veteran Governor Hillman is pictured with his great-grandchildren in 1968. From left to right are Derrick Hillman, Juan Quarterman, and Frankie Quarterman. (Courtesy Claudia Mae Hillman.)

Nine

PACESETTERS

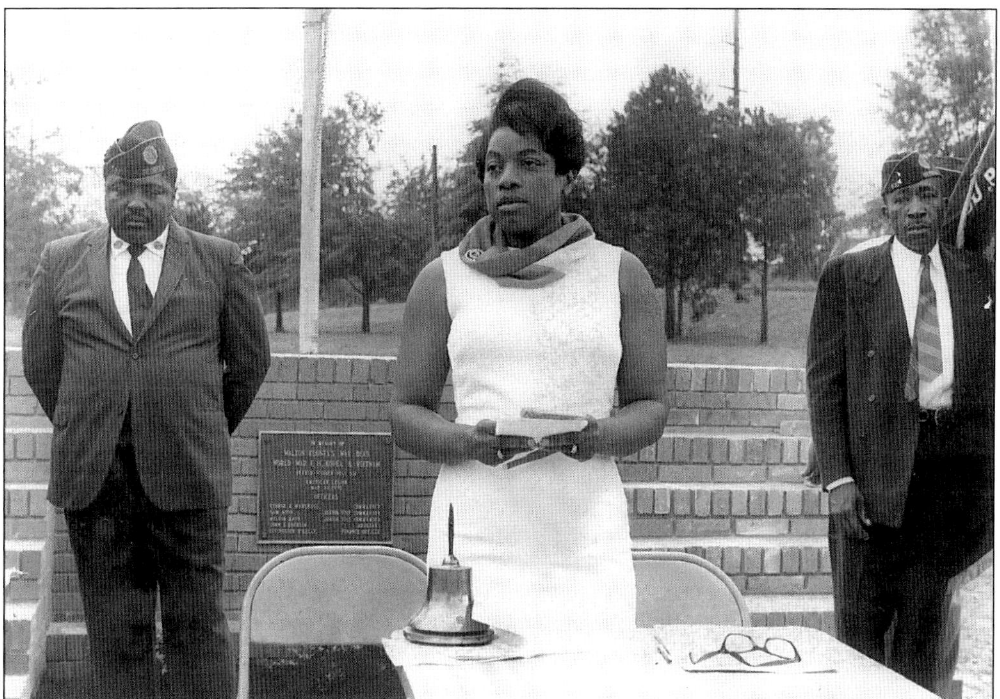

Mrs. Olia Pitts, center, was an educator in Walton County for many years. She began teaching colored children in Walton County in 1950, and was known for her classroom structure and non-questionable discipline. She was well respected in and out of the classroom. Mrs. Pitts is shown here during a ceremony dedicating the flagpole at the American Legion Post 531. (Courtesy George Marshall.)

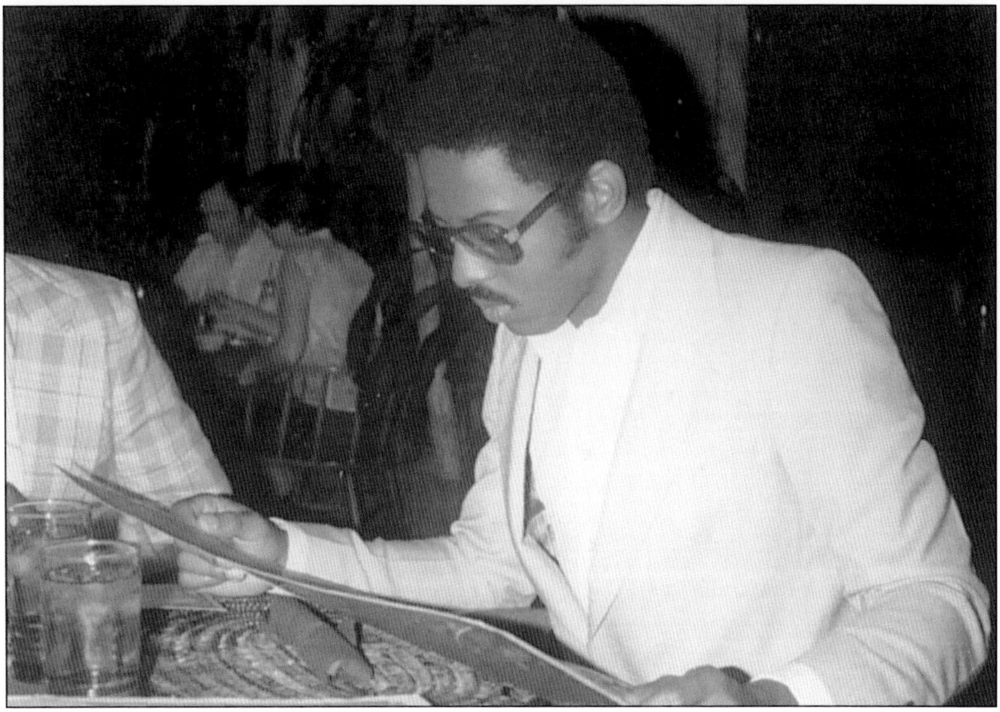

Michael DeRand Hill was sworn in as an attorney in Walton County in 1978. He served on the Walton County Board of Education from 1989 to 1993 and was chairman from 1990 to 1991. Hill is also an original member of the Moore's Ford Memorial Committee and has served as the organization's treasurer since its inception in 1997. Hill operated a private law practice in Monroe for 22 years and is now supervising attorney in the Fulton County District Attorney office in Atlanta. (Courtesy Olia Pitts.)

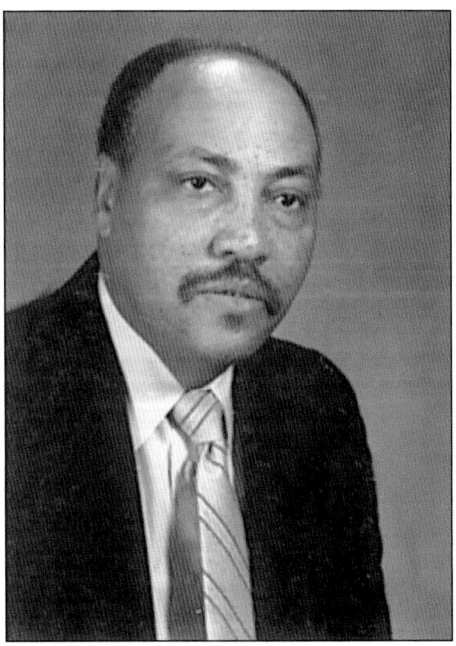

Donald Hector was born and raised in Walton County and has made numerous contributions to the community. Hector taught in the Walton County public schools for 32 years and was honored in 1972–1973 and 1977 as one of the Outstanding Elementary Teachers of America. He received special recognition by the *Atlanta Journal-Constitution* as an Unsung Hero in 1982. He received the Human Relationship Award 1983–1984; Teacher of the Year 1990; Who's Who Among America's Teachers 1990, 1992, and 1996; Most Outstanding Elementary Teacher 1995–1996; and was nominated into the Presidential Ward of Excellence for Science and Math Teachers. A member of Spring Hill A.M.E. Zion Church, Hector has served his church in many capacities. Now retired, he runs the one-on-one after-school program in Monroe. (Courtesy Donald Hector.)

Sarah Nell Knox Syphoe was born and raised in Social Circle. She taught school in nearby Newton County for 30 years and was honored as Teacher of the Year in 1970. She has been an active member of Mars Hill Baptist Church for over 60 years, where she works with the youth and is director of music. She is also an active member of Golden Link Chapter of the Order of the Eastern Star and serves on the board for Keep Covington Beautiful. Since retiring from teaching in 1988, Mrs. Knox is a tutor and a musician for a group at Riverside Nursing Home and the Senior Citizens of Turner Lake Center. (Courtesy Sarah Nell Knox Syphoe.)

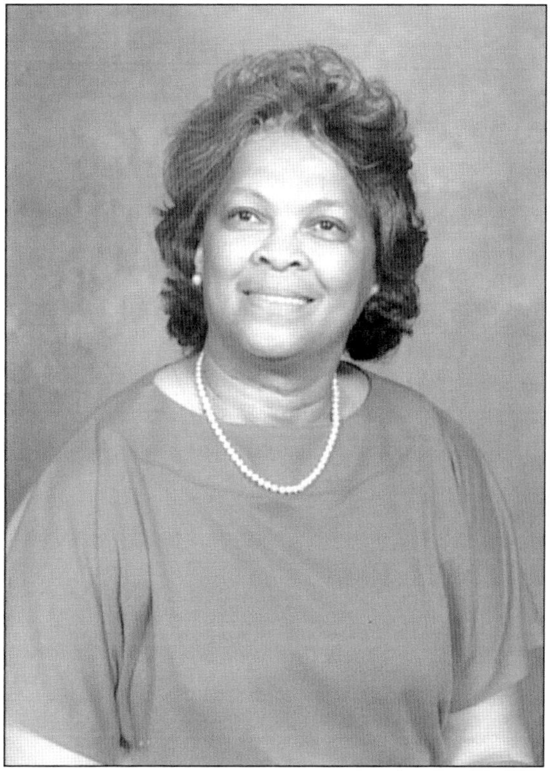

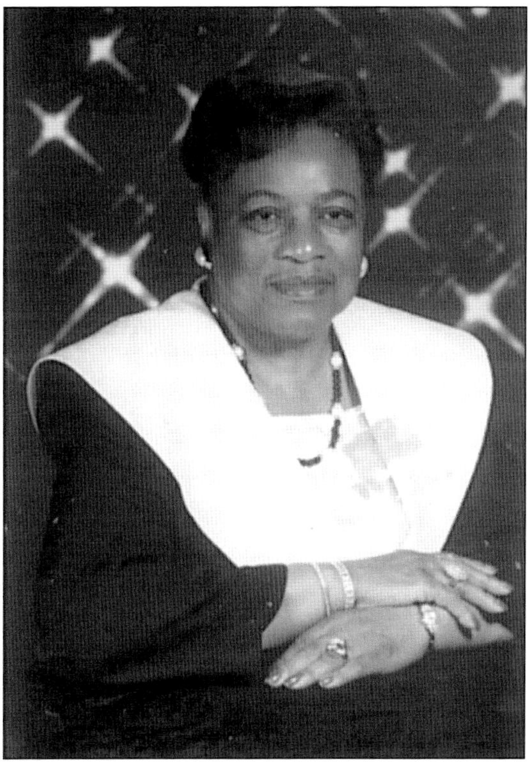

Olia Pitts taught students in the Walton County public school system for 37 years. She was recognized as Teacher of the Year at Carver Middle School in 1974. After she retired she did 12 years of continuous substitute teaching. Mrs. Pitts was and still is a volunteer for the Red Cross for 20 years, providing service to military families. She is a volunteer with the Hospital Auxiliary of Walton County Medical Center. An active member of Browns Hill Baptist Church, she is a Deaconess and member of the Caring and Sharing Ministry. She was the church clerk for 25 years and president of the usher board for the last 25 years. Also a member of Zebulon Star Chapter #166 of the Eastern Star for 21 years, she is secretary and Worthy Matron of that organization. (Courtesy Olia Pitts.)

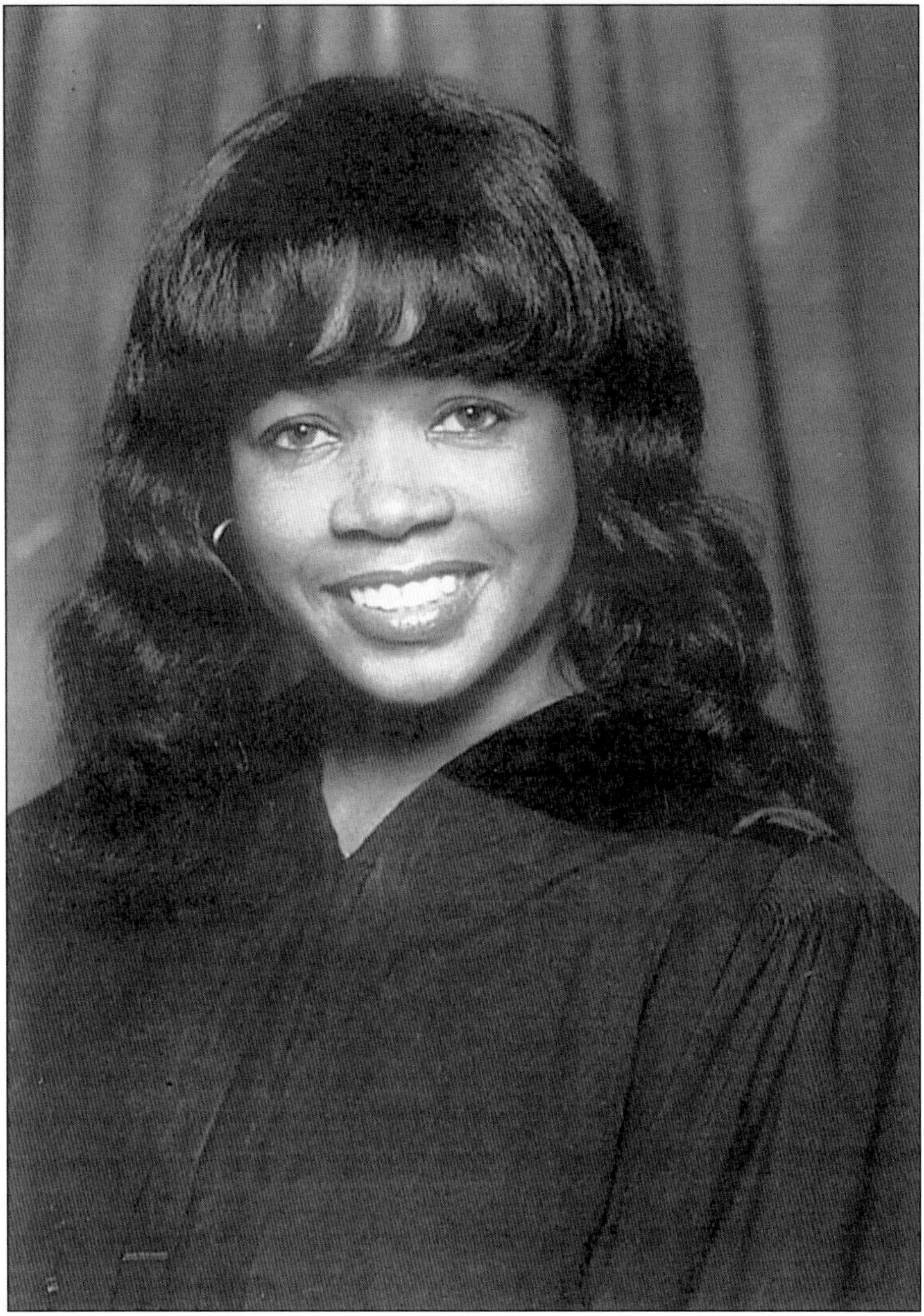

Jacqueline A. Gibson is an associate judge for the Fulton County Juvenile Court as well as an attorney with her own private practice. Gibson, who grew up and received her elementary and high school education in Walton County, is now responsible for conducting hearings, trials in juvenile cases, and civil and criminal litigation. Gibson holds memberships in the Gate City Bar Association, Georgia State Bar Association, Texas State Bar, Georgia Association of Black Women Attorneys, Georgia Association of Women Lawyers, and the American Bar Association. (Courtesy Jacqueline A. Gibson.)

Daryl G. Bloodsaw was born and raised in Monroe and is the son of Linda Jones. After graduating from high school in Monroe and the University of Georgia, Bloodsaw moved to New York. He has become a politician and grass roots organizer in his community. He is a member of Board 9 and the 30th Precinct Community Council; is program co-director of the Blue Nile Rites of Passage, Inc. (mentoring black youths in the Tri-State area); marketing advisor for the Harlem 5-Mile Classic; and is founder of Blacks for Political Accountability. He is also a past member of the National Black Child Development Institute. Daryl believes that his ultimate success in life lies in how he can help strengthen his community. In 2001 he ran for city council in upper Manhattan. (Courtesy Linda Jones.)

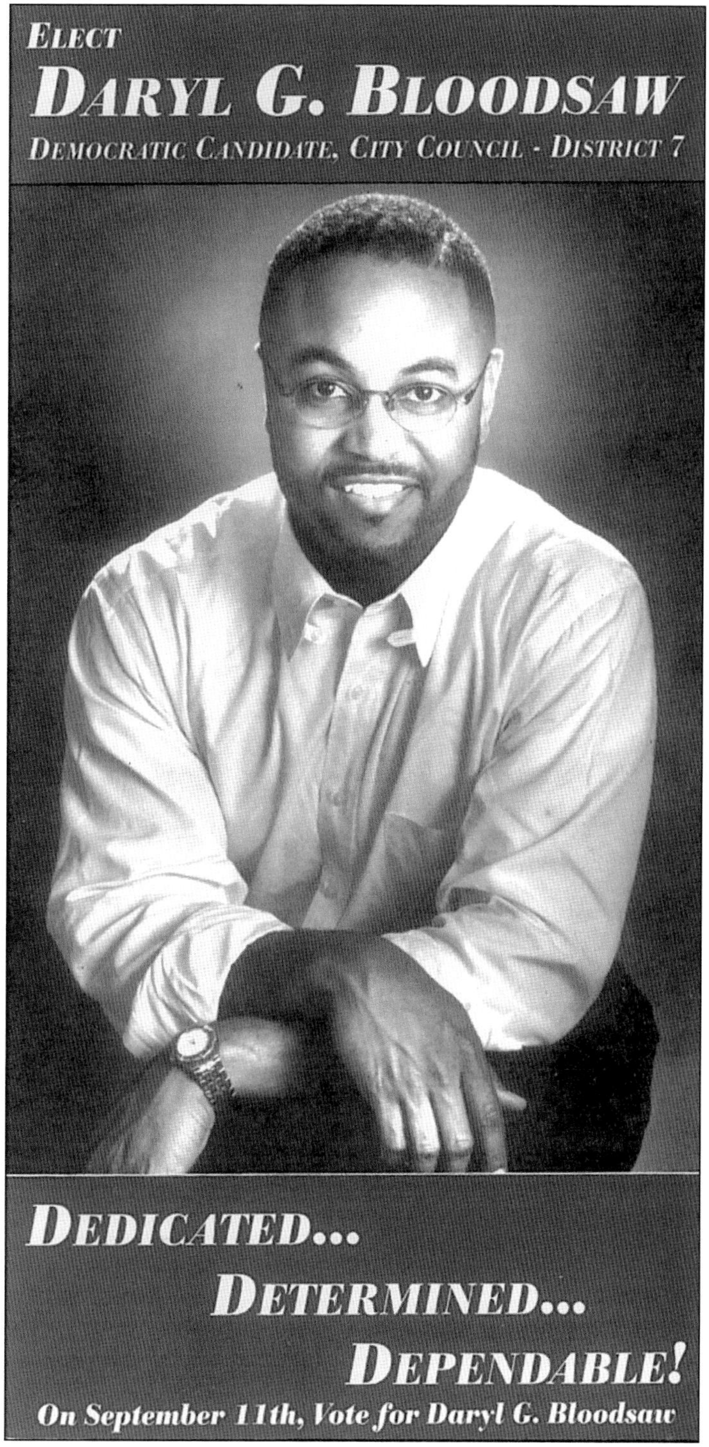

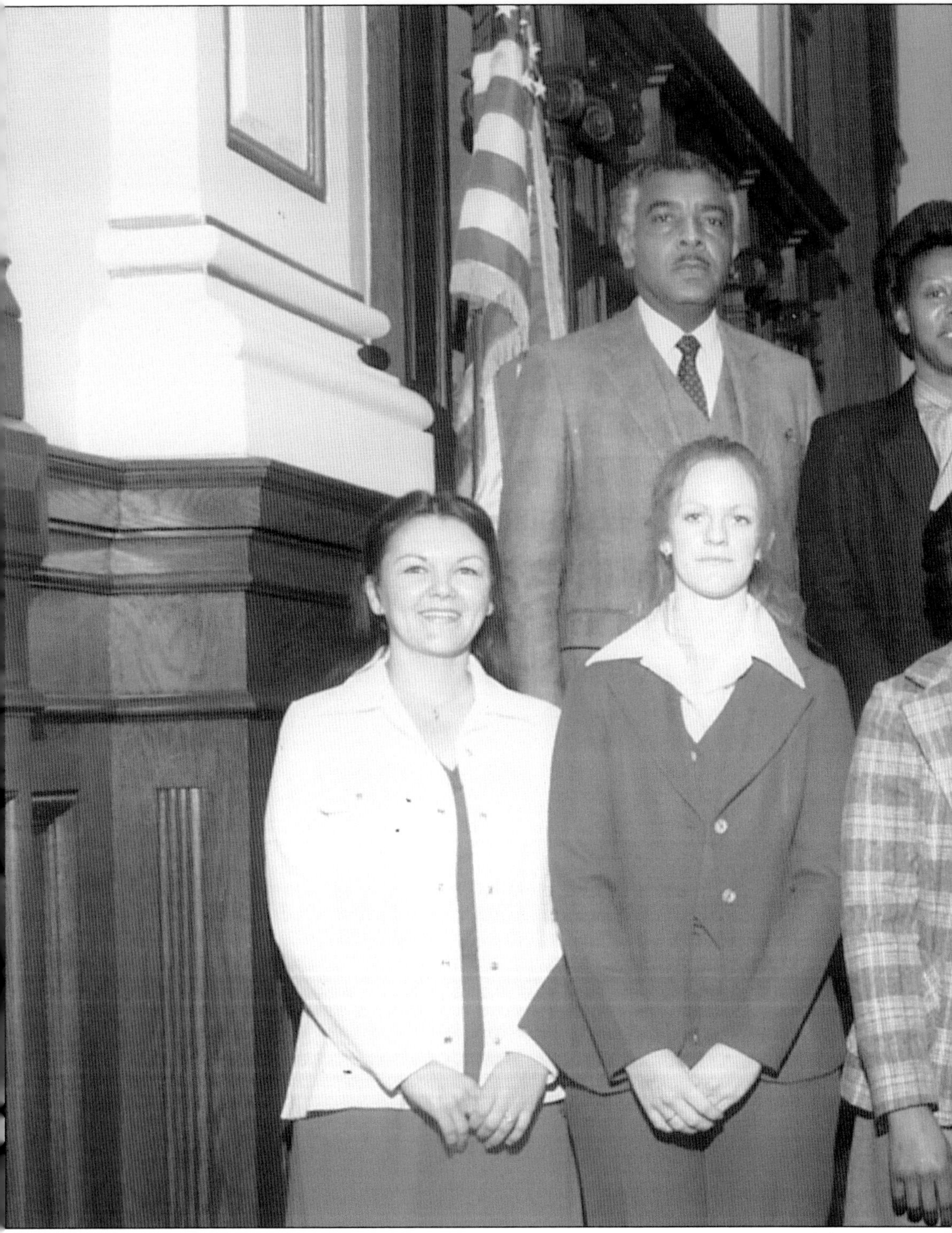

Sandra Kay Locklin (back row, third from left) is pictured with Horace Tate (left, next to flag) and Zell Miller (back row, right). She was employed by the Georgia Department of

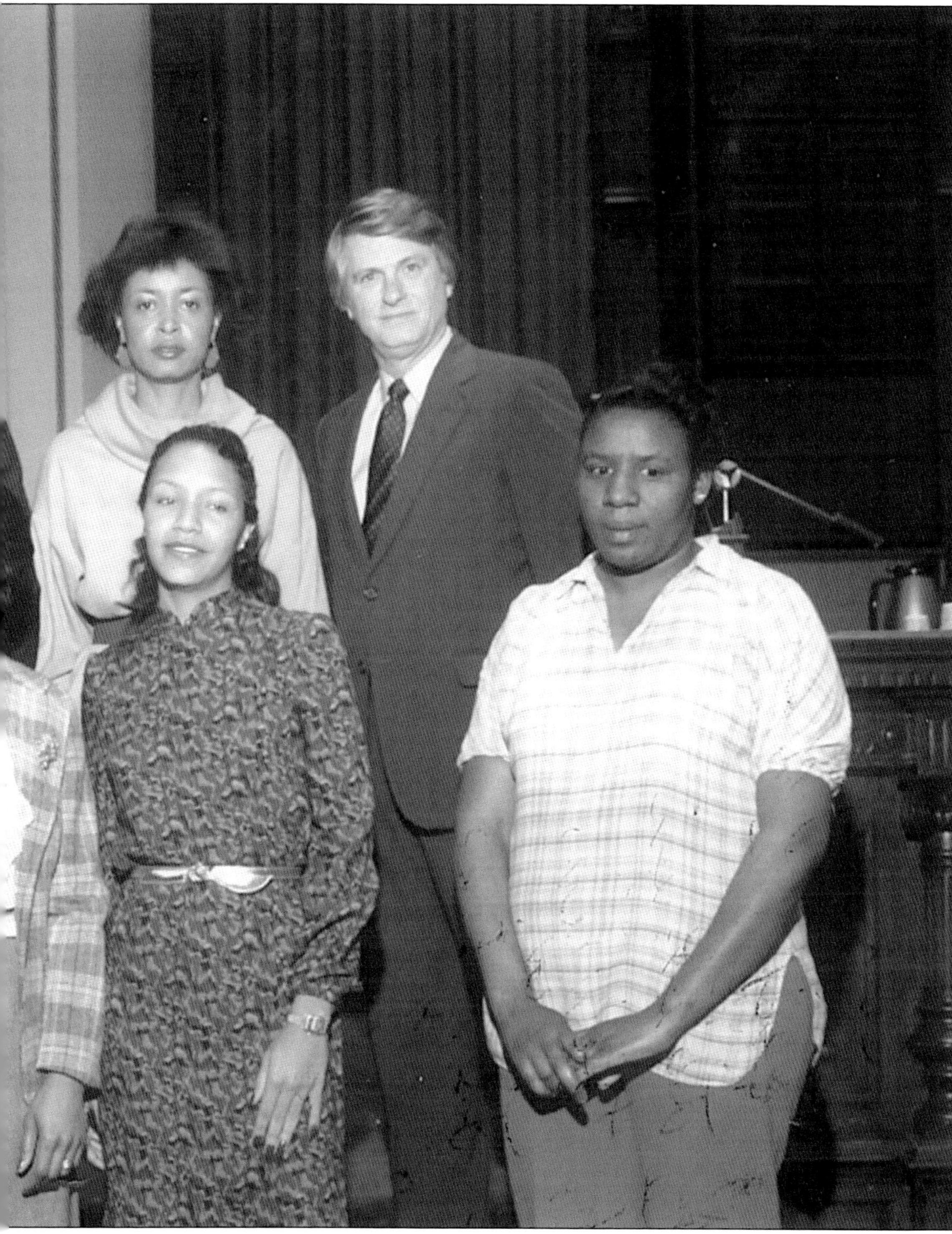

Corrections. (Courtesy Geneva Locklin.)

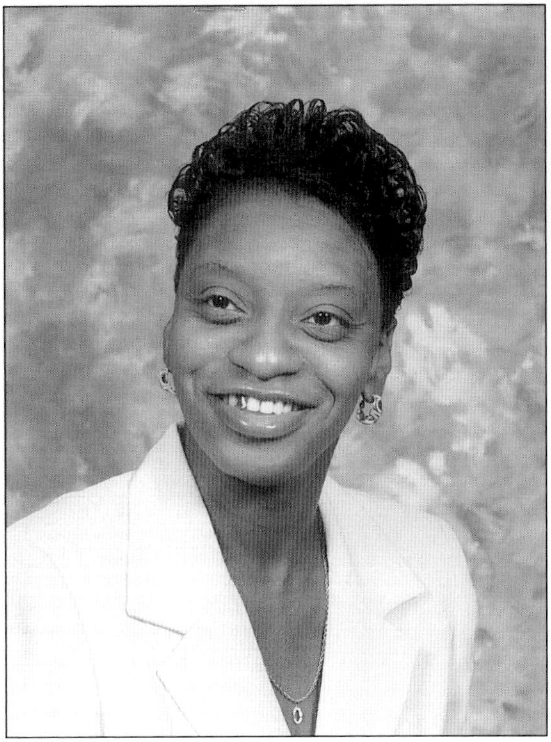

Dr. Olivet James was born and raised in Social Circle. She graduated from Social Circle High School in 1986, received a B.S. from Fort Valley State College in 1990, an M.S. from Fort Valley State University in 1992, and an Ed.D. from the University of Georgia in 2001. With 12 years of experience in education, she is currently the principal of Union Point Elementary School. (Courtesy Dr. Willie Enus.)

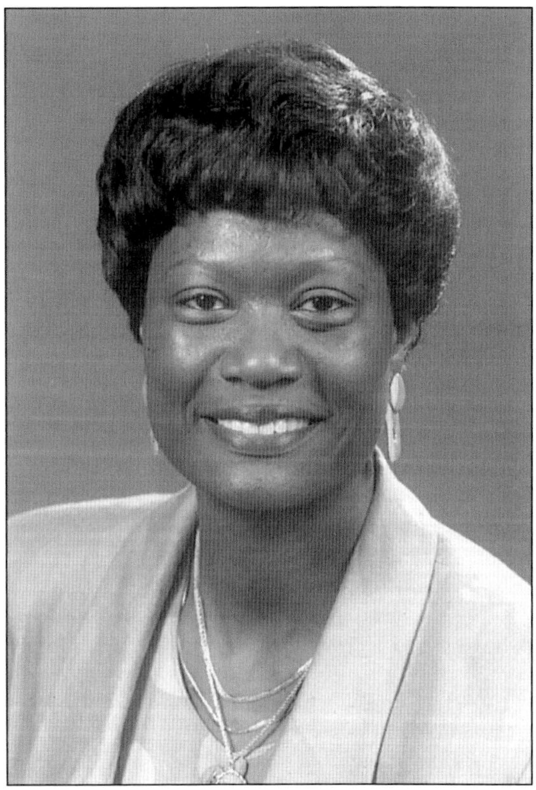

After leading the Monroe Lady Hurricanes to numerous championships, Trish Roberts went on to become a 1976 Olympian in women's basketball and was named All-American at the University of Tennessee. She continues to use her exceptional talent as collegiate head coach at Stony Brook. The Basketball Coaches Association of New York (BCANY) selected Roberts as Division I Coach of the Year in 2000, the top selection of more than 17 head coaches. She was inducted into the Women's Basketball Hall of Fame in 2000. (Courtesy Cherry Lee Roberts.)

After a very successful career in the military and law enforcement, James H. Vaughn, now a minister, founded Now House, Inc. in 2000 and opened the first house for boys in 2001. Now House provides underserved youth an opportunity for success by providing loving environments with guidance and direction. Now House provides a network of services including behavioral therapy, vocational training, education, workplace skills, and alcohol and drug assessments. (Courtesy Robbie Mapp Vaughn.)

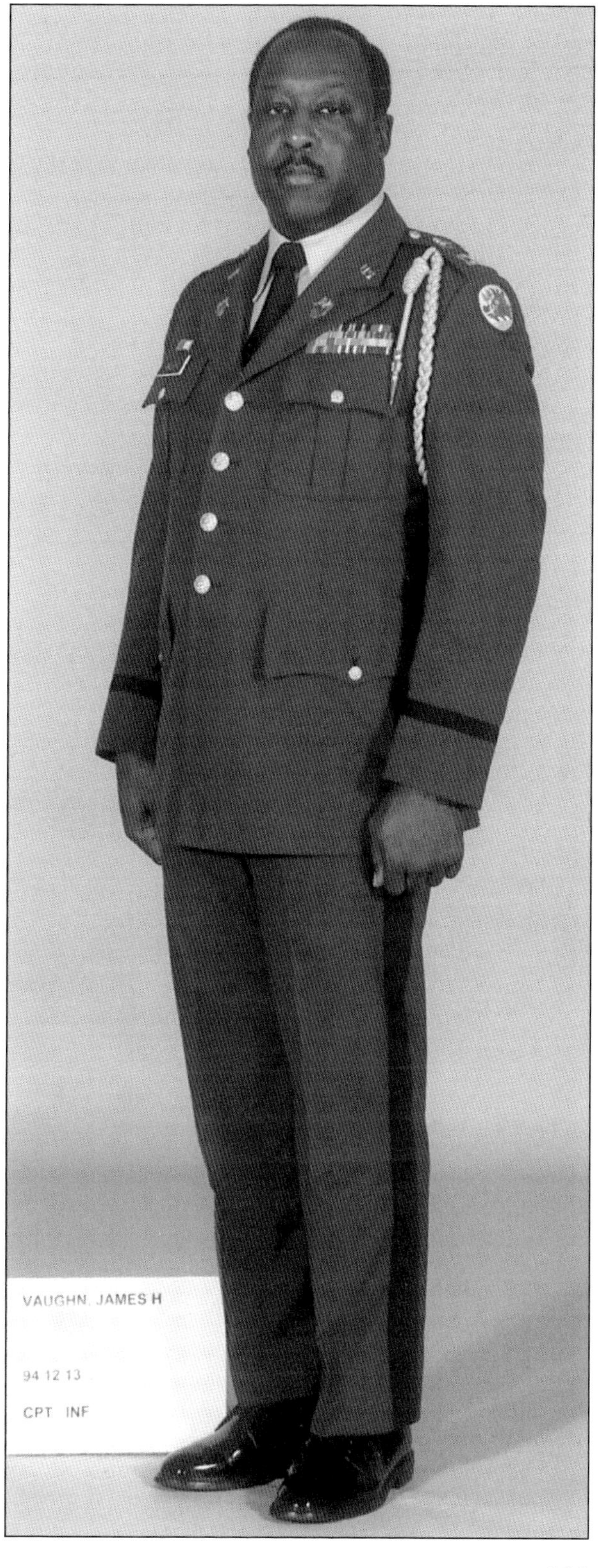

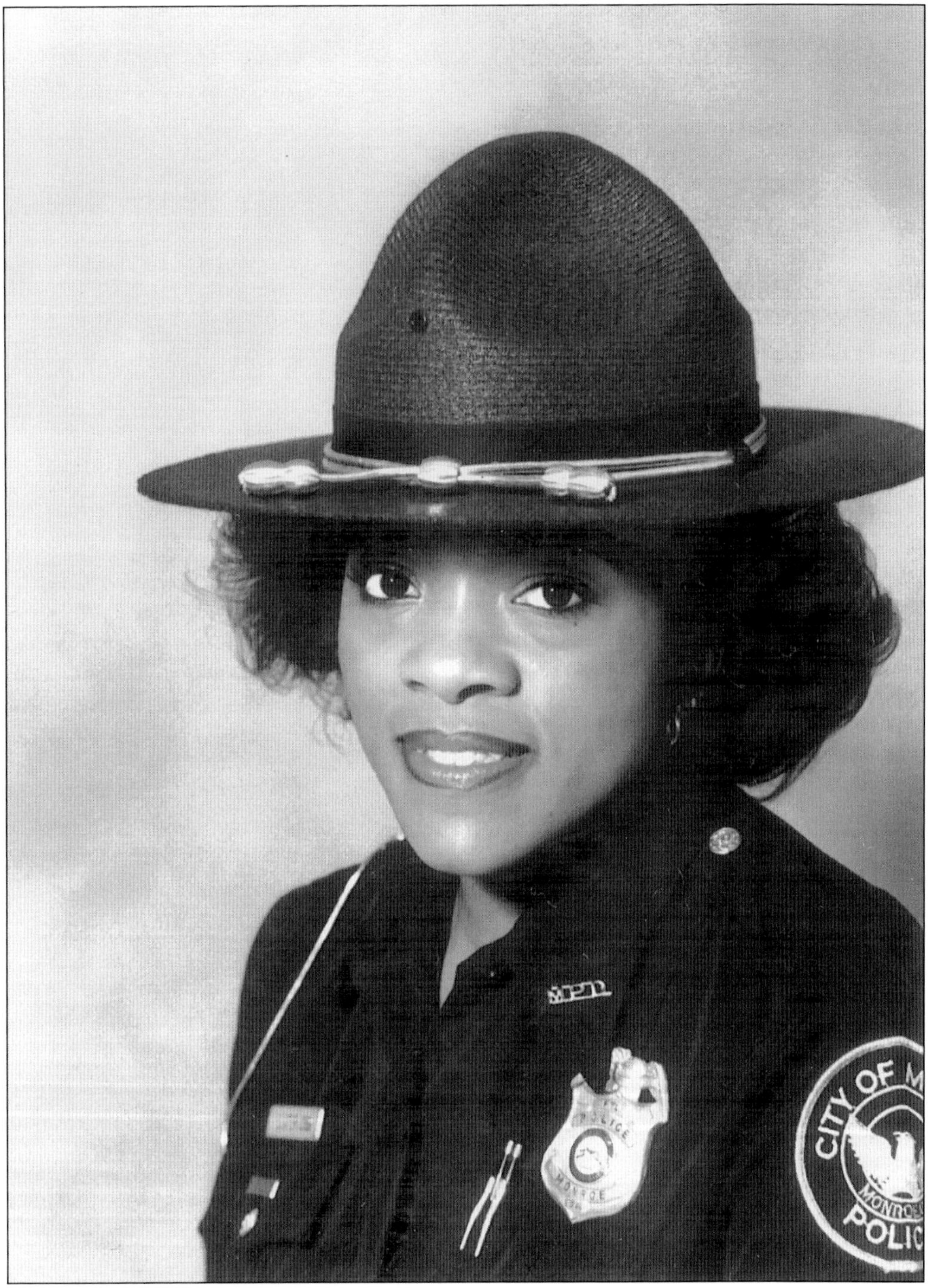

Emily Mapp Hunter became the first female police officer to patrol Monroe in 1975. Her male coworkers respected her as a competent police officer who could "hold her own." Since retiring from the police department, Ms. Hunter opened Now House, Inc. for girls in 2000. (Courtesy Robbie Mapp Vaughn.)

Ten

The Moore's Ford Lynching

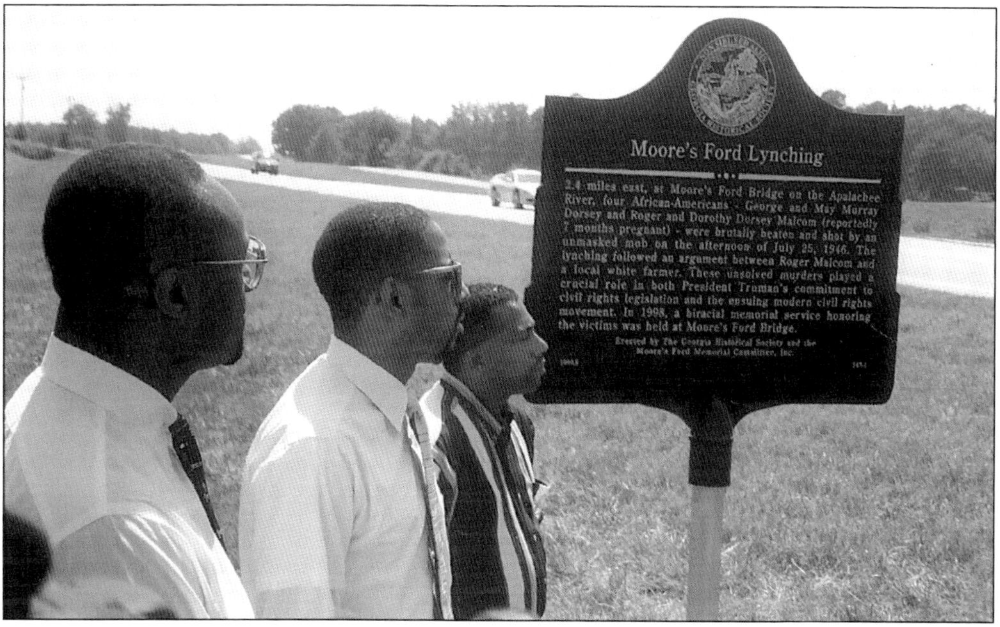

J.L. Nunnally (left), chairman of the Moore's Ford Memorial Committee, Michael Hill (center), and Waymon Mundy (right) look at the Historical Marker on Highway 78. The sign reads: "2.4 miles east at Moore's Ford Bridge on the Apalachee River, four African Americans—George and May Murray Dorsey and Roger and Dorothy Dorsey Malcom (reportedly 7 months pregnant)—were brutally beaten and shot by an unmasked mob on the afternoon of July 25, 1946. The lynching followed an argument between Roger Malcom and a local white farmer. These unsolved murders played a crucial role in both President Truman's commitment to civil rights legislation and the ensuing modern civil rights movement. In 1998, a biracial memorial service honoring the victims was held at Moore's Ford Bridge. Erected by the Georgia Historical Society and the Moore's Ford Memorial Committee, Inc." (Courtesy Lynn Camp.)

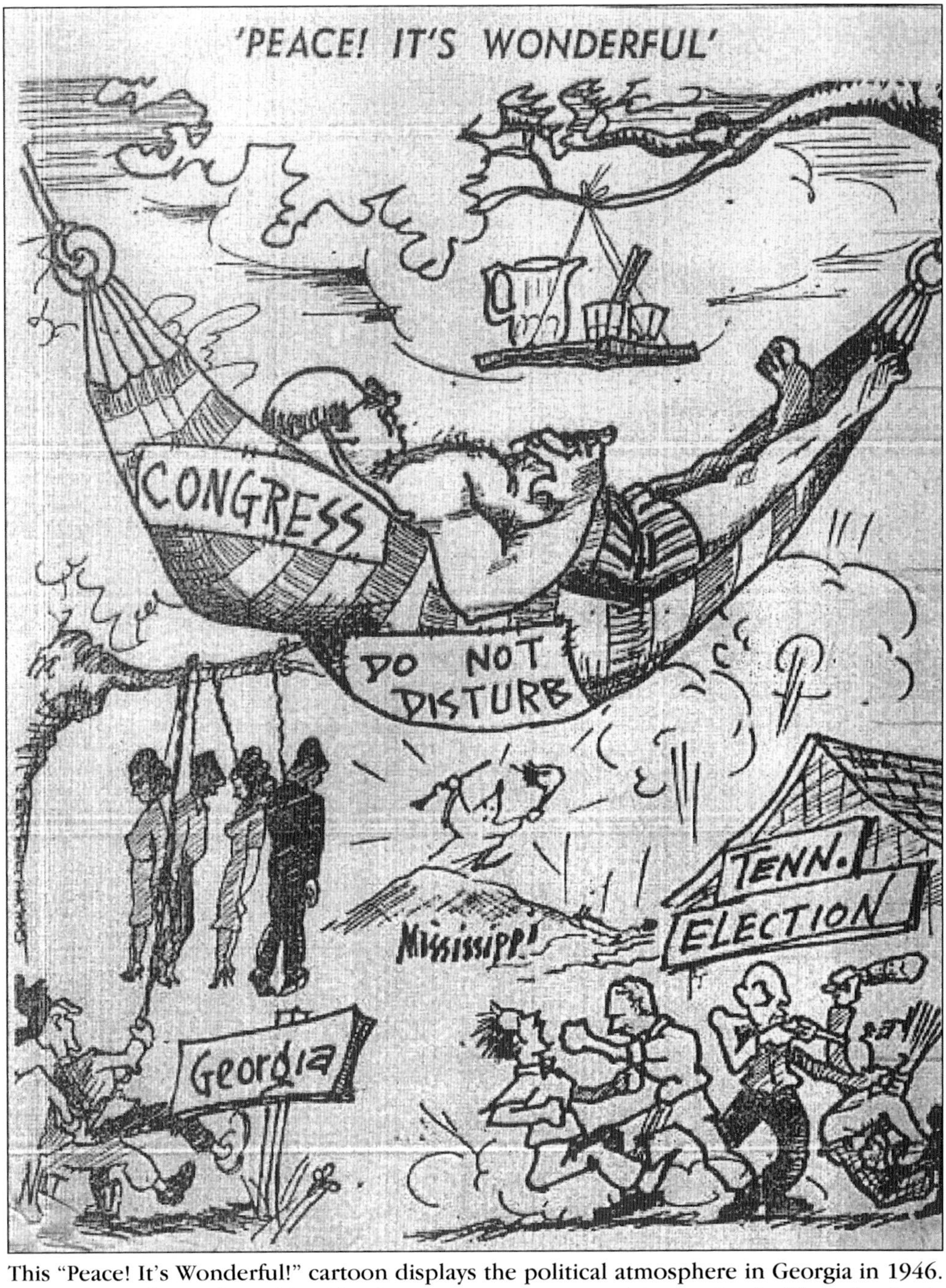

This "Peace! It's Wonderful!" cartoon displays the political atmosphere in Georgia in 1946. It was drawn by Nathaniel Barkley Brown Sr. and appeared in the *Louisville Defender* in Louisville, Kentucky in 1946. (Courtesy Elsa Barkley Brown and the family of Nathaniel Barkley Brown Sr.)

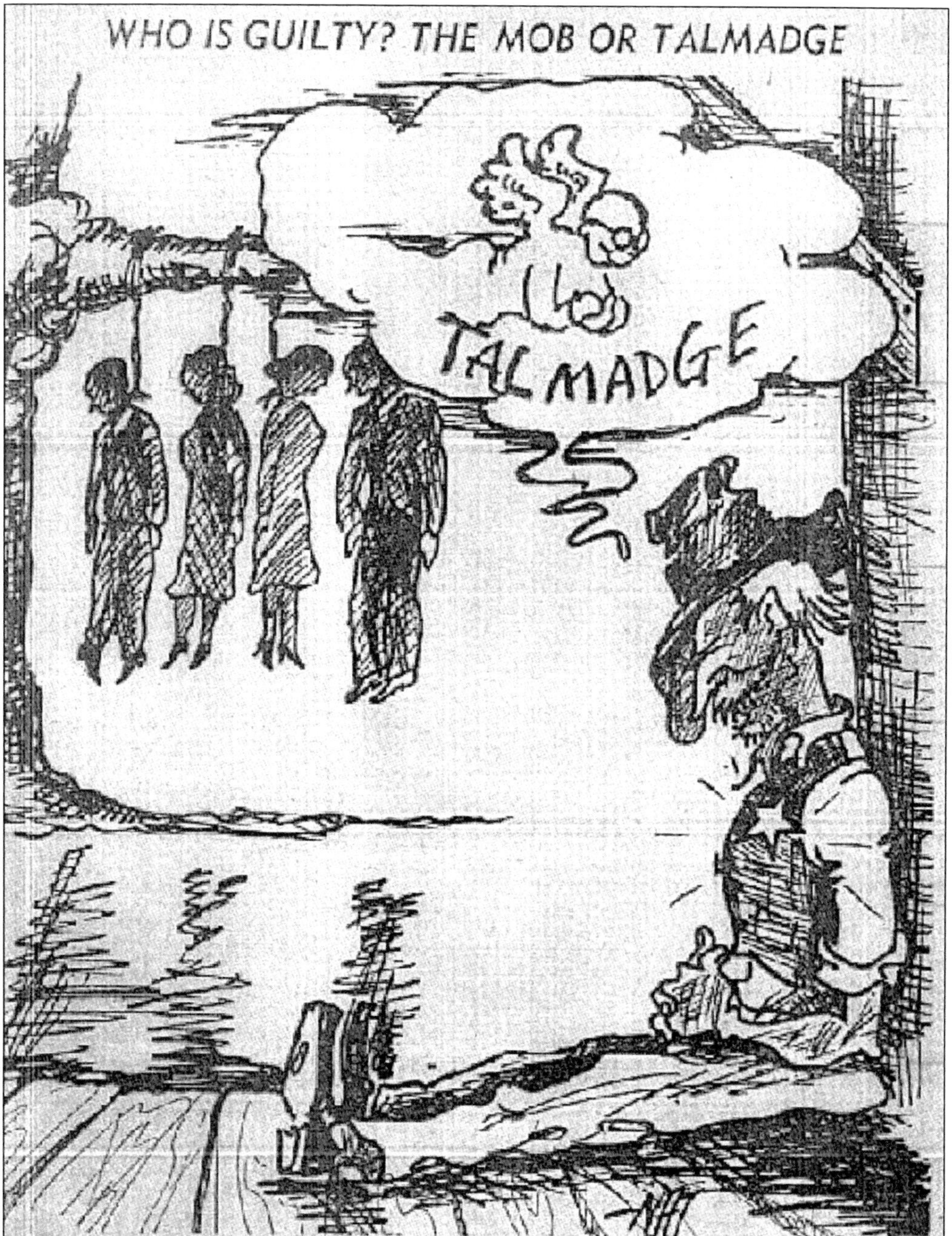

Another political cartoon by Nathaniel Barkley Brown Sr. appeared in the *Louisville Defender* in Louisville, Kentucky in 1946, reflecting on the Moore's Ford Lynching. "Talmadge" refers to Georgia governor Herman Eugene Talmadge. (Courtesy Elsa Barkley Brown and the family of Nathaniel Barkley Brown Sr.)

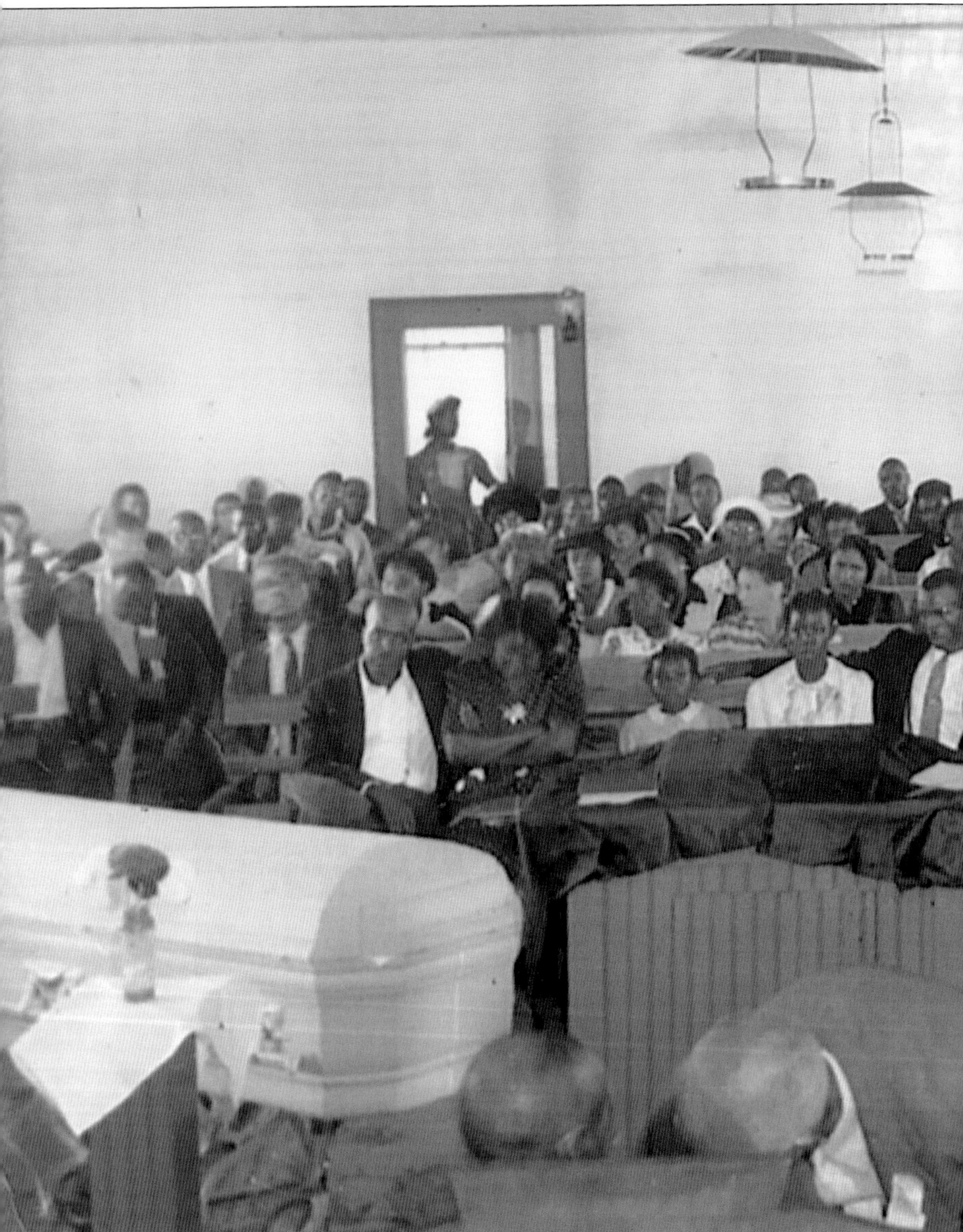

On July 28, 1946 friends and relatives gathered at Mt. Perry Missionary Baptist Church for the funeral of brother and sister lynching victims, World War II veteran George Dorsey and

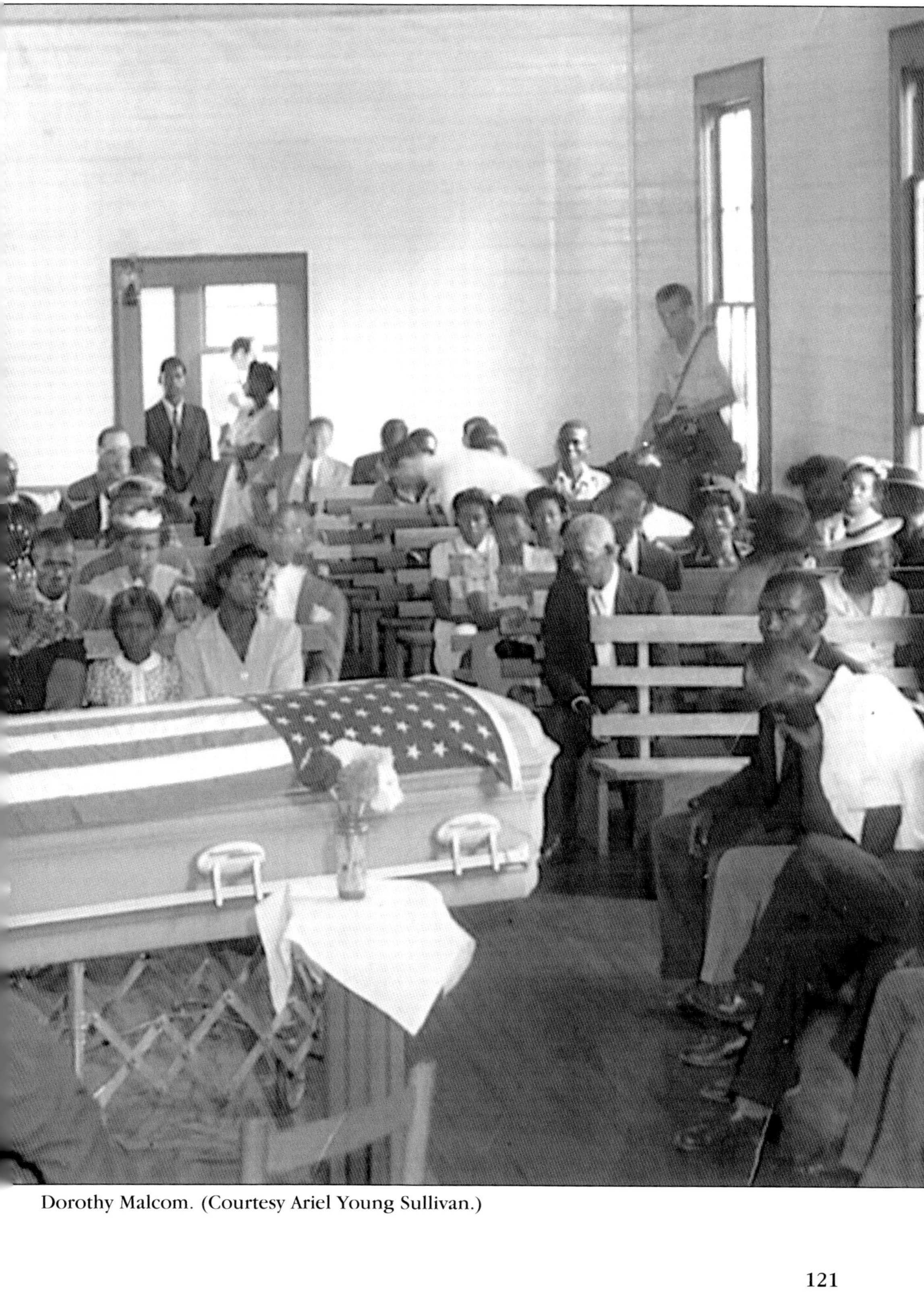

Dorothy Malcom. (Courtesy Ariel Young Sullivan.)

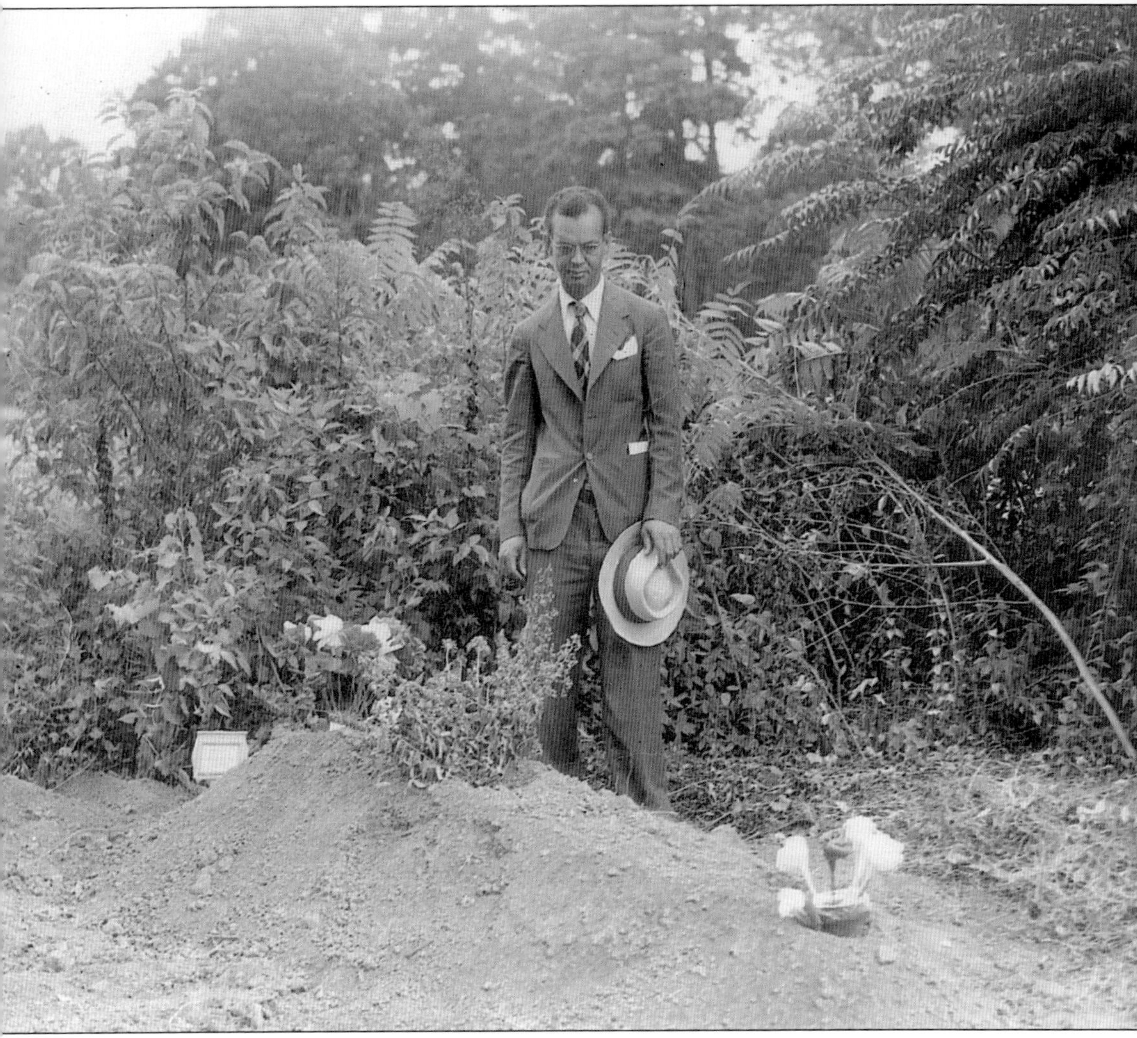

Mortician Dan Young stands at the graveside of his cousin, Mae Murray Dorsey. Young, owner of Young Funeral Home, was in charge of the funerals for all four victims. (Courtesy Ariel Young Sullivan.)

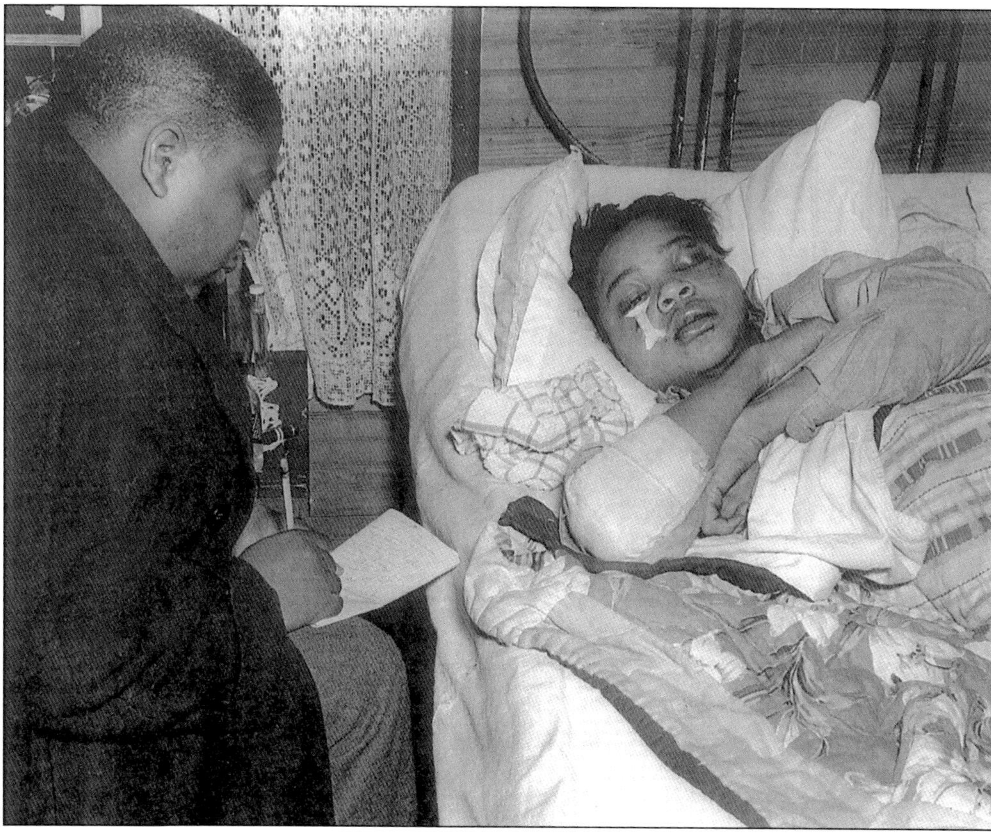

Five months after the Moore's Ford lynching, Lamar Howard testified before a grand jury in Athens. He was beaten afterwards by two brothers who admitted to their actions in court but were acquitted. Howard exiled himself from Walton County, returning only to visit close relatives. In 1999 he attended the memorial military service for George Dorsey and afterwards accepted a resolution passed by the Georgia House of Representatives commending him for his courage. (Courtesy *Atlanta Daily World*.)

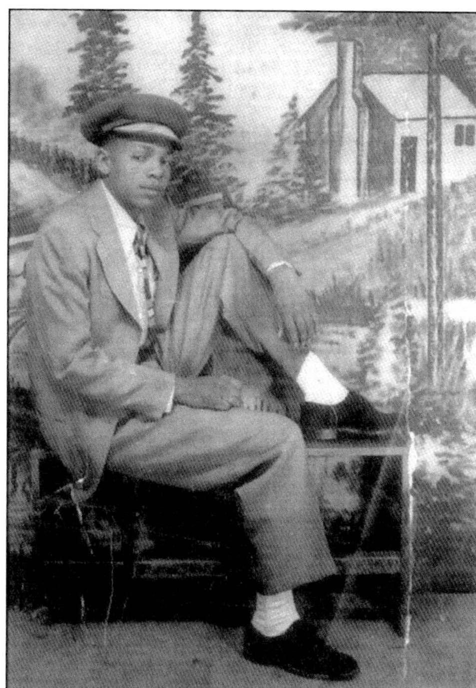

Lamar Howard was 19 years old in 1946. He was working at the icehouse where he witnessed men cleaning guns and practicing tying nooses prior to the lynching. (Courtesy Lamar Howard and Catherine Jones.)

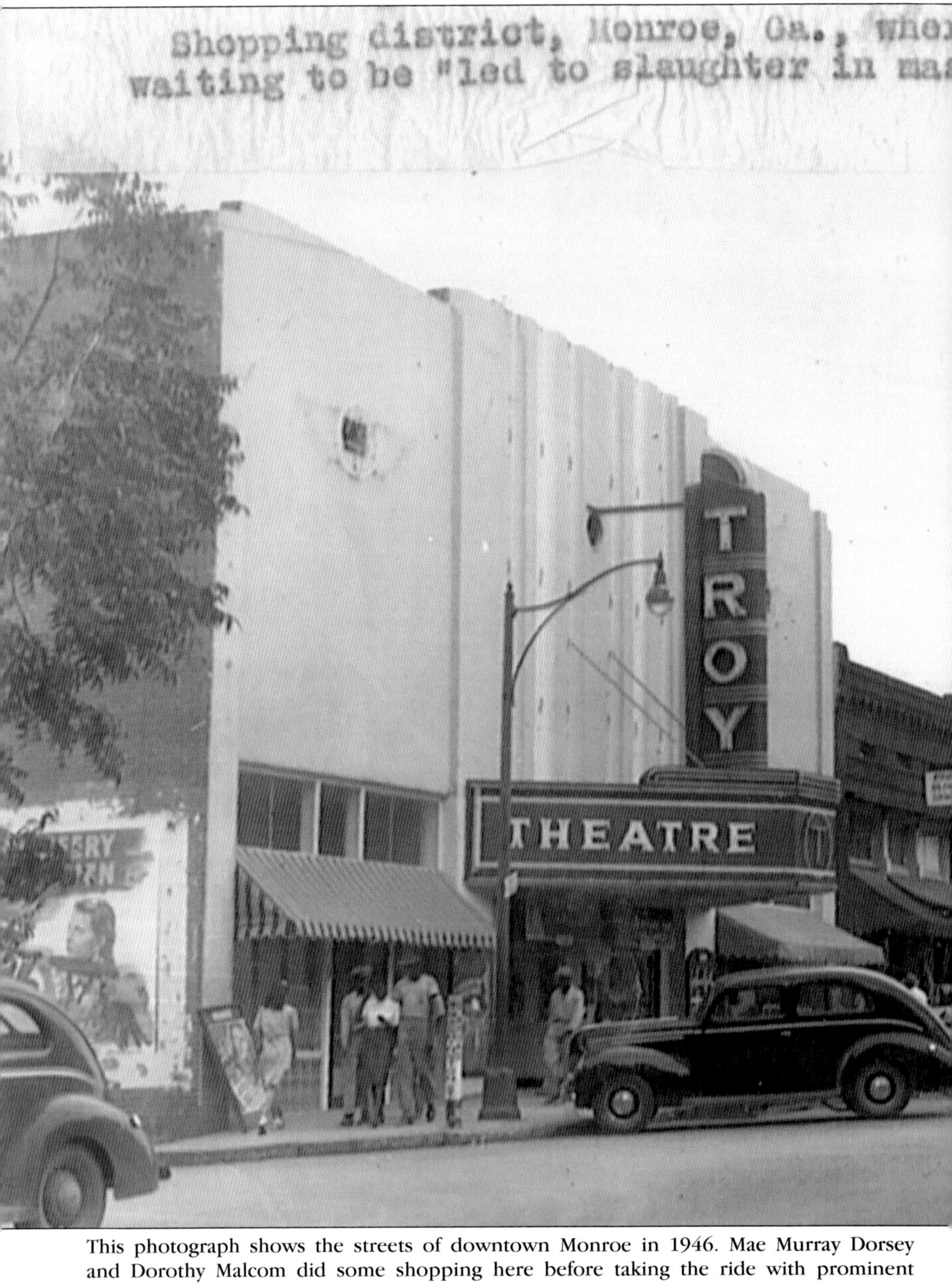

This photograph shows the streets of downtown Monroe in 1946. Mae Murray Dorsey and Dorothy Malcom did some shopping here before taking the ride with prominent

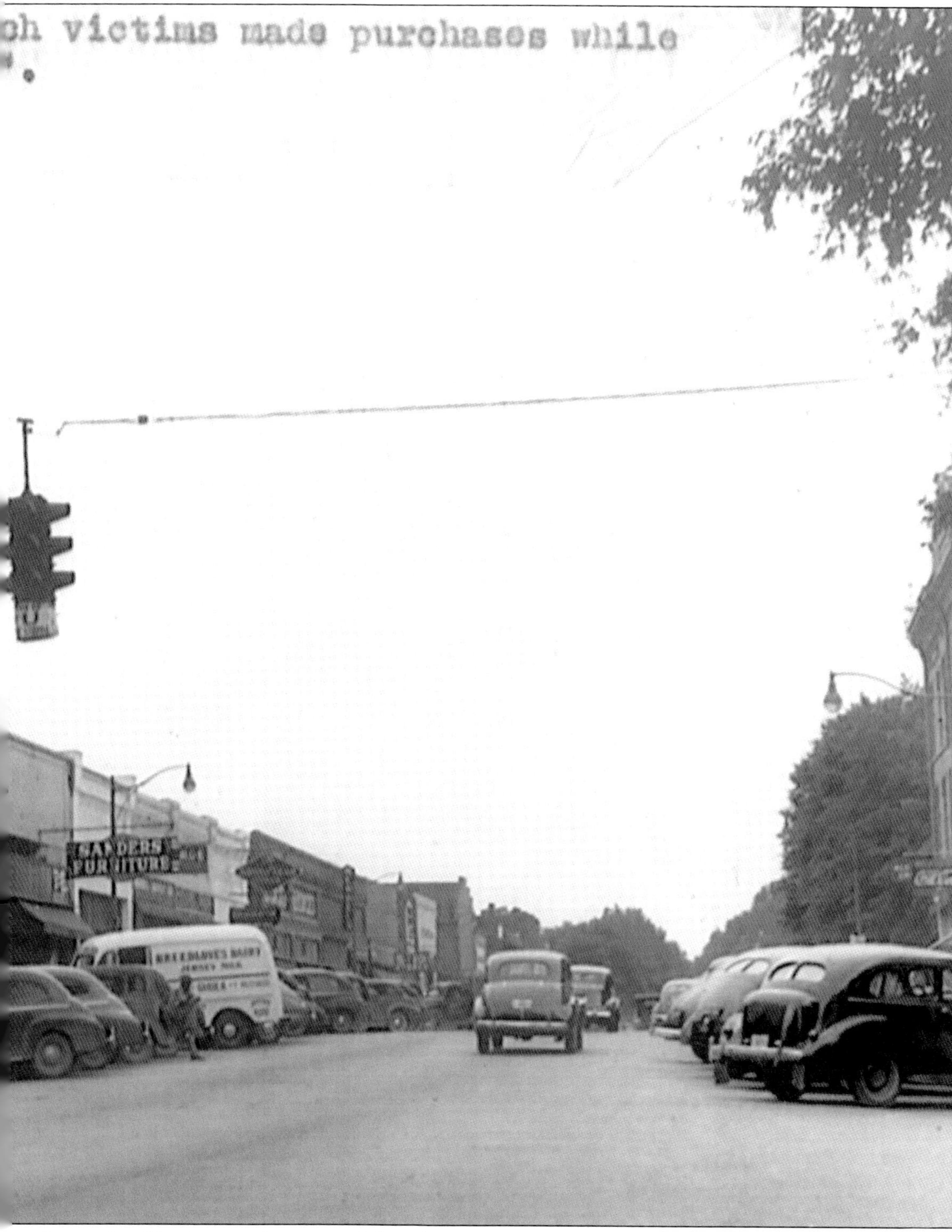

farmer Loy Harrison to the scene of their lynching. (Courtesy Ariel Young Sullivan.)

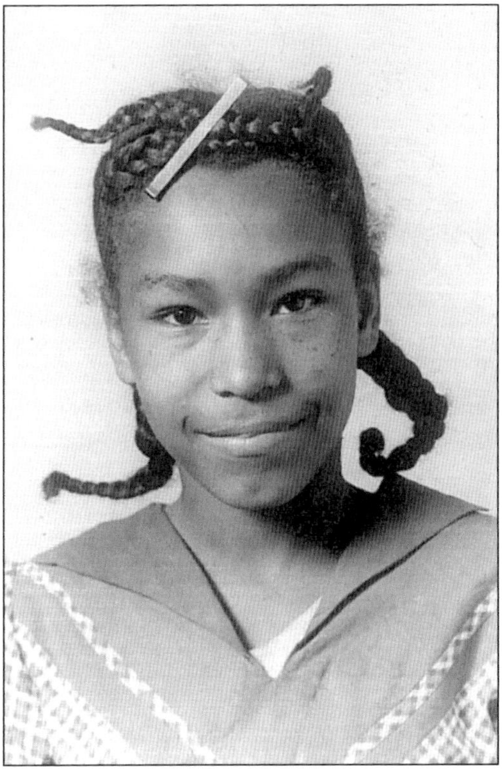

Betty Ansley was seven years old when her cousin, Mae Murray, was killed. Foster said she never will forget that night when one cousin was killed and a set of male twin cousins were born. (Courtesy Betty Foster.)

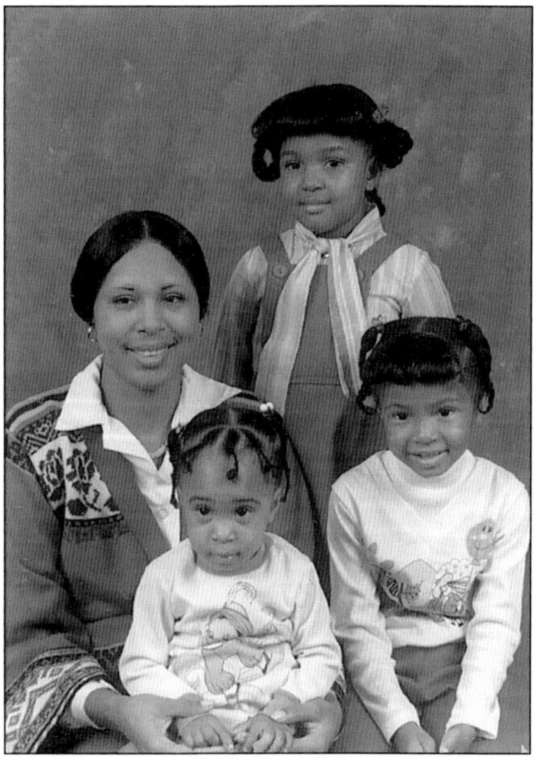

Teressa Sorrells and her daughters Tamla, Larynee, and Errica are cousins of Mae Murray, seen in 1976. Teressa is a special events consultant, floral designer, and freelance artist whose drawings are featured in this book. (Courtesy Lynn Camp.)

Sarah Maddox was a teenager when her cousin Mae Murray was killed. Maddox had her first child on July 25th, four years later. (Courtesy Sarah Maddox.)

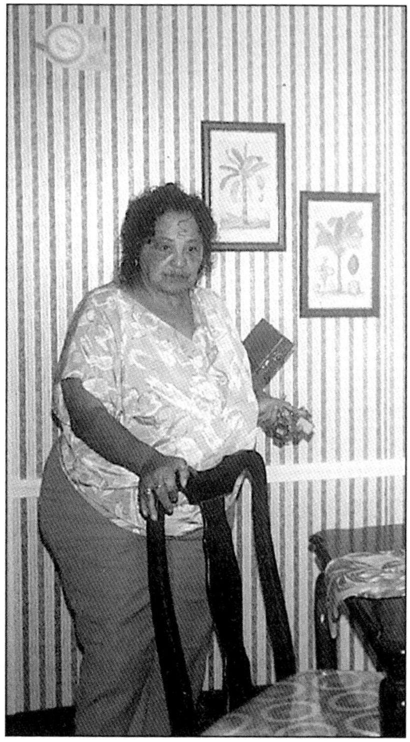

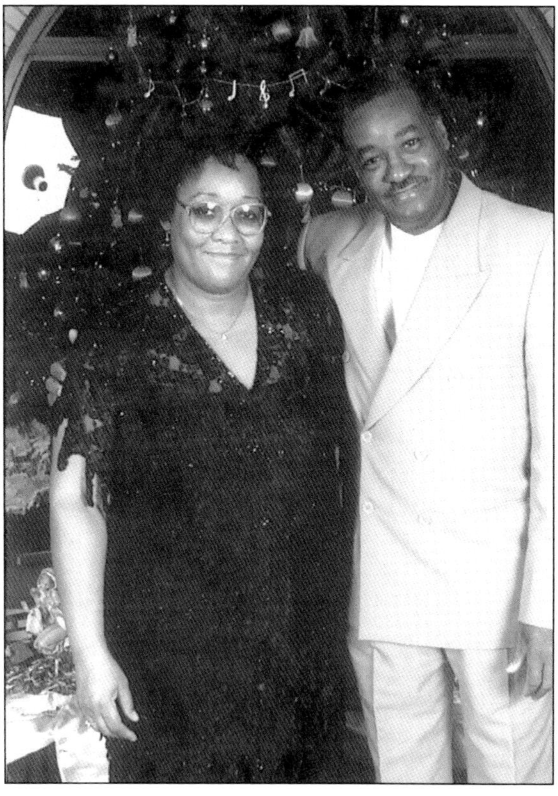

Roger M. Hayes Sr. and his wife Anita Hayes have attended several memorial programs held by the Moore's Ford Memorial Committee. Hayes was two years old when his father, Roger Malcom, was killed. (Courtesy Roger M. Hayes Sr.)

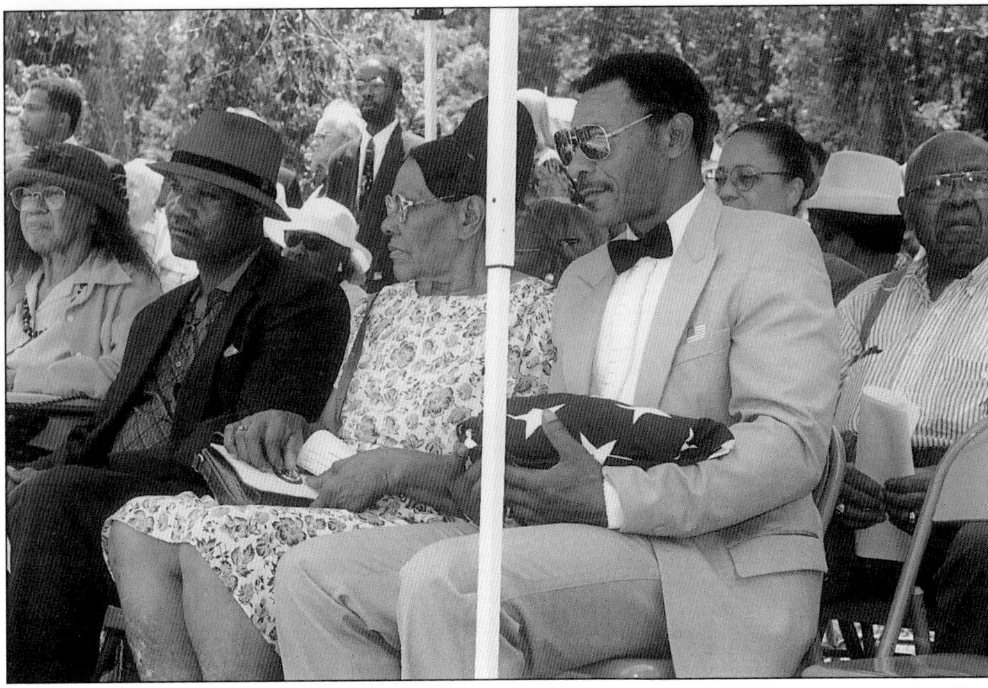

Relatives of George Dorsey attended the memorial military service and received the flag. From left to right are nephew (and namesake) George Dorsey, sister-in-law Ruby Dorsey, and nephew Columbus Dorsey. (Courtesy *The Walton Tribune*.)

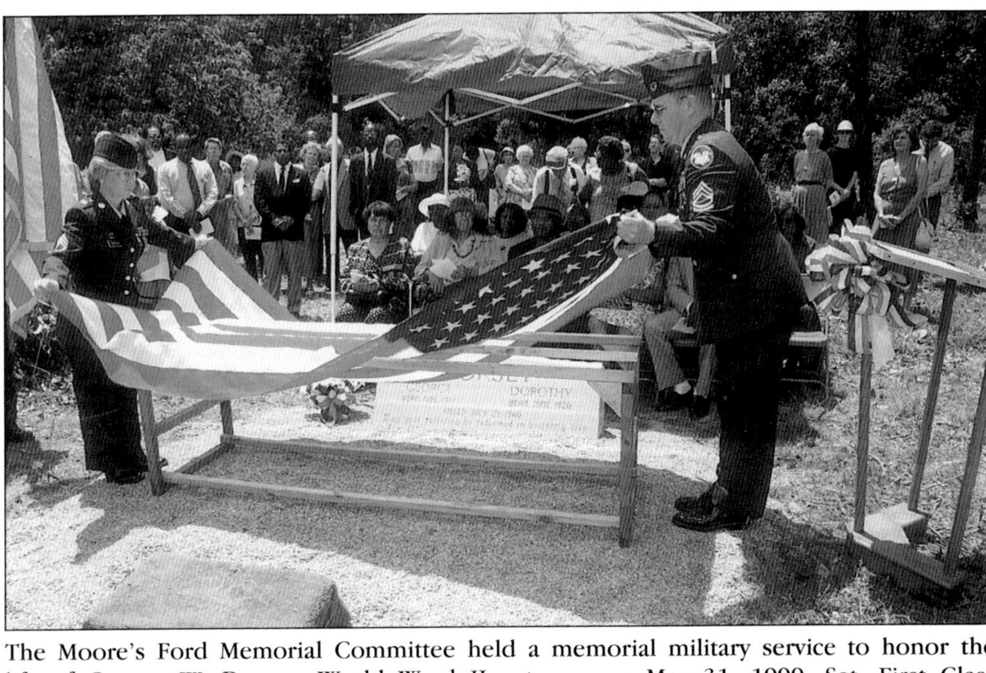

The Moore's Ford Memorial Committee held a memorial military service to honor the life of George W. Dorsey, World Ward II veteran, on May 31, 1999. Sgt. First Class James Payton and Staff Sgt. Antoinette Wheeler are shown folding the flag. (Courtesy *The Walton Tribune*.)